T0094688

Advancing U.S.-Nordic-Baltic Security Cooperation

Adapting Partnership to a New Security Environment

Daniel S. Hamilton, Andras Simonyi, Debra L. Cagan
Editors

Center for Transatlantic Relations
Paul H. Nitze School of Advanced International Studies
Johns Hopkins University

Hamilton, Daniel S., Andras Simonyi, Debra L. Cagan, eds. *Advancing U.S.-Nordic-Baltic Security Cooperation*.

Washington, DC: Center for Transatlantic Relations, 2014

Center for Transatlantic Relations
The Paul H. Nitze School of Advanced International Studies
The Johns Hopkins University
1717 Massachusetts Ave., NW, Suite 525
Washington, DC 20036
Tel: (202) 663-5880
Fax: (202) 663-5879
Email: transatlantic@jhu.edu
http://transatlantic.sais-jhu.edu

ISBN 13: 978-0-9907720-0-2

On the cover: upper—The Arctic Circle (courtesy NOAA); lower left—LNG terminal, Lithuania (courtesy AB Klaipedos Nafta); lower center—F15 fighters during an air policing exercise over Lithuania, April, 2014 (U.S. Air Force photo by Airman 1st Class Dana J. Butler/Released); lower right—A U.S. Navy MH-60R Seahawk helicopter (U.S. Navy photo by Mass Communication Specialist 3rd Class Walter M. Wayman/Released)

Contents

Introduction

Daniel S. Hamilton, Andras Simonyi, and Debra L. Cagan

The Nordic-Baltic region holds a special place when it comes to the resilience of free and democratic societies. Today, more than ever in the last 25 years, the integrity of the "West" is at stake. Nordic-Baltic-U.S. security cooperation is at the heart of the future of the region. The Nordic-Baltic countries remain strong partners for the United States, sharing values and norms and a commitment to pragmatic cooperation, and as net contributors to economic growth, foreign policy management, development assistance and security. The Nordic-Baltic region shows that market democracy works, human rights and the rule of law can be respected, a positive outward vision of the world is still possible, and that transatlantic cooperation remains indispensable to tackle many challenges.

When Cold War tensions faded, the countries of the region turned from being security importers to being security exporters. Now, a whole new set of challenges to a Europe whole and free has emerged.

In the aftermath of the Russian invasion of Crimea and eastern Ukraine, the Nordic-Baltic region has again moved to the forefront as a critical region for all transatlantic partners. There is a unity in this region of Europe that is unmatched elsewhere on the continent. These are strong relationships forged over the last several decades resulting in unprecedented economic development, security and defense ties, and political cooperation. As countries and collectively, the Nordic-Baltic region and the United States are more operational, integrated and interoperable than at any time in history. The transformation of security forces in this region and the level of cooperation among Nordic-Baltic countries are clearly outpacing the rest of Europe.

Enhancing the Nordic-Baltic partnership in cooperation with the United States and Europe is an opportunity to enhance relationships with stable and like-minded partners who can help tackle global problems as part of the guarantor of security for a Europe whole and free.

With these dynamics in mind, the Center for Transatlantic Relations has been exploring the opportunities to enhance security cooperation among the United States, the Nordic states and the Baltic countries. Our initiative was intended to give life to goals set forth by President Obama, together with Nordic and Baltic leaders, to advance mutually supportive efforts on a range of security-related issues.

During the course of our project we engaged directly with senior officials and convened the best policy minds to focus on cooperative possibilities to enhance U.S.-Nordic-Baltic security cooperation. We asked experts from throughout the Nordic-Baltic region and from the United States to offer recommendations.

Our discussions covered a broad agenda, reflective of the diverse issues addressed by Nordic-Baltic-U.S. cooperation. We looked at integrated approaches to preventive diplomacy and security. We considered more effective ways to cooperate to advance our common vision of a Europe whole, free, and at peace, particularly in light of Russia's forceful and illegal annexation of the Crimean region of Ukraine, its continued intrusions into Ukraine, and its tactics of intimidation, cyber attacks, use of energy dependence, and control of media assets to influence countries throughout Europe and Eurasia. We looked at ways to strengthen Nordic/Baltic defense capabilities and how they might affect U.S.-Nordic-Baltic defense cooperation. We also looked at alternative NATO partnership architectures and other important issues such as energy security and prospects for U.S.-Nordic-Baltic cooperation on issues related to the Arctic and the High North.

Throughout our deliberations we focused on the changing nature of U.S. engagement in northern Europe and the continent more broadly, and offer recommendations regarding the future U.S. role in Europe.

We wish to thank our colleagues Hans Binnendijk. Erik Brattberg, Miriam Cunningham, Sylvia Staneva and Charlotte Cunningham for their engagement and hard work on this project. We are also grateful for the generous support provided by the Foreign Ministry of Sweden for this project. All authors write in their personal capacity, and their views do not represent any government, institution or organization.

Our policy recommendations are our own, and do not necessarily reflect the views of all authors on every subject.

Daniel S. Hamilton
Andras Simonyi
Debra L. Cagan

Center for Transatlantic Relations
School of Advanced International Studies
Johns Hopkins University

Executive Summary

The Nordic-Baltic region holds a special place when it comes to the resilience of free and democratic societies. Today, more than ever in the last 25 years, the integrity of the "West" is at stake. Nordic-Baltic-U.S. security cooperation is at the heart of the future of the region. Sharing values and norms and a commitment to pragmatic cooperation, and as net contributors to economic growth, foreign policy management, development assistance and security, the Nordic-Baltic countries remain strong partners for the United States. The region shows that market democracy works, human rights and the rule of law are respected, a positive outward vision of the world is still possible, and that there is still important work ahead for transatlantic cooperation. When Cold War tensions faded, the countries of the region turned from being security importers to being security exporters. For over a decade these countries proved their ability to deploy and conduct operations a long way from Europe, in Afghanistan.

Now, a whole new set of challenges to a Europe whole and free has emerged. Northern European insecurities have returned, sparked in particular by Russia's illegal annexation of the Crimean region of Ukraine; its active support for Ukrainian separatists; deployment of thousands of troops into Ukraine and on the Russian-Ukrainian border; cyber attacks in Estonia; provocative military activities towards the Baltic states, Finland and Sweden; and efforts to intimidate Baltic and other European energy consumers. Greater uncertainties also beset the High North, with its shared borders and special neighborhood, due to the rapid rate of climate change, the pace of natural resource development, the nature and rate of public and private investments, changing transportation patterns, and potential security challenges presented by Arctic and non-Arctic states alike.

These new challenges and opportunities call for enhanced U.S.-Nordic-Baltic security cooperation. Our key recommendations are noted below, followed by a more detailed summary of the book:

- **Emphasize NATO's eastern flank and northern borders** by enhancing its command structure; deploying sustained (perhaps even permanent) multinational ground forces in the Baltic states and Poland; prepositioning equipment for additional forces in those countries; and training and exercising to make NATO more resilient and better able to respond to strategic surprises and disruptive shocks. The 2014 NATO Summit took important steps in this direction. But more should be done.

- **Move forward with a new phase of NATO partnership relations for Sweden and Finland.** Sweden and Finland should declare their intention to join the Alliance. The region is stronger as a whole than it can ever be as individual countries with separate defense pacts. Short of this step, Sweden and Finland should become Premier Interoperable Partners (PIP)—a level of engagement beyond what was offered at the 2014 NATO Summit.

- **Revisit the meaning of deterrence for the High North,** including enhanced diplomacy, routine communication channels and a military presence with greater national military capabilities and regional multinational training and exercises, which will in turn reduce chances of misunderstanding and conflict.

- **Create a common Nordic-Baltic energy market and increase cooperation and integration with the United States on energy security.**

- **Maintain the Arctic commitment to environmental stewardship and enhance the Arctic security architecture through links to NATO and increased maritime and security operations.**

- **Push for the early conclusion of TTIP to ensure economic prosperity and a more secure transatlantic relationship.**

Security and Defense Challenges

Develop a NATO with full spectrum capability

- *Boost deployable combat capability as a first step.* Longer term, tie higher defense expenditures to efficiency improvements and critical means that can enable a full spectrum capability.

- *Implement NATO's Readiness Action Plan* to counter across the spectrum of contingencies, from hybrid attacks to rapid mobilization.

- *Equip the Alliance to be more resilient to strategic surprises and disruptive shocks.*

- *Strive for a common view of the regional patterns of Russia's behavior and its future intentions.*

- *No-excuses burden sharing.* The United States expects Europe to take more responsibility for its own security. If allies and partners want a United States committed to the security of the High North and Europe, they must do more to share the burden. It is unacceptable to point to development aid or other non-military contributions as an offset against an adequate defense commitment.

Reform NATO's Command Structure

Increase the regional focus of the NATO Command Structure and define geographical areas of responsibility for the two Joint Forces Commands. Ensure a closer link between NATO's command structure and national headquarters; a Norwegian initiative to strengthen the link between Norway's national headquarters outside Bodø in Northern Norway and NATO's command structure could lead the way.

Bolster NATO's Focus on its Eastern Flank

- *Reassess and test on a regular basis NATO's contingency plans for the collective defense of the Baltic states and Poland via robust and complex exercises.* Such exercises should regularly bring Allied troops to the Baltic countries, especially from the U.S. and larger European allies.

- *Commit to a sustained multinational presence of NATO forces— including but not limited to U.S. troops in the region—*focused on specialists with skills in, *inter alia*, intelligence, electronic and cyber counter-measures, air-to-ground fire support, anti-tank and anti-air defense systems and host nation support, rather than on large troop formations. These forces should also engage in regular exercises with regional allies and partners.

- *Establish Host Nation Support (HNS) arrangements in the Baltic states* to facilitate a rapid Allied response to unforeseen and quickly unfolding events. NATO infrastructure funds should be used to build up the needed facilities. In each country, local manpower should be recruited, trained and exercised.

- *Pre-position military equipment,* fuel and lubricants, as well as different kinds of ammunition to raise the deterrence threshold and bring Allied troops faster into their operations areas.

- *Develop and extend NATO's Framework Nation Concept* to both force development and operations; Multinational Corps Northeast (MNC-NE) could become a model of an enhanced regional NATO command to the East.

- *Encourage increased defense spending by Poland and the Baltic states.*

- *Continue to focus on missile defense.*

- *Bolster Baltic states' national defense quickly through donations of excess equipment or through favorable conditions to purchase such equipment.*

Extend NORDEFCO to the Baltic States

This new Nordic Baltic Defense Cooperation (NORBALDEFCO) would cement the prominent role of Sweden and Finland as premier partners of NATO; strengthen the NATO aspect of Nordic-Baltic security; enable greater interoperability among regional forces; facilitate security cooperation with the United States; and open opportunities for greater cooperation with Poland, Germany and other allies.

- *Upstream focus:* defense planning; professional military education cooperation; training facilities.

- *Downstream focus:* training and exercises; defense capacity building in third countries.

Revisit the Meaning of Deterrence with Regard to the High North

- Enhance diplomacy, regularized communication channels and routine military presence to reduce chances of misunderstanding and conflict.

- Define the threshold for defensive action.

- Consider greater national military capabilities and presence.

- Emphasize multinational training and exercises in the High North.

Develop Preparedness and Responsiveness

The NATO Response Force should place more emphasis on collective defense, deterrence and reassurance. Enhance the relevance and usability of standing naval forces.

Increase Situational Awareness

The Alliance needs better political and military situational awareness regarding the environment in which it has direct responsibilities, as well as turbulent regions to its east and south. Allies and willing partners need to continue work to improve geographical expertise, update threat assessments, and facilitate closer intelligence cooperation. These assessments must also consider Russia's political, economic and societal influence in NATO and EU member states that may limit independent action and threaten governmental stability.

Improve Contingency Planning

Update existing contingency plans and develop new ones to ensure that the Alliance can perform its core tasks. Turn strategic guidance into concepts of operations and ultimately develop corresponding national plans. Host nation agreements, command and control arrangements and logistics are key to operationalization and implementation.

NATO and Partners

NATO's current partnership framework has run its course. 25 years since the fall of the Iron Curtain, the challenges of both European and global security have evolved considerably—as have the nature, needs and opportunities of partnership.

Sweden and Finland Should Join NATO

- The most straightforward way to strengthen Nordic-Baltic defense capabilities and to enhance security throughout northern Europe is for Sweden and Finland to join NATO. Each country would be more secure as a full NATO member, and NATO would be better with Sweden and Finland as members.

- Sweden and Finland also add geographic space to the Alliance, which would enhance NATO's credibility with its Baltic members.

- Nordic-Baltic defense cooperation would become more effective and efficient in both development and use of capabilities. Alternatives to membership offer only more circumscribed means for less effect.

- Membership for Sweden and Finland underscore that NATO's door remains open and that partnerships really mean something.

Short of such a step, as outlined below, Sweden and Finland should become Premier Interoperable Partners (PIP)—going beyond the 2014 NATO Summit offerings—and exploit to the fullest extent a new NATO opt-in model.

NATO's Partnerships should Evolve *from a hub-and-spokes model to a non-hierarchical network of partnerships linked via five nodes or clusters.*

- ***A basic cluster of partners engage in political dialogue*** with NATO to improve mutual understanding, avoid misconceptions, and find common areas of interest. This could constitute the entry point for new partners.

- ***A second cluster should consist of NATO working with partners who wish to develop their capabilities and their interoperability,*** in order to be able to contribute to peace support operations and other activities.

- ***A third cluster should be a special track for those countries that have declared their intent to join the Alliance.***

- ***A fourth cluster would consist of international organizations*** partnering with NATO.

- *The fifth cluster—which would hold special significance for U.S.-Nordic-Baltic cooperation—would consist of Premier Interoperable Partners (PIP).*

This would include leading countries that are both willing and able to contribute to NATO efforts beyond the PfP norm. Countries such as Sweden, Finland or Australia, for instance, have in recent years formed deep partnerships with NATO. They have a serious military track record on par with many of the most capable NATO allies, and are already largely interoperable with NATO. The 2014 NATO Summit offered a new Interoperability Platform for these three countries, plus Georgia and Jordan. But this model would go further.

- Criteria for eligibility might include a partner's military capability, its degree of military interoperability, its history of participation in military operations and exercises led by the Alliance, as well as its participation in programs such as the Planning and Review Process; the Operational Capabilities Concept Evaluation and Feedback; and forces such as the NATO Response Force.

- PIP should not be viewed as a substitute for membership, nor is it aimed at replacing the need for membership action plans. It is a tool to promote partners' work towards becoming more able to contribute to addressing the challenges facing them and NATO. It will become increasingly difficult to discern a PIP from a member, save for the critical and sensitive issue of collective defense.

NATO Should Offer Premier Interoperable Partners (PIP) a New Opt-In Model

- *Provide for structured and regular consultations at the political, military and intelligence levels* with the North Atlantic Council (NAC), the Military Committee, the International Staff and the International Military Staff. This would occur routinely on all levels, including ministerials and summits. These would not be plus-one models, but a practical and regular part of doing business at NATO headquarters, the Supreme Headquarters Allied Powers Europe (SHAPE) and at the Allied Command Transformation (ACT) in Norfolk. Consultations would cover all relevant matters related to operational connectivity, capability development, capacity building as well as prevention and thematic issues of political significance;

- *Offer early involvement in policy discussions relevant to operations, a role in planning and decision shaping relating to exercises, education and training, and full access to NATO Smart Defense programs and to the Connected Forces Initiative;*

- *Offer opportunity to participate in the NATO Response Force*, which would be used as a facilitator for continued interoperability and force integration;

- *Offer opportunity not only to participate, but to have a role in planning related to force rotations and related operations;*

- *Offer opportunity to opt-in or opt-out of exercises, education, training and operations* and to make recommendations for exercises, training and education and even for potential operations.

Lift and Extend the e-PINE Agenda

Cooperation between the United States and Nordic-Baltic countries is facilitated by the Enhanced Partnership in Northern Europe (e-PINE), a unique vehicle for honest discussion on most relevant regional and global issues between like-minded countries. Yet e-PINE could be better utilized:

- *Strengthen current e-PINE dialogues by annual ministerial consultations.*

- *Extend e-PINE consultations by including other relevant ministries and agencies beyond foreign affairs ministries.*

- *Keep Eastern Partnership countries at the top of the e-PINE agenda.* The most effective counter to Russian intrusion into Ukraine, for instance, is to work with Ukrainians to make their transition to a more representative, effective and prosperous democracy a success. Baltic states offer relevant experience in open society transition; Nordic states and the United States offer extensive expertise in championing democracy and human rights around the world.

- *Pioneer Transatlantic Cooperation to Enhance Societal Resilience.* Transboundary arteries carrying people, ideas, money, energy, goods and services criss-cross modern societies and contribute significantly to economic growth and prosperity. They are essential sinews of open societies, daily communications, and the global economy. Yet this dynamism also creates vulnerabilities that can lead to intentional or accidental disruption of such critical functions as transportation, energy flows, medical services, food supply chains and business systems, communications, cyber links and financial networks. Governments are accustomed to protect their territories; now they must protect their society's critical functions, the networks that sustain them, and the connections those networks bring with other societies. These developments call for private-public partnerships and close interactions among governments, the private sector, the scientific community, and non-governmental organizations.

As leading democratic knowledge economies, the United States and its Nordic-Baltic partners are at the forefront of efforts to forge greater societal resilience in the face of such challenges. They also share a keen interest in ensuring the societal resilience of other countries, particularly on their borders, since strong efforts in one country may mean little of neighboring systems are weak. Russia's hybrid tactics used to subvert Ukrainian authority is but the latest example of this growing security challenge. The U.S. and its Nordic-Baltic partners should share experience and pioneer new approaches to societal security, both among themselves and also with a view to "projecting resilience forward" to others.

- *Baltic states should design and execute complex comprehensive security plans* that would engage civilian and military authorities together to sustain and defend the vital functions of society.

- *U.S., Nordic and Baltic states should use the e-PINE framework to advance a Resilient Societies Initiative* to share good practice and pioneer new approaches to societal resilience, including possible new forms of diplomatic, intelligence, economic, and law enforcement cooperation; customs, air, and seaport security; data protection and information exchange; bio-resilience and critical infrastructure protection.

- *Project Resilience Forward.* E-PINE partners should make a concerted effort, together with other NATO and EU allies as appropriate, to work with Ukraine and other Eastern Partnership countries to improve societal resilience to corruption, psychological warfare, and intentional or natural disruptions to cyber, financial and energy networks and other critical infrastructure, with a strong focus on prevention but also response.

- *Pioneer a public-private Global Movement Management Initiative (GMMI)* as an innovative governance framework to align security and resilience with commercial imperatives in global movement systems, including shipping, air transport, and even the internet.

- *Facilitate U.S. engagement in regional projects* or initiate new forms of cooperation, especially related to energy, infrastructure, defense and security. Strengthen cooperation in information security and share research and expertise.

- *Priotitize enhanced maritime cooperation in the Baltic Sea.* As a seasonally ice-covered regional sea, the Baltic Sea holds a number of similarities to Arctic coastal waters. A full range of joint operations and exercises (for example, coastal naval operations, maritime law enforcement, search and rescue and environmental response focused on oil spills) can be held with full U.S.-Nordic-Baltic participation.

- *Pioneer a study of the Baltic Sea as an effective ship emissions control area.* A cooperative research effort, given the winter conditions in the Baltic Sea, could be focused on understanding oil spills in ice and the challenging aspects of winter cleanup in extreme cold environments. Knowledge of cold regions marine operations gained through joint exercises can enhance the regional readiness of the maritime agencies and coast guards and provide operational experience of value to future Arctic state responses.

- *Strengthen Unified Approaches within International Forums.* The U.S.-Nordic-Baltic relationship can prove fruitful within the International Maritime Organization (IMO), the World Meteorological Organization (WMO), the International Hydrogaphic Organization and other bodies. Unified approaches to a broad range of emerging issues can provide significant leverage with the global maritime industry.

- *Facilitate greater cooperation and sharing of good practice regarding e-governance*, including high quality government service delivery, anti-corruption transparency, citizen participation, and the use of state of the art technology in providing government services.

- *Raise the profile of inclusiveness issues.* The ultimate test of a healthy society is fairness, inclusiveness, equal citizen rights and equal opportunity. All nine countries face challenges of inclusiveness and the fair treatment of minorities, and have relevant experience to share and from which to learn.

- *Create and provide sustained funding for a joint U.S.-Nordic-Baltic Center*—virtual or actual—that would connect experts of the nine countries for purpose- specific tasks and solutions.

Energy Security

Create a Common Nordic-Baltic Energy Market

The Nordic-Baltic region has not worked together strategically on energy issues. Nordic-Baltic efforts to integrate their energy systems and diversify energy supplies will build resilience by diminishing vulnerability, ending the isolation of the Baltic region's energy sector, reducing Russia's ability to use energy coercion, and better managing future energy challenges.

- *Norway and Denmark should use their experience with off-shore oil and gas exploration* and seismic technology to assist the Baltic states in exploring their seabed for commercially profitable hydrocarbons.

- *Sweden, Denmark and Finland should fund and administer a robust program for wind and bio-mass production in the three Baltic states.*

- *Finland should take the lead in assisting Lithuania* to carry out a new analysis regarding the commercial viability of constructing a new nuclear power plant.

- *The Baltic states should speed up integration of their energy sectors*, including electricity, natural gas, renewables and efficiency standards.

- *The Nordic countries should build additional gas and oil storage*, thus bringing more energy supply redundancy for the three Baltic states.

- *Sweden and Finland should provide additional human and financial resources to the Cyber-security Center in Tallinn and the Energy Security Center in Vilnius.* The fragile power grids, refineries and pipeline pumping stations in the Baltic States should be made more secure so as to be able to sustain operations in the event of another cyber-attack from the East.

- *Norway, with its energy exports and massive foreign reserves, could use some of its oil and gas resources to provide competition to the Russian monopoly import role.* Furnishing a small amount of discounted oil and LNG might incentivize Russian companies to reduce their energy bullying and agree to more reasonable prices.

- *Promote regional cooperation in nuclear safety and security.*

- *Develop national capacities to prevent illicit trafficking of nuclear and radioactive materials.*

- *Transform NATO's Energy Security Center of Excellence (ENSEC COE)* based in Lithuania into a regional center focused on a more efficient conduct of operations and enhanced protection of critical energy infrastructure.

- *Extend to all Nordic-Baltic countries the 2013 Lithuania-U.S. agreement to counter nuclear smuggling.*

- *Support the EU's Third Energy Package* as a crucial element to connect Baltic energy sectors with the rest of Europe.

- *Finland and Estonia must sort out their interests and agree on the venue for a Baltic Sea regional LNG terminal* in a way that allows the project to receive EU financing.

- *The Baltic states must move faster to resolve existing disputes over energy issues,* for example, the sea-border dispute between Latvia and Lithuania should be resolved in order to attract foreign energy investors to the region.

- *The United States should open natural gas exports to Europe*—it would be a game changer.

Develop the U.S.-Nordic Security Dialogue. Elements of an agenda include

- *Step up consultations on Wider Europe.* Experience of Nordic countries in supporting those transitions in the Baltic states in the 1990s could provide valuable lessons for Ukraine, Moldova and Georgia;

- *Lift the importance of the Arctic and High North.* Maritime security and safety is one potential avenue for enhanced U.S.-Nordic cooperation;

- *Utilize the expertise of the Nordic countries in civilian crisis management*, particularly with regard to promoting civil-military ties in conflict settings.

Advance a U.S.-Nordic-Baltic Arctic Agenda

The U.S.-Nordic relationship will be central to maintaining such a stable and peaceful Arctic region. The Baltic states, located on a regional sea with heavy commercial marine traffic, also have key maritime security and environmental interests that are synergistic with an evolving maritime Arctic. The Arctic Ocean and the Baltic Sea are waterways that should be made safe, secure and open to all for trade.

Use the 2015-2017 U.S. Arctic Council Chairmanship to

- *Maintain the Arctic Council's priority focus on environmental stewardship.*

- *Promote the International Maritime Organization's mandatory Polar Code* for ships operating in polar waters during its implementation phase following agreement in spring 2015.

- *Further develop the new Arctic Economic Council* with a focus on sustainability issues.

- *Seek agreement among Arctic states to share marine traffic information to enhance Arctic maritime domain awareness.* Traffic data passed in real-time among the Arctic states can reduce the risks of potential incidents and facilitate maritime response while also providing an integrated, circumpolar view of Arctic commercial marine operations.

Hold the First Arctic Council Summit of heads of government in 2016, the 20th anniversary of the signing of the Ottawa Declaration that established the Council.

- *Seek agreement on modalities governing Arctic research, search and rescue and other possible areas.*

- *Reinforce the view that Arctic states are committed to protecting Arctic people and the environment, and to maintaining the region as a safe, stable and peaceful place.*

- *Use U.S.-Nordic-Baltic cooperation, outside the mandate of the Council,* to advance shared maritime interests, including joint marine and naval exercises in littoral waters, to forge a more effective network of capacity and resiliency.

- *Develop Arctic security architecture further, and link it more closely to NATO's defense and security policy.* Increased commercial activity in the High North does not necessarily create more tension and rivalry and should not in itself be considered a security policy challenge. Yet more activity increases the need for routine Allied military presence as a stabilizing factor, particularly with regard to surveillance and support to search and rescue operations.

- *Enhance Arctic maritime and security operations.* Focus joint Arctic maritime operations on joint search and rescue, emergency response and law enforcement. Selected operations closely related to civil functions could include Russia directly as a way to buid regional resiliency.

- *Conduct coastal Arctic naval operations* (on a smaller scale than full NATO deepwater operations) among Nordic and U.S. Coast Guard and Navy air and ship units. Leveraging this combined capability in Arctic littoral waters and in Baltic Sea waters provides enhanced competency and expertise in cold region war-fighting and possible future enforcement actions.

- *Joint testing of new technologies,* for example unmanned underwater vehicles for coastal mine laying operations in Arctic conditions, would benefit all partners.

- *Using the icebreaking capacity of Finland, Sweden and Estonia in joint training exercises would be a unique contribution* to understanding real-time operations in ice-covered waters.

Security and Prosperity

Economic prosperity is one of the greatest guarantors of a Europe whole and free. Strong economic performance underpins U.S. and European capabilities and commitments to common security.

Use U.S.-Nordic-Baltic Cooperation to Push Early Conclusion and Ratification of the Transatlantic Trade and Investment Partnership (TTIP).

- TTIP promises to unleash significant opportunities to generate jobs, trade and investment across the Atlantic, but TTIP is far more than a free-trade agreement, and is likely to have an outsized positive impact on US-Nordic-Baltic cooperation, offering significant geopolitical potential as a values-based, rules-based initiative likely to

  - strengthen Western economic and social cohesion

  - offer a second transatlantic anchor to NATO

  - stimulate U.S. investment and reinforce the U.S. commitment to Europe

  - strengthen transatlantic energy ties

  - contribute to greater attractiveness of the Western model

  - spark greater links among U.S.-Nordic-Baltic knowledge economies

  - bolster the resilience of central and east European economies

  - resonate across Wider Europe, especially Ukraine, Moldova, Georgia, even Belarus and Russia.

Push back against the Kremlin's "active measures," which include tactics of pressure and intimidation, to derail the TTIP within the EU, while indicating a readiness to engage with Russia economically on the basis of the rules and procedures being advanced through the TTIP.

Defense Trade

Consider a US-Nordic-Baltic Initiative for joint development of an unmanned maritime system (UMS), focused on such missions as mine clearing and anti-submarine operations

There is currently no future year United States Navy program funding to produce and field a next-generation system. A UMS project that could induce the U.S. Department of Defense and the U.S. technology release community to work more cooperatively with Nordic and Baltic governments; enhance the overall technology transfer environment; and send a significant and potent message to Moscow about the unity of the transatlantic relationship.

Produce an industry-led "shadow TTIP" agreement for the defense sector

The U.S. and EU have excluded the "sensitive defense" industry from TTIP negotiations. Yet TTIP can be a test vehicle to discuss bigger transatlantic defense market issues. Nordic defense industries have unique technological niches in certain areas that could be of interest to U.S. industries. Nordic countries are open to transatlantic defense integration and already have strong bilateral relations with the United States. They should initiate this effort.

Chapter 1

Security Challenges in the High North: Norwegian Perspectives

Ine Eriksen Søreide

Look North more often. Go against the wind. You will get redder cheeks. Find the rugged path. Keep to it. It's shorter. North is best. Winter's sky of flames. Summer nights' sun miracle. Go against the wind. Climb mountains. Look North. More often. This is a long country. Most is North.

"North," Rolf Jacobsen

Any security assessment must take geography, distance and resources into account. Norway's extensive coastline, facing the North Atlantic, the Barents Sea and the Arctic Ocean creates an enormous expanse of territorial waters and a vast economic zone, especially large in comparison to our population of five million. Norway has jurisdiction over about one million square miles at sea, which is seven times larger than our mainland territory. Norway is a maritime nation. We have Europe's longest coastline. Our prosperity is closely linked to the sea, with considerable reserves of petroleum, natural gas, minerals and seafood. We are the world's second largest fish exporter and we are the third largest energy exporter. We also have one of the world's largest merchant fleets.

The *High North*, defined as the European Arctic, is a key priority for the Norwegian government. Although the High North is an elastic concept and open to interpretation, I prefer the traditional definition that refers to the northern parts of the Nordic countries and Russia. This includes the oceans and islands from the Kara Sea, including the archipelago of Svalbard, to the southeastern shores of Greenland. This is part of the wider "circumpolar North," or the "Arctic region," which also includes the United States, Canada and Greenland. While the High North is and will remain Norway's core area of interest in the north, Norwegian policy also has a broader Arctic perspective.

The North Atlantic Treaty Organization (NATO)'s area of responsibility stretches all the way to the North Pole and one of Norway's most important contributions to our allies is, as such, to safeguard the High North. While the wider Arctic region is largely a question of "soft" security challenges—such as handling environmental issues, sabotage, smuggling, illegal trafficking and transportation accidents— the High North is also a matter of "hard" security. Although the High North is a relatively peaceful, stable and secure part of the world, it is not immune to conflict. Norway works actively to safeguard stability and security and one measure is Norwegian and Allied military presence. Through presence, we acquire situational awareness and local knowledge, which serves as a basis for prudent decision making.

I would like to use this opening chapter to discuss challenges and opportunities for the High North, emphasize the implications for Norwegian defense and security and recommend a set of steps that NATO should take to become a more capable and better prepared Alliance. I strongly believe that we need to reinvigorate NATO: we need to recommit ourselves to the common values that have kept the Alliance strong and relevant since its inception; restore confidence in the transatlantic relationship; and refocus on ability to plan, lead and execute collective defense missions. This formula underpins the very purpose of the Alliance: to safeguard the freedom and security of its members through political and military means. For the Alliance to be politically credible, it needs to be militarily capable.

The Growing Importance of the Arctic

The changing climate—melting polar ice and thawing tundra—has led to increased interest in the Arctic. The average temperature has risen at twice the rate of the global average in the last 50 years. We are still talking low temperatures and harsh conditions, but there is greater access to natural resources, longer sailing seasons for maritime transport and growing commercial activities. For example, ships going from the Netherlands to Japan can reduce the distance of their voyage by 4,500 miles if they travel via the Northern Sea Route north of Russia rather than through the Suez Canal, and their cargo will not be subject to the canal's draft limits, thus also increasing their cargo load.

The Arctic holds a considerable mass of undiscovered recoverable oil and gas resources. Most of it is offshore. Fisheries, extraction of oil, gas and minerals, maritime transport and safety and tourism are significant industries. Although shorter transportation routes—real and potential—are being explored, in-and-out commercial activities have already increased markedly. Consequently, countries near and far from the Arctic see new political, economic and military opportunities. As a result, we see new players entering the region. China, India and Japan are among the countries that have increased their presence in the Arctic.

Russia and the High North

Among the five littoral Arctic states—Canada, Denmark (Greenland), Norway, Russia and the United States—Russia is the only non-NATO member. It is a great power and it has more Arctic land, coastline and waters than any other nation. Given Russia's size and location, it plays a prominent role in shaping the security environment in the High North and the wider circumpolar North. Moscow is a determined player with high ambitions in the Arctic, and core realism is an important feature of Russian strategic culture.

The High North undoubtedly will remain important in Russia's maritime and nuclear strategy. It contains ports with ice-free waters throughout the year and is the home of the Northern Fleet, which includes the majority of Russia's ballistic missile submarines. Russia has modernized its armed forces considerably the last few years and uses this region as testing ground for new weapons systems, military training and large-scale exercises. Russia's airborne nuclear capability is another important element of the strategic environment of the North. The strategic bombers of Russia's Long Range Aviation represent the core of that capability. In 2007, Russia resumed regular strategic flights over the Arctic and started to make more extensive use of bases in the north. We do not regard these activities as aimed directly against Norway or any other state, but the important point is that the High North is a region where various political, economic and military interests come together.

Norway seeks a constructive relationship with Russia. We have enjoyed a thousand years of peaceful coexistence and we conduct practical and pragmatic cooperation in the High North. However, the

Norwegian government strongly condemns Russia's recent violation of Ukraine's sovereignty and territorial integrity. We consider the actions a clear breach of international law. Using military force— might over right—to redraw national borders is unacceptable. These actions challenge the notion of a "Europe whole and free" and our values of democracy, individual liberty and the rule of law. Russia's illegal *de facto* annexation of Crimea and destabilizing efforts in Eastern Ukraine have reshaped the geopolitical map of Europe and derailed cooperation between Moscow and the West for years to come.

Mechanisms for Cooperation

Although we see increased activity, any conception of fierce and uncontrolled competition over resources in the region is misleading. The area is well-regulated and the legal framework is clearly spelled out. By signing the *Ilulissat Declaration* (2008), the five Arctic littoral states committed themselves to settle unresolved issues of jurisdiction and sovereignty diplomatically through existing legal mechanisms. The United Nations Convention on the Law of the Seas (UNCLOS) constitutes the legal basis for activities in the region. In order to secure stability and predictability with new players in the region, we should strengthen the legal framework in areas in which existing regulations may not be sufficient.

In the historical Maritime Delimitation Treaty (2010), Russia and Norway solved their unresolved maritime boundaries after 40 years of negotiation. Under the agreement, the disputed area of 68,000 square miles was divided into two parts of approximately the same size. In addition to establishing the delimitation line, the agreement contains provisions that ensure the continuation of Norwegian-Russian fishery cooperation as well as provisions concerning exploitation of any transboundary hydrocarbon deposits.

There is a high degree of common understanding, constructive dialogue and increasing cooperation among the various actors in the High North. A number of cooperation fora have emerged in the last two decades. The Arctic Council is the most important forum for political discussions on Arctic issues. It includes the eight Arctic states (Canada, Denmark, Iceland, Finland, Norway, Sweden, Russia and the United States). Canada currently holds the two-year chairmanship and the United States will take over in May 2015. Norway, which hosts the permanent secretariat in Tromsø, remains a supporter of inviting observers. Currently, 12 non-Arctic countries have been admitted (France, Germany, Italy, the Netherlands, Poland, Spain, the United Kingdom, China, Japan, South Korea, Singapore and India), in addition to nine inter-governmental and inter-parliamentary organizations. Inclusion of non-Arctic stakeholders is increasingly important as more and more nations seek footprints in the North.

Another important forum is the Barents Euro-Arctic Council, which seeks to promote business development, protect the environment and maintain settlement patterns. Members are the five Nordic countries and Russia, and the permanent international secretariat is in Kirkenes, Norway. In addition to regional governance, local authorities work closely together to make the best use of human and natural resources in the Barents region and beyond.

The High North offers an example of how small and big nations can work together within international accepted legal frameworks. It is also an example of nations coming together to find common ground in an area of strategic importance. We seek to strengthen consultative and cooperative mechanisms. The Arctic security architecture needs to be developed further, and we would like to link it more closely to NATO's defense and security policy.

Perspectives on Norwegian Security

Increased commercial activity in the High North does not necessarily create more tension and rivalry and should not in itself be considered a security policy challenge. At the same time, we believe that more activity increases the need for routine Allied military presence as a stabilizing factor. It is in everyone's interest to maintain safety and security in this harsh and vulnerable area. Military assets are a key element with regard to surveillance and support to search and rescue operations. Military forces at an appropriate level should be considered a natural actor in the High North.

Norway sees no immediate threats to its sovereignty or territorial integrity, neither in the High North nor on Norwegian soil, but maintains armed forces capable of deterring and defending against pressure, assault and attack on Norwegian territory and adjacent areas. This is not only paramount to Norwegian sovereignty, but an important contribution to the security of NATO. NATO and Norwegian national presence in the High North seek to promote stability and predictability and demonstrate resolve.

Norwegian military presence in the High North is not directed at any state; rather, it reflects the fact that Norway has important assets and interests worthy of protecting and defending. This includes executing sovereignty and authority over the Svalbard archipelago in accordance with the Svalbard Treaty of 1920.

The Norwegian Armed Forces play an important role in the High North. The Norwegian Joint Headquarters has been established in Bodø, just north of the Polar Circle. We have invested in AEGIS frigates, coast guard vessels and maritime helicopters. Our acquisition of new fighter aircraft, the F-35, is also a part of this overall investment. Military platforms are important, but at the end of the day these are operated by men and women. We also have started a major personnel reform to ensure that we have the right people at the right place at the right time—now and for the foreseeable future.

NATO is the cornerstone of Norwegian security and defense, and stability in the High North is best secured through the NATO Alliance. If serious threats of attacks were to occur, these must be handled within the framework of NATO's collective defense. When we scramble our F-16s to identify or intercept Russian military aircraft, we do this to protect our sovereignty and territorial integrity. But we also do it on behalf of the Alliance. We do it because preserving the integrity of NATO airspace is a collective task. The High North is not "out of area". It is "in area".

NATO's crisis-management operations, from the Balkans to Afghanistan, have been important for our collective security. Norway is a strong supporter of partnership programs in their various forms, be it defense and security sector reform or integrity building. We need to continue this work. But we must also ensure that the Alliance has the ability to plan, lead and execute the collective defense mission, in accordance with the Washington Treaty of 1949, particularly Article 5 of the Treaty. After all, NATO's most important task is to prevent an attack on Allied nations, to deter and dissuade a potential aggressor from contemplating any military action against NATO territory and populations and to defend our people should it come to that. Our deterrence posture is closely linked with the credibility of our collective defense capability and the ability to provide reassurance to Allies. Although the Arctic is mostly a matter of soft security challenges that are on the margins of the core obligation, the Alliance needs to think of possible "spillover effects" and strengthen the mechanisms for handling them before they develop into hard security encounters.

Norway has a long-standing tradition of hosting allied training and exercises. We consider it important to improve interoperability and cooperation on strategic, operational and tactical levels. The biannual Exercise Cold Response is an excellent example: in 2014, 1,000 troops from 16 nations operated together in icy weather and low temperatures. Norway will continue actively to facilitate a wide range of allied and partner training also in the future. We also have a well-established system for cross-border training with Sweden and Finland, and we work at strengthening military exercises and training between Nordic, Nordic-Baltic, and NATO programs. Part of this is formalized in Nordic Defence Cooperation (NORDEFCO), and together with Finland, Sweden and Denmark we seek to strengthen further our relationship with Estonia, Latvia, and Lithuania. I would like to see a further strengthening of the Nordic-Baltic relationship.

A NATO More Capable and Better Prepared

What makes NATO unique and sets it apart from all other alliances and organizations is the combination of its integrated military structures, collective defense planning, collective capabilities and its permanent political decision-making mechanisms. This makes it the only multinational organization that can carry out high-intensity operations on short notice. Such an ability must be maintained and developed. This requires serious, sustained, long-term political and financial commitment from Allies. But NATO is more than a military alliance. It is also a political alliance based on common values and shared security interests. This makes NATO a source of stability in a complex and rapidly changing security landscape.

As we draw down our forces in Afghanistan, Norway is arguing that this is the time to refocus more efforts on NATO's ability to do collective defense. It is not a matter of either crisis management operations *or* collective defense, but rather a need to strike the right balance between these core tasks of the Alliance. Norway, therefore, proposes a set of measures aimed at a more credible and better prepared Alliance. These measures are also formulated in a policy paper written together with the United Kingdom and Poland, released to NATO in June 2014. The recommendations are generic in nature, but applicable to the entirety of NATO's territory, acknowledging that each member state has a special responsibility for its own region and vicinity. This applies to the Baltics, the Black Sea, the Mediterranean and the High North. The new policy paper is an update and revision of the Norwegian Core Area Initiative from 2008.

1. *Increase Situational Awareness.* The Alliance needs better political and military situational awareness. We need better insight into, and knowledge of, the environment in which we have responsibilities, and which might be threatened. The actions in Ukraine—and experiences from Georgia, Libya and Syria—illustrate the importance of understanding security challenges in our close vicinity. We need to continue work on geographical expertise as well as updated threat assessments. It is as such, important to facilitate closer intelligence cooperation between nations and NATO, and nations should consider ways to strengthen their intelligence-sharing mechanisms.

2. *Reform NATO's Command Structure.* We need a robust and effective command structure that can conduct the whole spectrum of NATO's tasks. We must increase the regional focus of the NATO Command Structure and define geographical areas of responsibility for the two Joint Forces Commands. This would improve and strengthen NATO's command structures as a whole. A closer linkage between NATO's command structure and national headquarters is critical. We offer to strengthen the link between our national headquarters outside Bodø in Northern Norway and NATO's command structure.

3. *Improve Contingency Planning.* We need to update existing contingency plans and develop new ones to ensure that the Alliance can perform its core tasks. We need to start with

strategic guidance, then turn these into concepts of operations and ultimately develop corresponding national plans. Host nation agreements, command and control arrangements and logistics are key elements for operationalization and implementation. These strategic documents and plans should be used to identify high-end capabilities required to meet future challenges. The Connected Forces Initiative is very promising and should be realized. We are pleased to note the ongoing work in NATO on contingency plans.

4. *Emphasize Training and Exercises.* Contingency plans will provide the framework required to ensure that training and exercises are conducted as realistically as possible. The motto "train as we fight" is just as valid now as it has been in the past. To deter hostile actions in the High North, to prevent a crisis from developing into armed conflict and to defend our population and interests should it become necessary, we need to train and exercise in the region. Multinational exercises, particularly live exercises, are important to NATO for both political and military reasons. Politically, high visibility exercises show the NATO flag and are important for public awareness. Militarily, multinational exercises are important for maintaining and improving interoperability of people, equipment and concepts of operations. Multinational exercises validate contingency plans, sharpen and prepare our forces, reassure allies and partners, and demonstrate capabilities and commitments to potential adversaries. Smaller national exercises can be incorporated into the larger NATO exercise schedule.

5. *Develop Preparedness and Responsiveness.* These two elements are critical to a credible defense posture. This entails having the right kind of forces that are available, deployable and sustainable, when and where needed. As a first step, we want to see a NATO Response Force with more emphasis on collective defense and ability to provide deterrence and reassurance. We also need to enhance the relevance and usability of our Standing Naval Forces. Maritime capabilities will be a vital element of the Alliance's future deterrence posture. A core element in this regard is to ensure that "high-end forces" are

used for "high-end tasks". A broadly composed flexible force readily available to provide reassurance to Allies on short notice would be a useful tool to signal NATO commitments, cohesion and determination. The German-led Framework Nation concept and the UK-led Joint Expeditionary Force initiative are worthy of further exploration and operationalization.

6. *Strengthen the Transatlantic Rrelationship.* A strong and sound relationship with North America is key to maintaining stability in Europe. U.S. engagement and leadership and a Europe that is willing to assume more of the burden for collective security are essential. We fully understand that the United States expects Europe to take more responsibility for its own security and with that give priority to their defense budgets (and on what they actually spend their budgets). We need a United States committed to the security of the High North and Europe, and we will do our part to improve the burden-sharing.

In short, two factors are essential to a secure, stable and prosperous future: continued and sustained U.S. engagement and leadership in Europe; and a strengthening of the European pillar in NATO. These two factors are both interconnected and mutually dependent. It is important for Norway that we ensure a capable and credible Alliance for the 21st century. This requires leadership, organizational coherence and a military capacity that underpins the pillars of deterring threats from external actors and providing reassurance to member states. We need to put collective defense higher on the agenda, we need to identify and find measures against emerging threats (conventional and non-conventional, regular and otherwise) and we need to think globally about security (events in the Greater Middle East and the Asia-Pacific region can also affect our immediate region). This may well challenge the "in-area" and "out-of-area" definition and the grey area between soft and hard security.

Conclusion: Look North More Often

In closing, we need to adapt to changing circumstances and develop a NATO that can respond to present and future challenges. For two decades, NATO has to a large degree focused on international crisis management operations. Returning from more than a decade of operations in Afghanistan, we face a different world and a more complex security situation than when the operations started. We need to get back to basics and think anew at the same time. We need common priorities and a common vision. We need to agree on what is worth fighting for. For the High North, we need to revisit what deterrence really means and define our threshold for defensive action. We seek cooperation with Russia, expanding relations with the Nordic countries and maintaining a strong link with the United States. On the military side, we need national capabilities and presence—predictability, stability and communicating areas of interest, which are significant elements to avoiding misunderstanding of intent in the High North. Through diplomacy and routine of military presence in peacetime, we reduce the chance of misunderstanding and conflict. The Russians have grown accustomed to Norwegian maritime patrol aircrafts and the coastal guard operating in the High North. The military, used correctly in peacetime, strengthen our relations, but prepare us for the worst.

We believe that the key to a more capable and better prepared NATO lies in increasing situational awareness, reforming NATO's command structure, improving contingency planning, emphasizing exercises and training, developing preparedness and responsiveness and strengthening the transatlantic relationship. These six steps are relevant for safeguarding the High North and for strengthening NATO as a whole.

I am fully aware of the challenges NATO member states and partners are faced with—each region has its own set of problems—but let us not take for granted that the High North will remain forever peaceful, stable and secure. We must have a wide perspective, no doubt, but we must also "Look North More Often".

Chapter 2

Europe Whole and Free: A Baltic View

Linas Linkevicius

It isn't enough to talk about peace. One must believe in it. And it isn't enough to believe in it. One must work at it.

Eleanor Roosevelt

In the spring of 2014, Estonia, Latvia and Lithuania celebrated the 10th anniversary of their membership in the North Atlantic Treaty Organization (NATO) and European Union (EU). This historic event merits not only a celebration, but also a steady reflection on what has been achieved already and what challenges lie ahead of us.

Whenever I discuss with a euro-skeptic who doubts the success and meaning of the European project—the European Union—I am always reminded of a joke that was probably born in a similar discussion: 'a euro-skeptic asks the euro-enthusiast, "So, in the end, what has Europe given you?" The euro-enthusiast answers, "It has given me— and you—peace." The euro-skeptic is not satisfied. "What else?" "Prosperity." The euro-skeptic does not give up. "Is that all?"

The joke ends here, for there is nothing more to say. Peace is a reward in itself. For those who believe that is insufficient, there is nothing more to discuss.

It is crucial that we recall European values of peace and prosperity so that we are not taken back to days when, as President John F. Kennedy said, we could secure peace only by preparing for war. What-ever we are facing now, whatever is being lost in it, or born out of it, Europe needs to address new challenges. The Baltic states, having been through a great historic ordeal, and the Nordic states, labeling themselves as world "problem solvers," have a lot to say on these issues.

Let me start with the Nordic—Baltic region as a part of a Europe whole and free.

The region has approximately 30 million inhabitants and a combined GDP of close to 1.5 trillion dollars, which makes it the tenth or twelfth economy in the world (depending on different rankings) and fifth in Europe.

The region boasts relatively low levels of corruption, ease of doing business, as well as a high level of development and possibly the cleanest environment. Enjoying close geographical proximity, bordering the Baltic Sea and sharing many similar features, these small, yet dynamic, Nordic-Baltic countries almost 25 years ago made a choice of regional cooperation, keeping to this choice throughout Europe's big steps—whether it was EU or NATO enlargement.

Nordic-Baltic cooperation since the 1990s has taken so many forms and levels that going through the list would take another article. Numbers say it all: there are more than 50 regional meetings among Nordic and Baltic officials every year and twice as many bilateral consultations; there are dozens of regional organizations; the region accounts for up to one-half of its countries' exports; the lion's share of investments to the Nordic-Baltic countries comes from within the region; and finally, Nordic-Baltic states are interconnected by a network of banks, communication and IT enterprises. Additionally, the Nordic-Baltics share a single financial regulatory and supervisory framework; they are joined by the Schengen passport-free zone and place equal importance on high value-adding products. Besides, we all call beer ale.

Drivers of regional integration are obvious:[1] greater effectiveness and more capability to solve practical challenges, increased influence on European, transatlantic, and global issues, deeper Baltic integration in Europe, strengthened security relations between NATO and EU members.

Following the path of integration, the Nordic-Baltic countries seek to belong to a single cluster within the joint EU energy market, and massive projects have already commenced.

---

1. Damon Wilson and Magnus Nordenman, "The Nordic-Baltic Region as a Global Partner of the United States," Atlantic Council of the United States, 2011.

At the end of 2015 two medium-sized towns—Klaipėda on the eastern Baltic coast and Nybro on the western Baltic coast—will become connecting points for a 280-mile long underwater electricity cable NordBalt, enabling two-way energy flow between Sweden (Nordic states) and Lithuania (Baltic states). It might take another five years, but we are certain that all the countries of the region will eventually belong to a synchronized electricity system. Besides, a Lithuanian-Polish gas interconnection will ensure we are a part of a broader energy system. With diversified gas and oil supply channels we will finally become a cell, not an island, in the European map of energy.

That will mean a lot: first, independence from unpredictable suppliers (right now 100% of Lithuania's gas imports and 99% of its oil imports comes from a single source); and second, it will mean better prices, better planning and better business. That is why the name we chose for a liquid natural gas floating terminal that is being built for Lithuania in South Korea by a Norwegian-run company—the "Independence"—was more than symbolism. This is very real for us. All of these measures could become an example—and an answer—to other countries that struggle with energy dependence and yet do not take full advantage of regional cooperation prospects.

Whether regional cooperation is fostered by opportunities afforded by deeper economic integration, the advantage of belonging to a like-minded club of partners, or the need to address common threats and challenges, there is also a strong geopolitical incentive that makes the region unique and requires even greater achievements. That is why we turn our gaze to the Atlantic.

The transatlantic link has been essential for the region's accomplishments in the last decade.

Cooperation between the United States and the Nordic-Baltic region is established through the Enhanced Partnership in Northern Europe (e-PINE). Today, this forum provides a unique possibility for honest discussion on most relevant regional and global issues between like-minded partners and friends. Eastern Partnership countries remain at the top of our e-PINE agenda. Besides, this framework has a lot of potential in areas such as cyber security, operations and energy security.

A well-concerted economic network is another pillar that enables the region to grow. The Nordic and Baltic states fully understand the importance of the Transatlantic Trade and Investment Partnership (TTIP). United States-European Union trade is worth an estimated two billion euros per day or one third of global trade flows.

By removing tariffs and non-tariff barriers, the TTIP will create the largest free trade area. It means facilitated trade, improved standards, developed framework for international supply chains and new economic opportunities, particularly for small and medium-sized enterprises, which comprise two-thirds of all private sector jobs in Europe.

Nordic-Baltic companies are already closely linked economically with the United States. Therefore, the region is a strong supporter of TTIP. Tariff liberalization and regulatory coherence will notably improve trade in most important sectors of the region, especially for processed foods, chemicals, manufactured goods, transport equipment and motor vehicles.

But that is just one layer of the cake: TTIP also means U.S. investments in the region; an equal and non-discriminatory basis for public procurement; participation in the U.S. market; reduced costs for exporters; and, most importantly, access to U.S. energy resources, which are extremely important for the region.

The crisis in Ukraine confirmed that additional efforts are needed to reinforce the security and diversification of energy supply. Therefore, we should support ambitious energy provisions as part of TTIP, including elimination of U.S. export restrictions. Once concluded, TTIP will bring significant benefits and new opportunities for further expansion of trade and investment relations to all the Nordic–Baltic countries.

The third pillar of cooperation besides energy and trade is the most decisive for the region. Events in our neighborhood show that our countries are facing the same challenges, including to our security, despite, or perhaps exactly because, six of the region's eight countries are NATO members. Nordic countries, referring to the Stoltenberg report, have made a strong commitment to stand for one another in case of necessity. NATO contingency plans have been set for Baltic defense.

However, within the backdrop of today's tensions involving European borders, there is more the region can do, and do it together. Cooperation in the security domain is crucial and urgent.

The path has been already set: in 2011, NORDEFCO (Nordic Defence Cooperation) invited the Baltic states to join one of the format's COPAs (cooperation areas) related to human resources, including veterans issues, advanced distributed learning and gender issues. It was also decided that the Baltic states will take part in the annual NORDEFCO Military Coordination Committee. NORDEFCO, as well as the U.S.-Nordic security dialogue established in 2013, provides many opportunities to increase practical regional cooperation, starting from training and exercises, joint contributions to international operations, joint capability formation and many others.

Together with the Nordic countries and Ireland, the Baltics will soon belong to one of the EU Battle groups. As of 2015 Lithuania will contribute to the Nordic Battle group by providing a force protection platoon.

Finally, it is worth mentioning that our Nordic partners are always invited to take part in regional training exercises, such as Amber Hope, Baltic Host, Baltic Spirit, Open Spirit and Saber Strike.

The latter one is a long-standing, multilateral, multifaceted, U.S. Army Europe-led security cooperation exercise primarily focused on the three Baltic states, but also involves approximately 4,700 personnel from ten countries.

This year's exercise, completed on June 20, 2014 included participation from the United States, Canada, Denmark, Estonia, Finland, Latvia, Lithuania, Norway, Poland and United Kingdom. This was the first time Denmark and Canada have participated in the exercise.

We also have a solid record of joint training activities in our airspace, namely the Baltic Regional Training event, one of NATO's key air training events, which focuses on enhancing air interoperability among NATO and regional partners (Sweden and Finland). This training has been successfully conducted over the past five years in the äiauliai air base.

Using these activities as stepping stones, I suggest that we establish even broader joint air training activities, which would include a U.S. Air Force aviation detachment in Poland, and NATO Air Policing mission in the Baltic States, and our regional partners. This would contribute to our interoperability and strengthen our sense of solidarity.

Cyber security is another key area of cooperation identified in the 2013 U.S.-Baltic and U.S.-Nordic Summits. Indeed, cyber security is an increasingly important part of the regional agenda: two Nordic-Baltic cyber expert seminars have been held in Estonia (the first country among the Baltics to have opened NATO Cooperative Cyber Defense Center of Excellence in 2008) and in Lithuania, which has a new Center for Cyber Security, which could become a part of a larger network in the future.

We should also consider practical regional cooperation in nuclear safety and security. Nordic-Baltic cooperation and EU solidarity are especially important to ensure that nuclear energy in our common neighborhood is developed in a most responsible way and in compliance with the highest international safety and security standards. The EU has recently issued a strong message to neighboring countries in the framework of the Espoo Convention.[2]

Seeking to develop national capacities to prevent illicit trafficking of nuclear and radioactive materials, Lithuania established the Nuclear Security Center of Excellence (NSCE) in 2012 and signed the agreement for cooperation on countering nuclear smuggling with the United States in April 2013. We believe that NSCE has the potential and ambition to become a regional center.

Nordic-Baltic efforts to integrate their energy systems and diversify energy supplies will result in diminished vulnerability and will bring added value to the EU and to NATO, thereby managing future energy challenges. NATO's Energy Security Centre of Excellence (ENSEC COE), established in Lithuania in 2012, is working on a more efficient

---

[2]Convention on Environmental Impact Assessment in a Trans-Boundary Context (Espoo Convention).

conduct of operations and enhanced protection of critical energy infrastructure. Since ENSEC COE is open to NATO allies and partners, it can provide a stable ground for further cooperation of all Nordic-Baltic countries and the United States in this important area.

However, our gaze extends beyond the Atlantic. It is in our joint interest to have a stable, democratic, and prosperous eastern European neighborhood that is on the way to closer political association and deeper economic integration with the EU. The complicated situation between Russia and Ukraine clearly demonstrates that crises emerge when countries do not have a clear place in Europe's contemporary structure. In the absence of a clear vision and perspective on the larger European structure, peace is destined to be fragile.

It is important not to lose the momentum that has been built through the Eastern Partnership. It is of vital importance to raise and maintain the world's awareness of the situation in Ukraine and to assist its stabilization process. Signing the EU Association Agreements with Moldova and Georgia in June 2014 has opened a new phase for those countries. We have to deliver on EU commitments and further engage Eastern Partners and their societies.

The decision to join NATO ten years ago made us stronger, more secure and more confident. Today, in the face of the crisis in neighboring Ukraine, we stand better prepared to defend ourselves and to offer assistance to others. This experience has made us strong believers in the continued worth of maintaining solid NATO instruments—Partnerships and NATO's Open Door policy—directed at achieving a Europe whole, free and at peace.

Keeping the door open for those willing to contribute is a necessity in such tumultuous times.

At the same time, international security and stability cannot be achieved without our partners' involvement. Cooperative security is one of the key objectives of the Alliance. All available instruments must be used to maximize the Partners' interoperability with the Alliance, especially those who share the same values and are ready and willing to contribute to our missions. Enhanced involvement of dedicated partners like Sweden and Finland in NATO's activities would significantly contribute to our capabilities, while also providing another step toward deeper cooperation of Nordic-Baltic countries and the United States.

Additionally, we believe that EU-NATO cooperation also needs to be strengthened: the unexpected events in Ukraine have been a wake-up call for us to re-examine the core structures and make them stronger, faster and more united.

Last, but certainly not least, let me mention the need for European defense to be effective and relevant. We need to do our best to maximize available resources. Europe has already demonstrated its potential to be an effective security player successfully handling situations in Libya and Mali and carrying out active counter-piracy campaigns.

In times of economic difficulty and financial restrictions, security can only be ensured by combining strategic partners' resources and capabilities. Therefore, we need to foster closer EU-NATO cooperation, especially taking into account NATO's Chicago Summit conclusions that NATO's Smart Defense and the EU's Pooling and Sharing initiatives are complementary and mutually reinforcing. Smart Defense solutions are the key to making Europe a strong player in its immediate neighborhood as well as in other parts of the world. Nordic-Baltic countries demonstrate leadership by discussing a possibility for joint acquisitions of ammunition or setting joint sea surveillance cooperation, aimed at integrating navy-led surveillance systems, or nuclear emergency simulations, aimed at improving level of coordination among dozens of institutions.

Finally, the last pillar upon which we could build our cooperation is information security. We are witnessing unwelcome and growing Russia information activity in the region. The challenge that needs our smart response is information "attacks", which aim to question and challenge our values and way of life, especially among less informed part of our societies.

We have seen the damaging effect of falsified and misleading information in the media over the course of 2013 and 2014 in Ukraine. We need to join efforts in order to protect our information, thereby increasing security in the region. The first step to a shared position is a shared understanding of the situation, where information plays a crucial role. Hence, Nordics, Baltics and the United States could join forces in monitoring the rising threats and in establishing a common area of research and expertise. We could certainly do more against the biased, militant and self-serving media frenzy that we are witnessing today, right across our borders.

Let me sum up the following steps to further advance U.S-Nordic-Baltic partnership:

- Acknowledge the perspective of the region in becoming a key partner to the United States;
- Push for the the full implementation of TTIP as a new global business reality;
- Extend the e-PINE agenda to include both the structural dimension (presence and attention of high-level officials) as well as a well-coordinated, "no topics left behind" content;
- Promote greater engagement of the United States in regional projects or initiate new forms of cooperation, especially related to energy, infrastructure, defense and security;
- Strengthen cooperation in information security, sharing research and expertise;
- Create a joint U.S.-Nordic-Baltic center—virtual or actual— that would connect experts of the nine countries for purpose-specific tasks and solutions. Having our own transatlantic "cloud" for ideas would perfectly reflect today's reality—the region would be protected not only by NATO fighters and partnerships, but also by a strong "firewall of principles".

I strongly believe that Europe will stand whole and free by enabling each of its regions to follow the example set by the Nordic-Baltic countries. However, Europe will not advance based on lines of division, dominance, threat or elusive "zones of vital interest" as some countries tend to think. Instead, future challenges will require cooperation in every possible area: becoming a grand energy network; ensuring unhampered trade and business growth; and reaching out to the Atlantic partnership. Securing our values and ideas leads to what we call a general message for the rest of the world. The message is simple—cooperation pays off.

Chapter 3

Europe Whole, Free and at Peace: A Washington View

Michael Polt

Sometimes Moody Partners

> If we've learned anything from the century drawing to a close, it is
> that if America is going to be prosperous and secure, we need a
> Europe that is prosperous, secure, undivided and free.

These are the words of President Bill Clinton on the evening of
March 24, 1999, announcing U.S. engagement in NATO airstrikes
designed to stop Serbian ethnic cleansing in Kosovo, less than ten
years after Secretary of State James Baker announced that the United
States had "no dog in the fight'" of Yugoslav dissolution.

The United States can be a moody partner. These contradictory
declarations of U.S. policy on a conflict in Europe are the reality of
the Washington view of Europe, whole, free and at peace. It is the
reality of the Marshall Plan and of the pivot to Asia. And it is the reality of the Cold War Baltic "captive nations" policy and the reduction
of U.S. forces in Europe from a Cold War high of over 400,000 to less
than 60,000 today and decreasing.

Contrary to the arguments of our critics, as a nation and as a people, Americans have always been extremely reluctant to engage American blood and treasure beyond our borders. Former U.S. Secretary of
State Colin Powell said in 2003 that "We have gone forth from our
shores repeatedly over the last hundred years ... and put wonderful
young men and women at risk, many of who have lost their lives, and
we have asked for nothing except enough ground to bury them in, and
otherwise we have returned home to seek ... our own lives in peace...."

Most often, when discussing transatlantic relations, we tend to refer to security challenges, ranging from the Cold War to NATO's Afghanistan engagement and today, Russia's incursions into Ukraine. But while security issues are certainly immensely important, they still are but one element of a deeply interwoven and hugely beneficial relationship between Europe's democracies and the United States. Ours is a relationship that not only provides mutual security to some 500 million people, but also produces more than half the world's GDP.

Our intertwined economies are a given, and so should be transatlantic security cooperation. With the tremendous human and material capital on both sides of the Atlantic, joint creative efforts across a full range of 21st century challenges and opportunities should equally be a no-brainer. And yet we seem never to tire of U.S.-European debates over differences that pale in comparison to our common interests. Some of our most important joint opportunities beyond our traditional security partnership lie in e-governance, energy security, information technology and cyber security, infrastructure modernization and of course the further liberalization of trade (i.e. the promise of the Transatlantic Trade and Investment Partnership—TTIP), to name just a few. The collaborative success in these areas forms the progressive edge of American and European shared interest in a Europe whole and free.

To give all elements of transatlantic success new strategic direction, I suggest we stop talking about pivots, rebalancing, redirection and redistribution of U.S. global assets. We should signal that the United States is fully committed to maintaining and enhancing an already exceptionally strong relationship with Europe, while also realizing new opportunities and meeting challenges elsewhere. The indicators of the strength of the U.S. commitment in Europe must be our security, economic, social, emotional and creative presence. Massive reductions in NATO military forces, maintenance of old barriers to trade and mistrust in our common fight against terrorism do not signal such a commitment.

At the same time, of course, our relationship and Europe's security and democratic future cannot be more important to us than to our European partners. NATO is characterized by most European leaders as an essential organization. But actions on behalf of this essential organization have not always matched words. Only four Alliance members actually meet the common commitment to defense spending at the 2% of GDP level. American interests, and particularly American public opinion, demand an equal, across-the-board commitment, sharing both benefits and burdens of the relationship. Winning the Cold War together has been our most successful joint transatlantic enterprise. Our Nordic-Baltic partners have played a particularly important role in this success. Today the nations around and near the Baltic are some of the most creative, vibrant and accomplished friends and allies of the United States, whether in or out of NATO and the European Union (EU).

Unfortunately, the post-Soviet era, characterized by significantly expanded freedom in Europe, has not brought about the comprehensive goal we seek of an entire continent whole, free and at peace. Quite to the contrary, as we have seen in Georgia, and now Ukraine, Russia, rather than playing the role of a large and important country eager to build democracy at home and elsewhere, has done just the opposite. Resolutely advancing Europe whole, free and at peace in view of this sad reality is no less important today than it was during the depths of the Cold War. Sanctions imposed by us on Russia for its behavior will only have the desired impact if we in turn are willing to accept the full consequences of our principled position. There must be no special carve-outs for "special relationships" with Russia claimed by one or the other of us.

Together with Europe, the United States has been far too reactive to challenges to our principles, values and interests. We ask ourselves what Putin is up to in Ukraine. Germany worries about reliable gas supplies from the east and ever-rising energy prices. The United States is suddenly embarrassed that we depend on Russian rocket engines and vehicles to send our astronauts to the space station. On both sides of the Atlantic we should have prepared a new strategic direction as soon as we realized—certainly since the Georgian incursion—that our well-intentioned reset of relations with Russia did not work. Our German friends should have deliberated a bit more, together with us, before reacting somewhat precipitously to the nuclear plant accident in Japan and before allowing themselves to become ever more energy dependent on Russia. And we should have come up with a U.S.–European Space Agency (ESA) alternative to a long-term contract for cheap Russian rocket engines.

The Baltics and the Balkans

Since I served as Ambassador to Serbia and Montenegro as well as to Estonia, I am often confronted with comparisons between two regions. Both the Baltics and the Balkans are blessed with wonderful, intelligent and creative people. Both experienced a traumatic shift of fortunes following the collapse of an old regime. And then their ways parted dramatically. While both regions share a deep sense of their past, both painful and positive, much of the Balkans found itself mired in 16th century regrets, while the Baltics aimed headlong for a new millennium.

My good friend Vuk Draskovic, as Foreign Minister of Serbia, once compared Serbia's approach to seizing future success to the challenges of a bird flying backwards. In Tallinn, a former Estonian Prime Minister once revealed to me the secret of Estonia's free market success: "I read Milton Friedman's book, gave it to my ministers and said this looks good, let's just do that!" These contrasts, involving very different outcomes, speak to the rationale for greater U.S. engagement with our Nordic-Baltic friends, the "let's just do it" crowd, on behalf of a Europe whole free and at peace.

Championing a No-Nonsense Approach

In the global competition of ideas and entrepreneurial energy, enhanced by today's global networks, size does not matter. That said, during my years in Estonia from 2009-2012, among my greatest challenges was gaining sufficient Washington attention for our small, but amazingly accomplished and most steadfast ally. My colleagues in Riga and Vilnius had similar experiences. We often sought collective success in engaging with Washington, including by reaching out to our ambassadorial colleagues in the Nordic countries.

When I was successful in spotlighting my hosts, we achieved solid results: a joint U.S. Marines–Estonian armed forces amphibious landing exercise north of Tallinn demonstrated capabilities and commitment to the defense of NATO's borders. Formal U.S. accession to the Tallinn-based Cyber Center of Excellence contributed to the publication of the "Tallinn Manual"—the first ever study of the applicability of international law to cyber conflict and cyber warfare. A serious U.S. look at Estonian oil shale energy production encouraged a U.S. oil shale property purchase by Estonia's oil company and the planned opening of a new energy source using vast American oil shale deposits.

The "let's do it" attitude in Estonia, Latvia and Lithuania vaulted all three of the Baltic States to "Tiger" status in the early and mid 2000s. Interrupted by the global financial crisis in 2008, all three of these tigers are now back and on an even more sustainable path. Close cooperation and open borders and markets among all three states and their Nordic neighbors has created a 30 million people zone of political, economic and social stability and a model of success for the rest of Europe and the United States.

Reinvigorating the Transatlantic Narrative

There is no lack of verbal or written commitment to U.S.-Nordic-Baltic cooperative efforts. Since the freeing of much of Europe after the Soviet collapse, we have initiated multiple initiatives between the United States and the Nordic-Baltic states. In 1997, we kicked off the Northern Europe Initiative culminating in Baltic state membership in NATO and the EU. In 2003, we launched the successor Enhanced Partnership in Northern Europe (e-PINE) to deepen our cooperation with the Baltic region, and as late as 2013, the United States, together with Denmark, Sweden, Norway, Finland and Iceland, issued a joint summit statement recommitting to cooperation on U.S.-Nordic-Baltic security. The 2011 Open Government Partnership, to which all eight Nordic-Baltics and the United States belong, rounds out a full plate of commitments and assurances.

This set of commitments now needs consistent, long-term action, dedicated resources and whole-of-government efforts. What follows is a short list of seven recommendations that would leverage Nordic-Baltic and U.S. strengths to advance a Europe whole and free. Rather than adding new language and process, the broad e-PINE categories provide a perfectly useful organizing framework.

Cooperative Security

> The United States will use military force, unilaterally if necessary, when our core interests demand it—when our people are threatened; when our livelihoods are at stake; when the security of our allies is in danger.

A principle reasserted by President Obama in his May 28, 2014 West Point Commencement Address.

Boots, Boats and Planes

The time has come for the long-term placement of NATO security assets in the Baltic Region. The European Reassurance Initiative announced by President Obama on June 3, 2014 is a step in the right direction, but needs to be followed by a permanent adjustment in Alliance stationing architecture to include the Baltic States. The projected 1 billion dollars in security resources announced by the U.S. President should be leveraged to invite similar commitments by our European allies and partners. After Ukraine, any pretense of Western reluctance in crossing Russia's comfort threshold regarding western security arrangements close to its borders must be dropped. Clearly there is no such reluctance on the part of Vladimir Putin in crossing our comfort zone as he acquires territory of sovereign states along his country's western border.

Prior to Russia's most recent western incursions, NATO's security activity in the Baltic region was in unrelenting decline. Alliance and bilateral exercises were scaled back or reduced to desktop exercises. U.S. participation became little more than token. Mobile U.S. prepositioned forces in Europe were withdrawn to the United States, and U.S. troop levels in Europe dedicated to European security have declined to less than 60,000.

During my three years in Estonia I had to inform the government twice about a lowering of the number of U.S. combat brigades stationed in Germany. A joint amphibious landing exercise of U.S. Marines together with Estonian military forces was scheduled to be the last of its kind for the indefinite future. While post-Ukraine there has been an uptick in NATO's exercise tempo and Baltic Air Policing, the withdrawn permanent U.S. assets in Europe are not scheduled to return.

Without questioning the logic of reshaping and restructuring U.S. military forces, there is little logic in not including the Baltic region in such a restructuring. The three Baltic NATO states, together with NATO partner Poland, share a nearly 600 mile border with Russia. Yet, aside from Baltic Air Policing, there are no Alliance assets stationed in the Baltic states. Selected modestly sized units, drawn from U.S. and European NATO forces, forward deployed in the Baltic States, are sustainable and would lend much needed visibility to Article 5 commitments. European participation in such stationing would be essential to make the U.S. contribution acceptable to a combat fatigued American public. All three Baltic countries have already contributed substantial national resources to provide military facilities in support of a long-term NATO presence and would almost certainly be willing to add even more.

Such deployments, even if not part of standard U.S. military doctrine, must become part of the full tool kit of U.S. and Alliance security diplomacy. Not only would such a move address important and justifiable regional security concerns after Ukraine, but it would also signal—more than any verbal assurances—the categorical inclusion of the vulnerable Baltic states in our commitment to a Europe whole and free. We should also encourage the continued informal, but visible partnership with our non-NATO Nordic friends in securing the region.

Securing Virtual Space

In addition to such traditional defense enhancements, cyber security cooperation should be taken to the next level in the Nordic-Baltic space. In 2007, following the transfer of a Soviet military statue from downtown Tallinn to a military cemetery outside the city center, Estonia was the first country ever subject to a national cyber attack. In the process, the Estonians gained much experience in defending against such attacks and preparing for future incursions in cyber space. Estonia's NATO Cyber Center of Excellence was established in 2008. I finally raised the U.S. flag signifying our membership three years later in 2011. Estonian membership in this important institution deserves more NATO and U.S. support, as do similar Centers of Excellence in

Latvia and Lithuania on strategic communications and energy security, respectively.

Healthy Societies

State-of-the Art Governance

E-PINE sees Baltic nations contributing lessons in open society transition and Nordic States sharing extensive expertise in championing democracy and human rights around the world. Here the United States should engage energetically in a key element of modern good government, part of the Open Government Partnership, and a highly developed skill in the Nordic-Baltic countries: e-governance. E-governance includes high quality government service delivery, anti-corruption transparency, citizen participation and the use of state of the art technology in providing government services. All eight countries in the Baltic region have an impressive record in this area. They don't all share the same philosophy on the role of government in society. What they do share is high quality and efficient government services based on the latest technology, available at the tap of an iPad. Estonians can vote on the internet and complete their income tax returns in minutes. Latvia and Lithuania have deployed similarly advanced e-government systems and like Estonia have shared their skills with other European partners. One Baltic leader told me recently that more e-governance assistance would have a major transformative impact in Ukraine today. Similarly, adoption of rigorous accounting and statistical standards practiced among the eight could avoid future surprises in the euro zone.

Celebrating Diversity

The ultimate test of a healthy society is fairness, inclusiveness, equal citizen rights and equal opportunity. Both the United States and our Nordic-Baltic friends are challenged by issues of inclusiveness and the fair treatment of minorities. For the Baltic states, with large Russian minorities inside their borders, this takes on special political meaning, not least of why because they provide significant opportunities for the kind of mischief and interference, of which Vladimir Putin is so fond, having declared himself President of all Russians.

Despite many challenges, Tallinn, Riga and Vilnius have done a remarkable job of creating healthy societies that draw on the full diversity of their populations, regardless of ethnic heritage. All three countries share the experience of living under Soviet occupation. They understand better than their U.S. or European partners the full impact of extreme Russian nationalism. And they have dealt successfully, peacefully and constructively with such nationalist fervor in their countries. Sharing the Baltic experience with other countries struggling with the consequences of Soviet history is a significant contribution to healthy societies all over Europe.

Building New Stakeholders

New U.S. and European consular facilities focused on public diplomacy and business development in the major eastern cities of Estonia and Latvia could help national efforts as important platforms for growing relationships with minority communities, sharing western perspectives and building economic and commercial ties.

Vibrant Economies and Common Security

Modeling the No-Nonsense Economy

Virtually every U.S. congressional delegation visiting Baltic countries during my time in Estonia was suitably impressed by the region's startling economic performance, including the overall ease of doing business and the availability of broadband internet access. This reality, along with strategic location, EU membership and connections to the east, and of course the Nordic space, has not escaped the attention of the competition. China has ramped up its presence in and attention to the region. The Baltic states are a most attractive business launching platform, especially for small and medium businesses. Successful conclusion of a TTIP agreement, already embraced enthusiastically in all three states, would enhance that status even further.

Strong economic performance underpins U.S. and European capabilities and commitments to our common defense. Even as visions of peace dividends quickly evaporated after the end of the Cold War, both European and U.S. leaders have been eager to invest in domestic prosperity rather than defense. The 2008 world financial crisis brought guns and butter considerations into sharp relief, with many European countries planning deep cuts in defense expenditures, including the Nordic states. The United States is planning its own downward adjustments. Estonia, Latvia and Lithuania, to varying degrees, instead built up their militaries literally from scratch since regaining independence. All three countries have fully demonstrated their commitment in blood and treasure to Alliance missions, including in Iraq and Afghanistan, even while under significant economic pressure at home. Austerity measures on both sides of the Atlantic have not been restricted to defense expenditures. Social outlays have also been on the chopping block, making it difficult to argue an unqualified defense exemption from budget cuts. In the end, the only way to afford a more robust defense posture is to grow the country's economic pie. The Nordic-Baltic region's economic growth record as a consequence of a solid record on free trade, fiscal responsibility and competitive capitalism suggests emulation by others.

No Excuse Burden Sharing

Burden sharing in defense is still the only effective and fair way to keep NATO convincingly strong. Estonia and the United States are among the minority of members who meet or exceed the Alliance's agreed 2% of GDP level of defense expenditures. In seeking to justify lesser contributions, it is unacceptable to point to development aid or other non-military contributions as an offset against an adequate defense commitment. Neither the United States, nor any other ally, is prepared to become the mercenary element of the Alliance while others make "soft" contributions.

In the End, Does Any Part of Europe Still Matter?

However important, U.S.-Nordic-Baltic relations are of course a subset of the U.S. relationship with Europe as a whole. In that context, I spoke to students and faculty at Tallinn Technical University in September 2011 on the provocative question: Does Europe still matter? And more specifically, does it still matter to the United States? At that time, in pre-Ukraine Europe outside the Nordic-Baltic region, and to an extent in the United States, the conviction had certainly started to take hold that European issues had somehow been solved, that "whole and free" had at least in large measure been achieved.

I had read an op-ed by CFR President Richard Haass entitled "Why Europe No Longer Matters" in the June 17, 2011 edition of the *Washington Post*. In it, Haass describes the decline of a common U.S. and European set of interests that in the past had been based on historical patterns of American elites that traced their ancestry to Europe. Today's broader elite in the United States, he argues, relates to African, Asian and Latin American roots and does not share the emotional or intellectual ties to Europe that defined transatlantic relations in the 20th century. Haass posits that if NATO didn't exist today, no one would feel compelled to create it. Inadequate European financial and physical commitments to Alliance actions are a case in point, along with what he calls the emerging European cultural norm of not accepting any casualties in the prosecution of a war. He concludes that old alliances and relationships are dead or on their death-bed: "Europe and the United States have changed. The world has changed."

I share many of Haass' concerns about the U.S.-European relationship. Former U.S. Secretary of Defense Robert Gates in his farewell speech to NATO in Brussels in June 2011, voiced his concern that NATO could become "a two-tiered alliance that is split between those willing and able to pay the price and bear the burdens of Alliance commitments, and those who enjoy the benefits of NATO membership but don't want to share the risks and the costs." Most of our Nordic–Baltic Alliance partners would belong in tier one in such a case, as on so many other issues occupying the U.S.–European dialogue.

I also agree that American elites are much more diverse today than in the mid-1900s. But I would contend that a Chinese-American raised in San Francisco has far more in common with an individual from Tallinn, Riga or Copenhagen than he does with a Chinese citizen raised in Beijing. The American and European belief in democracy, individual freedom and open markets transcends ethnic heritage and will continue to bind Americans to Europeans, even if we sometimes disagree on details. I do not concur with the assertion that with the entry of other power players into the new international (dis)order, existing participants are by definition marginalized or, worse, sidelined completely. NATO remains the only Alliance that wields an extremely powerful punch, matched by no one. And 40% of all world economic activity still takes place between Europe and the United States.

Admittedly, Europe today is not the singular center of America's universe. But it never really was. America, since its inception with powerful European roots, has steadily continued to develop its global vocation. Our ties to Europe form a critically important partnership that has hardly been characterized by full and consistent harmony. France kicked out NATO's headquarters in 1966 and did not return to the unified NATO military command until 2009. In 1983, Germans threw Molotov cocktails at the U.S. Embassy in protest over introduction of U.S. medium range nuclear missiles in Europe—for the defense of Europe! And yet an enlarged NATO stands today, enhanced by new members formerly part of the Warsaw Pact, and is reminded of its founding principles as it confronts Russia's renewed expansionism.

In June 2014 in Poland, President Obama called the Ukrainians of today the heirs of Solidarity. The Baltic states certainly share that same heritage since carrying out their "Singing Revolution." Together with their Nordic friends, who had helped to make the Iron Curtain a bit more transparent, they carried out a post-Cold War miracle that is today a model of democracy, rule of law and free market success. Now is the time to intensify our collaboration with these ready partners around the Baltic to reinvigorate and strengthen the transatlantic bond.

Chapter 4

From Neutrality to Solidarity?
Sweden's Ongoing Geopolitical Reorientation

Mike Winnerstig

The Baltic Sea area became a fairly peaceful region after the end of the Cold War. Many nations, including the Scandinavian countries, took this as a reason for reducing their military expenditures and lowering their military readiness. Russian aggression in Ukraine during 2014 has changed most of the parameters related to this, which is only now being fully perceived by the leading politicians of the Scandinavian countries.[1]

Sweden is currently in the midst of a profound reorientation of its security and defense policy, a lengthy process that started at least 20 years ago. Today the complexities of Swedish policy in this field are so many and so intricate that even seasoned Swedish diplomats have problems delivering a logical, coherent presentation of Swedish security policy to foreign and domestic audiences. The policy builds explicitly both on solidarity with "others," particularly its neighbors—including the military aspects of this—and on non-alignment, i.e., not being a member of the North Atlantic Treaty Organization (NATO). In the international press, this policy is currently questioned with some regularity.[2]

To explain this, one has to recall what could be called Sweden's "double identity" during the Cold War. Its then clear and straightforward "neutrality policy" was essentially composed of two different parts: isolationism at home—in the near abroad—and political solidarity far away—such as long-term support for the African National

---

[1] For a comprehensive assessment of this, see Niklas Granholm et al. (2014): *A Rude Awakening: Ramifications of Russian Aggression Towards Ukraine* (Stockholm: FOI), FOI-R-3892-SE.

[2] See, for a recent example, Charlemagne (2014): "What Price Neutrality?" *The Economist*, June 21, at http://www.economist.com/news/europe/21604586-russia-stokes-fresh-debate-among-nordics-about-nato-membership-what-price-neutrality.

Congress in South Africa under Apartheid and high-level criticism of the U.S. war against North Vietnam.

In terms of the former, military-political isolationism was a direct consequence of the Swedish neutrality policy first introduced in the early 19th century. As a non-aligned country in peacetime, aiming at neutrality in war, Sweden had to stay away from conflicts in its neighborhood. This also meant that Swedish politicians by and large never strived for a "Europe whole and free" during the Cold War. The superpower conflict was seen as an eternal one and anybody promoting change, for example by talking about the eventual independence of the Baltic states, was dismissed as a "dreamer" or, even worse, a "crusader." In essence, the logic of the neutrality policy demanded that Sweden should not be pressured by the "nearby superpower" (the Soviet Union), nor become a "threatening outpost" of the other superpower (the United States).[3] During this time, Swedish armed forces were among the strongest in Europe, at least in numerical terms. After mobilization, they could count on more than 800,000 troops, a very substantial air force and a relatively strong navy.

Today, the picture is very different, especially compared to the 1980s. Swedish political engagement with its neighbors—including the military sector—is the strongest since perhaps the late 18th century; European Union membership has turned the country away from isolationism and defense restructuring; and reform has left Sweden with less than 10% of its earlier manpower. Since its inclusion in NATO's Partnership for Peace program in 1994, the Swedish military is increasingly integrating into NATO military structures as well.

Thus, Swedish security and defense policy has been fundamentally altered. Not only is Sweden politically integrating in the West in a way not seen before the early 19th century, but also the size of its military is by default requiring almost immediate "assistance from abroad" in the event of an attack on Sweden. After the 2014 events in Ukraine, there is also a broad national consensus that the only possible direction of such a threat is from the Russian Federation under President Vladimir Putin.

---

[3] See Sverker Åström (1983): *Svensk neutralitetspolitik [Swedish Neutrality Policy]* (Stockholm: Svenska Institutet)

Strategically and geopolitically, these developments entail several important issues. Currently, Sweden does not argue that it can defend itself on its own. Quite the contrary, current official doctrine explicitly argues that Sweden should be defended "together with others." Furthermore, all the forms of EU and NATO integration that Sweden currently pursues, including future forms of "enhanced partnership" status as eloquently suggested by Johan Raeder in another chapter of this book, indicate that anybody (including Russia) wanting to act against NATO countries in the Baltic Sea region would have to regard Sweden as part of the enemy camp. When it comes to EU and Nordic countries, Swedish neutrality is not an option anymore.

On top of this, to defend Sweden rationally "with others" means that this has to be exercised in peacetime and that common defense plans have to be written in advance of a major crisis. This is very hard, if not impossible to do if the countries involved do not belong to the same military-political system, i.e. NATO. Thus, the new geopolitical realities, the dramatic restructuring of the Swedish armed forces and the Swedish political integration in the euro-Atlantic organizations (EU and NATO) that Sweden pursues, all point in the same direction: NATO membership is a necessary condition in the Swedish defense equation. Also, Swedish and Finnish membership would entail major benefits for all other EU and NATO countries around the Baltic Sea, as the lingering questions regarding what Sweden actually would do in the event of a major crisis or military attack in the area would disappear.

But, as was stated above, this is a slow process. There is no political leadership on the issue in Sweden, the current government is not explicitly working on preparing Sweden for NATO membership, the parliamentary opposition—poised to win the parliamentary elections in September 2014—is dead against it and public opinion is still against it as well, though there has been a steady uptick in support for Swedish NATO membership in the polls during the last year and a half.

At the same time, the debate on NATO membership is more dynamic than ever and there is rarely a month per year when the issue is not debated publicly, especially by former politicians, academics and editorial page editors. Lately, two former ministers of defense have been promoting NATO membership although their own party is largely silent on the issue.[4] To understand why this is the case, a historical background of Swedish security policy must be sketched.

Swedish "Grand Strategy" in Times of Geopolitical Turmoil

Security Policy Doctrine in Historical Context

Since the formation of Sweden as an independent nation-state in the early 16th century, the "grand strategy" of Sweden has changed fundamentally no more than roughly three times. Firstly, due to decisions of Gustavus Adolphus in the early 17th century, Sweden entered the 30 Years War and emerged as regional great power in Northern Europe.

Second, given the defeats of Sweden by Russia in the Great Northern War in the early 18th century and the end of the Napoleonic wars in the early 19th century, Swedish security policy was again altered fundamentally. After the loss of Finland in 1809, Sweden's grand strategy was based on two pillars: the "policy of 1812" and a policy of neutrality. Both were introduced by the French field marshal Jean-Baptiste Bernadotte, appointed crown prince of Sweden in 1810 and crowned as the King of Sweden in 1818. The policy of 1812 essentially declared that Sweden's position as a great power in Europe had ended and that the country now was to focus on its own core territory—though using Norway as an extension of this after a peace convention in 1814. The policy heavily emphasized a two-pronged approach: non-provocation toward Russia and implicit reliance on a Western power (essentially the United Kingdom) to counter Russian power in the Baltic Sea area, while at the same time staying outside of conflicts between Russia and the United Kingdom (UK). The policy also meant, by extension, that the Kingdom of Sweden stayed out of the Crimean war, the First and Second World Wars and formally also the Cold War.

---

[4]See Ivar Arpi (2014): "De låter som Bagdad Bob [They sound as Bagdad Bob]," interview with Mikael Odenberg, minister of defence 2006-2007, *Neo*, nr. 3, and Sten Tolgfors & Mike Winnerstig (2014): "Stabilare Europa med Sverige i NATO" [A More Stable Europe with Sweden as a NATO Member," *Göteborgsposten*, June 18. Tolgfors served as minister of defense from 2007 to 2012.

The additional policy of neutrality was never declared as a policy of permanent neutrality (which was the case for countries like Switzerland), but rather as a form of temporary, pragmatic neutrality aiming at supporting the objectives of the policy of 1812.

However, during the First World War, a substantial minority of the Swedish establishment wanted Sweden to join the German war effort. Several military measures favorable to Germany and highly unfavorable to the UK were also taken, such as the use of Swedish mines in the straits of Östersund (between Sweden and Denmark), effectively blocking the Royal Navy from entering the Baltic Sea.[5] Throughout the Second World War, Sweden essentially conducted a policy of appeasement first toward Hitler's Germany and, when the tides of the war had changed, toward the Western allied powers.[6]

Modern research shows that, during the Cold War, Sweden was in fact partially integrated in the Western (essentially NATO) defense planning against the Soviet Union and its vassal states within the Warsaw Pact.[7] Thus, it can be said that Sweden was never particularly true to the policy of neutrality. Due to spying and other efforts, it is also highly likely that the Soviet Union knew about these preparations and made counter-preparations for military actions against Sweden.[8]

In 1995, the third fundamental shift in Swedish grand strategy occurred since the era of Gustavus Vasa in the early 16th century: Sweden became a member of the then-European Community, now—the

---

[5]See Bo Siegbahn (1992): "Minnesruna över 'neutralitetspolitiken' [An Obituary of the 'neutrality policy'], *Svensk Tidskrift*, December, p. 123ff.

[6]See, for example, Christian Leitz (2000): *Nazi Germany and Neutral Europe During the Second World War*, (Manchester: Manchester University Press).

[7]See Robert Dalsjö, (2007): *Life-line Lost: The Rise and Fall of "Neutral" Sweden's Secret Reserve Option of Wartime Help from the West*, (Stockholm: Santérus) and Mikael Holmström (2011): *Den dolda alliansen: Sveriges hemliga Natoförbindelser [The Hidden Alliance: Sweden's Secret NATO relationship]* (Stockholm: Atlantis).

[8]The many reports of USSR submarines intruding in Swedish territorial waters in the 1980s might be proof of this. See Gordon H. McCormick (1990): *Stranger than Fiction: Soviet Submarine Operations in Swedish Waters* (Washington, DC: RAND). However, a Swedish scholar working in Norway has for years put forward somewhat wilder theories arguing that the submarines were in fact NATO vessels trying to appear as Soviet ones—sent out by the Western powers to install a more anti-Soviet mood in presumably neutral Sweden. See Ola Tunander (2004): *The Secret War Against Sweden: US and British Submarine Deception in the 1980s* (London: Cass Series: Naval Policy and History).

European Union. Since the early 1960s, the Social Democrats, the traditionally dominant party in Sweden, had considered this to be an impossible step to take, as around 80% of EU members were already members of a military alliance (NATO). Becoming members of the EC/EU would, thus, severely compromise Swedish neutrality policy. After the end of the Cold War, however, Social Democrats changed their mind and proposed a referendum on the issue in late 1994. This resulted in a majority, albeit rather small, for EC/EU membership, and Sweden joined the following year.

After joining the EU, though, the discourse of neutrality continued to dominate the Swedish debate; Swedish national identity seemed to be highly entrenched in neutralism and its inherent isolationism. Despite Sweden becoming a member of NATO's Partnership for Peace program in 1994, and despite the Swedish armed forces' increasingly close relationship with NATO, Swedish public opinion until very recently clearly favored the traditional neutralist/non-aligned stance. To many analysts, this had to do both with isolationist, realpolitik factors (NATO was seen as an organization potentially dragging Sweden into distant, foreign wars detrimental to Swedish security) as well as with identity issues; being a Swede was considered equivalent to being non-aligned and neutral.[9]

The "Solidarity Declaration" of 2009

When the EU's Lisbon Treaty entered into force in 2009, two kinds of mutual assistance clauses were included in the treaty: in the first place, a solidarity clause relating to mutual assistance in the event of a terrorist attack, a natural disaster or the like in a member state (art. 2.2.2). Secondly, a traditional defense assistance clause of the NATO Article 5 variety (art. 42.7 of the Lisbon Treaty) was included as well.

Partly as a result of this, the Swedish Parliament adopted a major defense bill in the summer of 2009. In this bill, two major changes of Swedish security policy were introduced. Firstly, the government stated, in fundamental contrast to the Swedish security policy doc-

---

[9]See for example Ulf Bjereld, "Fortsatt starkt NATO-motstånd i svensk opinion [Continued strong resistance toward NATO in Swedish opinion]" in Lennart Weibull, Henrik Oscarsson and Annika Bergström [eds.] (2013): *Vägskäl [Crossroads]* (Gothenburg University: The SOM Institute].

trine's main tenets since the early 19th century, that Sweden will not remain passive if a disaster or an attack should afflict another EU member state or Nordic country and that Sweden also expects these countries to act in the same manner if Sweden is attacked. Secondly, in order to operationalize this, the government tasked the Swedish armed forces to be able both to give and to receive military assistance.[10] Both of these issues, being affected by attacks on other states and being able to help them militarily as well as receive help from them in the event of an attack on Sweden, had been anathema for Swedish security policy decision-makers since 1812. A peculiarity of this new doctrine, labeled the "solidarity declaration" in Sweden, is its unilateral character; in announcing it, Sweden did not ask for any reciprocity, but instead seemed to rely on "expectations" that other countries would come to Sweden's assistance without any prior official endorsement of this doctrine, and vice versa. The new doctrine led to a few public critical comments in Sweden, especially by some theologists of the traditional neutrality policy,[11] but was in general accepted without much fanfare (and, one could add, much public knowledge of the doctrinal change). From a Swedish historical perspective its contents were actually revolutionary.[12]

The Defense Reform of 2009

The same 2009 defense bill also contained the framework for a major defense reform, including making conscription "dormant" and forming instead a small, all-volunteer force of less than 10% of the manpower available during the Cold War. In many ways, this was also a most revolutionary reform.

---

[10]Ministry of Defence (2009), *A Useful Defence*, The Swedish Government's Bill 2008/09:140, esp. p. 9. See http://www.regeringen.se/content/1/c6/12/29/57/853ca644.pdf.

[11]See, for example, Mikael Nilsson (2009), "Ny doktrin sätter freden på spel" [New Doctrine Puts Peace at Risk], *Svenska Dagbladet*, Dec. 2nd, http://www.svd.se/opinion/brannpunkt/ny-doktrin-satter-freden-pa-spel_3878379.svd.

[12]The Royal Swedish Academy of the War Sciences published a major study on the solidarity declaration in 2011, which was published in English the year after. This volume contained among other things some critical analyses of the practical abilities to sustain militarily the implicit promises of the solidarity declaration, but has so far not achieved a lot of public attention. See Bo Hugemark [ed.] (2012): *Friends in Need: Towards a Swedish Strategy of Solidarity with Her Neighbours* (Stockholm: Royal Academy of the War Sciences).

The defense force was to be drastically strengthened as compared to the situation in 2005, when the then government had implemented a series of major reductions in the peacetime military establishment, abolishing some 60 regiments over a ten year period. Most of the then available military forces, altogether not amounting to more than 30,000 troops, was also on very low alert and required at least a year's preparations to gain combat-ready status.

The new defense reform aimed at a combat-ready force of about 50,000 troops in total, half of which consisting of national guard-style units. The defense bill's main principle was that Swedish armed forces should be available and useful "here and now," which meant that the future force would consist of professional soldiers and officers as well as of contracted reservists.[13]

This force structure was considerably larger and more effective than its equivalent in 2005, when the role of the armed forces was fundamentally unclear and no defense planning at all for Swedish territory was made. However, people (both within the establishment and the population at large) still compared this to the Swedish armed forces of the 1980s. At that time, the conscription system made it possible for Sweden, then a country of some nine million people, to mobilize around 800,000 troops. This amounted to half the current active-duty force of the United States (a country of some 330 million people and the sole global superpower). On top of this, the general view in Sweden of the role of the Swedish armed forces was essentially inherited from the Cold War; only Swedish armed forces defend Sweden; and they defend the whole country all the time. Thus, the public viewed the defense reform with some skepticism.

What got the debate started, though, was an interview the Swedish supreme commander General Sverker Göranson (essentially the Swedish CHOD—Chief of Defense) published in early 2013. According to General Göranson, Swedish military war-gaming during the autumn of 2012 had revealed that the future structure of the Swedish armed forces, which was to be completed in 2019, would be able to defend Sweden against an attack against a limited target for about a week.[14]

---

[13]See Ministry of Defence (2009), *A Useful Defence*, The Swedish Government's Bill 2008/09:140. http://www.regeringen.se/content/1/c6/12/29/57/853ca644.pdf.

[14]Mikael Holmström (2013): "Försvar med tidsgräns [A Defence with a Time Limit]," *Svenska Dagbladet*, January 2.

In a NATO setting, this would not have been regarded as very strange or controversial; most NATO countries the size of Sweden have similarly sized defense forces and rely on reinforcements from other allies to defend themselves. But in Sweden, where public opinion still very much embraced the idea that the Swedish armed forces should be able to defend the whole country on their own, the CHOD's statement was sheer political dynamite. A huge number of politicians, commentators, members of parliament, journalists and members of the general public made statements showing their utter surprise as to where Swedish armed forces had been going.[15]

In another interview, General Göranson further noted that instead of planning for the defense of the entire country, the limitations of the future armed forces meant that military defense planning could only realistically be made for the five most important areas of the country and only one of these could be defended at any time. In the Swedish debate, this was seen as almost as dramatic as the CHOD's revelation of what quickly became called the "one-week defense." The drama did not end there, though; General Göranson went on sick leave for several weeks and legal authorities started investigating him for suspicion of leaking military secrets.[16] The defense debate temperature in Sweden was increasing rapidly, although the charges against General Göranson were dropped. His comments, however, indicated that a posture of isolationist non-alignment and neutrality was no longer a realistic option in the event of a conflict; a neutral country needs to be able to defend its own borders for its neutrality to be respected. If it cannot do this, there is no point in being non-aligned in peace, nor in aiming at neutrality in war, as its borders will most likely not be respected by the warring parties.

The Consequences for the Swedish Security Policy Debate

After the end of the Cold War, NATO membership became a moot point in the Swedish debate on defense and security. Although the membership debate in the Swedish defense establishment went back as far as 1997, most opinion polls from the end of the Cold War until 2012 showed that around half the population was against membership

---

[15]Ewa Stenberg (2012): "Uttalandet från ÖB är en politisk bomb [The CHOD statement a political bomb]," *Dagens Nyheter*, January 3.

[16]Mikael Holmström (2013): "Försvarsplan bara för fem områden [Defence plans only for five areas]," *Svenska Dagbladet*, January 26.

in the Alliance and less than 25% was in favor.[17] This meant that the issue was raised only by ideologically-driven smaller parties in the Parliament, essentially only the Liberal party. For the rest of the parliamentary parties, the issue was either a matter of perceived national identity (in the sense that being a Swede is to be non-aligned and neutral, making the idea of NATO membership almost repulsive), or something that in theory was desirable but in practice not worth fighting for (as was the case with the dominant center-right Moderate party, which has been leading the government since 2006).[18]

In recent years, only two of the four current Swedish governmental coalition parties (including the Moderate party of the Prime Minister, the Foreign Minister and the Defense Minister) have openly been promoting Swedish NATO membership. The other two, the Center (Agrarian) party and the Christian Democrats, have traditionally been strong supporters of Swedish non-alignment, but are now officially undecided and have demanded a full parliamentary investigative committee on the pros and cons of Swedish NATO membership.[19] The latter has partly been realized after the Swedish government recently appointed a senior, retired ambassador to set up a committee investigating "Sweden's military cooperation" with the Nordic countries, the EU and NATO.[20] This action was immediately criticized by the Social Democratic press, which strongly opposes NATO membership (together with the rest of the opposition: the Greens; the former Communist party; and the right-wing populist Democrats party).[21]

---

[17]See e.g. Mike Winnerstig (1997): *Alliansfrihet eller NATO-medlemskap? Sveriges och Europas säkerhet efter NATOs utvidgning [Non-Alignment or NATO membership? Sweden's and Europe's security after NATO's enlargement]* (Stockholm: Swedish Institute of International Affairs) for one of the earliest examples of a more in-depth discussion on Sweden and NATO.

[18]See Joakim Berndtsson, Ulf Bjereld & Karl Ydén (2012): "Svagt stöd för Nato-anslutning [Weak support for NATO accession]," *Svenska Dagbladet*, 26 maj, http://www.svd.se/opinion/brannpunkt/svagt-stod-for-nato-anslutning_7231251.svd.

[19]It is also worth noting that the youth organizations of both these parties have publicly demanded full Swedish NATO membership, not only an investigation of this. See Fredrick Federley et al. (2014): "Svenskt medlemskap i NATO ett måste [Swedish NATO membership a necessity]," *Svenska Dagbladet*, July 25, at http://www.svd.se/opinion/brannpunkt/svenskt-medlemskap-i-nato-ett-maste_3773898.svd

[20]Ministry of Defence (2013): Översyn över internationella samarbeten [Overhaul of international cooperative ventures]," December 28th, http://www.regeringen.se/sb/d/17014/a/231323.

[21]See e.g. Anders Lindberg (2014): "Vilket problem är Nato lösning på? [Which problem is NATO a solution to?" *Aftonbladet*, January 11, http://www.aftonbladet.se/ledare/ledarkronika/anderslindberg/article18158319.ab.

However, General Göranson's comments on the "one-week defense" had a deep impact on the debate. Additionally, Russian military exercises directed against Sweden became part of the defense debate as well. First, a Russian fighter-bomber formation flew against Swedish targets during Good Friday night in 2013. As this is a major holiday in Sweden, the air force crews were on leave and, thus, no Swedish planes were sent to meet the Russian ones (which did not enter Swedish territory proper). However, Danish F16s from NATO's air policing mission in Siauliai, Lithuania, went up against the Russian airplanes, which added insult to injury for the Swedish air force.[22] Later that year, a Russian intelligence ship sailed between the island of Gotland and the Swedish mainland in order to perform signals intelligence tasks related to a major international military exercise in Sweden that took place at the same time.[23] In the context of the *Zapad-13* exercise just after this incident, another mock air attack against Swedish targets was carried out by Russian air force units.[24]

All of this changed public opinion views on NATO membership. According to a poll in May, 2013, 32% of Swedes were in favor of Swedish NATO membership (up from 23% in 2012), whereas 40% were against it (down from 56% in 2012), with the rest being undecided. This poll was particularly interesting since it also revealed that some 24% of all Social Democrats and a majority, or 56%, of all Swedish Democrats were in favor of NATO membership. In another poll, performed within the German Marshall Fund's Transatlantic Trends project, 36% were in favor of NATO membership (up from 24% in 2012) and 56% were against it.[25] In yet another poll, published in January 2014, by the Swedish Civil Contingencies Agency (MSB),

[22]Mikael Holmström (2013): "Ryskt flyg övade anfall mot Sverige [Russian Aircraft Exercised Attacking Sweden]," *Svenska Dagbladet*, April 24.

[23]Mikael Holmström (2012): "Här spionerar Ryssland på Sverige [Here, Russia is spying against Sweden]," *Svenska Dagbladet*, September 21st.

[24]Olle Lönnaeus (2013): "Het militärhöst runt Östersjön [Hot military autumn around the Baltic Sea]," *Sydsvenskan*, November 9th, http://www.sydsvenskan.se/sverige/het-militarhost-runt-ostersjon/.

[25]See Claes Arvidsson (2012): "Känsla och förnuft—opinioner om NATO [Feelings and rationality—opinions about NATO]," in Karlis Neretnieks [ed.] *Nato—för och emot [NATO: Pro and Con]* (Stockholm: Kungliga Krigsvetenskapsakademien/The Royal Academy of the War Sciences), pp. 133 ff.

36% of respondents were in favor of Swedish NATO membership and 40% were against it, thereby indicating a statistical tie.[26]

In other words, the combination of a drastically altered defense structure, a partly and to an extent fundamentally changed security policy doctrine and a resurgent, rearming Russia, led to a substantial increase in Swedes' favor for NATO membership, to the point that the numbers of Swedes in favor and against membership are virtually the same.

It is, however, probably too early to tell how the effects of the Ukraine crisis will affect public opinion. One recent poll showed that the support for NATO membership has increased to 37% of the population, but that a majority (56%) still is against it.[27] Russian aggression in Ukraine might have two possible, and somewhat paradoxical, effects on Swedish views on NATO. Firstly, Ukraine is a country which is relatively distant and about which the average Swede knows very little. Thus, NATO's efforts to counter Russian actions might evoke old Swedish isolationist tendencies: why be involved in the conflicts of others with no tangible Swedish interests involved? On the other hand, Sweden's situation is actually very similar to that of Ukraine: both countries are non-aligned NATO partners and have for many years been increasingly integrating with NATO without enjoying a national consensus on eventual membership. The annexation of Crimea would never have been possible had Ukraine been a NATO member. Although a parallel to any Swedish contingency is far-fetched, similar actions could theoretically be taken against a non-aligned Sweden without generating a NATO response (or at least not a more substantive answer than the current policies of the West against Russia).

Conclusions: Security Policy at Road's End?

The difference between NATO partnership and NATO membership has been repeatedly underscored during the last few years. At a major Swedish security policy conference in January 2013, the Secretary Gen-

---

[26]See MSB (2014): Opinioner 2013 Allmänhetens syn på samhällsskydd, beredskap, säkerhetspolitik och försvar [Opinions 2013: The General Public's Views on Societal Security, Preparedness, Security Policy and Defence], http://rib.msb.se/Filer/pdf/27284.pdf, pp. 85ff.

[27]See http://wisemanswisdoms.blogspot.se/2014/06/gastinlagg-ingen-forandring-i.html.

eral of NATO Anders Fogh Rasmussen, a fellow Scandinavian and former Danish Prime Minister, explicitly stated that NATO has no obligation to assist non-members. This was partly an answer to a question as to whether Sweden could rely on military help from other countries along the lines of the 2009 Swedish unilateral Solidarity Declaration.[28] The then-Norwegian Minister of Defense essentially repeated this in an interview for Swedish public radio a couple of weeks later, adding that Norway does not have any troops available for defending anything but Norwegian territory together with NATO allies.[29]

At the same time, Sweden's increasing integration within NATO's structures is ongoing and the prospect of an enhanced partnership status seems to be on track. Thus, it might become more and more difficult to discern an "enhanced partner" from a member, at least short of really sensitive issues such as collective defense planning and territorial defense exercises.

However, faced with a revisionist and rearming Russia in the Baltic Sea region, the other countries involved, including the United States, will likely in the long run demand more clarifications about Sweden's plans for its own armed forces as well as its views on military cooperation in the event of a real crisis or military attack against other EU or Nordic states (all but Finland are also NATO members). This will most likely serve as yet another step of integration into NATO military structures; the alternative (i.e. Sweden returning to a policy of strict non-alignment and neutrality, refusing to cooperate with NATO, for example in terms of assisting NATO members around the Baltic Sea) is highly unlikely, to say the least.

This international context will also relate to the domestic debate, where the support for NATO membership has increased markedly without any noticeable political leadership. Should the latter appear, polls might shift even faster. What can be said with some certainty is that the old model of Swedish security policy, based on non-alignment and still alive in the mind of the general public, has come to the road's end.

---

[28]Mikael Holmström (2013): "NATO lovar inget ingripande [NATO does not promise any assistance]," *Svenska Dagbladet,* January 15.

[29]See interview with Anne-Grete Strøm-Erichsen, Norwegian Minister of Defense, on January 24, 2013, http://sverigesradio.se/sida/artikel.aspx?programid=83&artikel=5453467.

Chapter 5

Thinking of the Future of NATO Partnerships

Johan Raeder

The Origins of NATO's Partnerships

Neighbors Come Knocking—Starting the Dialogue

When the Berlin Wall was brought down in 1989 and Estonia, Latvia and Lithuania seceded from the Soviet Union a little less than two years later, hopes were raised that the confrontation of the Cold War was going to give way to a future based on a more peaceful and cooperative relationship between the countries of Europe. At the North Atlantic Treaty Organization (NATO) Summit in Rome in November, 1991, the North Atlantic Cooperation Council (NACC) was established as a forum for dialogue between NATO and these newly liberated states. The aim was to secure democracy and thereby also the security of the Alliance. In the communiqué, the Heads of State and Government said that they would support all steps in the countries of central and eastern Europe towards reform and give practical assistance to help them succeed in this difficult transition. "This is based," they said, "on our conviction that our own security is inseparably linked to that of all other states in Europe."[1]

Finding the Form—Entering into a Real Partnership

Only two months later, the Soviet Union itself had disintegrated. While to most NATO allies a new era of cooperation and peaceful relations with Russia seemed well within their grasp, several countries of the former Warsaw Pact, as well as the newly liberated Baltic states, were clear in their conviction that a secure future could, for them, only be guaranteed within NATO. A balance needed to be kept, felt perhaps most strongly in United States, between on the one hand fur-

---

[1]Press Communiqué S-1(91)86, Issued by the Heads of State and Government participating in the meeting of the North Atlantic Council in Rome 8th Nov. 1991, www.nato.int.

ther developing the relationship with post-communist Russia, and on the other hand supporting central and eastern European states in their pursuit of security and democracy. Russia's resistance to an enlargement of NATO meant that an alternative to membership was needed that could still be viewed as a step down that path for aspiring states. This need was even clearer as the aspiring states to a large degree lacked the capabilities and the interoperability to be easily integrated into the Alliance.

As an answer to this problem, it was suggested that a closer relationship between the Alliance and the participating states in the NACC should be established. The focus should be on practical cooperation and include combined efforts to increase transparency in defense planning, promoting democratic control of armed forces and building military capabilities in order to enhance the common ability to conduct peacekeeping operations.[2]

At the Summit in Brussels in January 1994, NATO reiterated its conviction that its "own security is inseparably linked to that of all other states in Europe."[3] At the meeting, the Partnership for Peace (PfP) was launched. The PfP Framework Document issued at that meeting makes it clear that it was created to "strengthen the ties with the democratic states to our east" and that PfP would, indeed, be a step on the way to membership. But NATO's invitation was broader than that. The intention was "to forge a real partnership—a Partnership for Peace." NATO, therefore, also invited other Commission on Security and Cooperation in Europe (CSCE) countries, which were able and willing to contribute.[4] In doing this, NATO underlined its "conviction that stability and security in the Euro-Atlantic area can be achieved only through cooperation and common action."[5]

---

[2] Ronald D. Asmus, *Opening NATO's Door: How the Alliance Remade Itself for a New Era*, Columbia University Press, 2002, p. 35

[3] Declaration of the Heads of State and Government participating in the meeting of the North Atlantic Council ("The Brussels Summit Declaration"), 11 Jan. 1994, www.nato.int.

[4] Partnership for Peace: Framework Document, issued by the Heads of State and Government participating in the Meeting of the North Atlantic Council, NATO Headquarters, Brussels 10-11 Jan. 1994, www.nato.int.

[5] Ibid.

Partners Aiming Only for Partnership— Sharing Interests, Combining Efforts

The opening up of PfP to include countries other than those participating in NACC meant that PfP now contained two distinct groups of countries: those who saw PfP as a way towards membership and those who had other reasons for their participation.

Sweden cited as its starting point its interest in participating in the development of a common European security order. Sweden also put great emphasis on the opportunity afforded by PfP to take part in increasing the effectiveness of international peacekeeping operations.[6] This was an obvious need based on the experiences from the United Nations-led Protection Force (UNPROFOR) mission in former Yugoslavia. PfP offered a framework for increasing interoperability in future operations. This would not only increase operational effectiveness, but it would also increase the security of the personnel deployed. The latter was all the more important since it was clear that the international community was entering into a new era of increasingly more complex military engagements. The concept of peacekeeping operations was evolving into a concept of peace support operations, meaning that part of the task would, in the future, be to actually make the peace that was then to be kept.

Sweden also referred to the aim of supporting democratic control of armed forces and greater transparency in defense planning. It stated its clear intention to contribute to this work. Specifically, it stated its intention to contribute to concentrated efforts to build peacekeeping capabilities primarily in the Baltic States.[7] This became the starting point for substantial support, which on Sweden's part was to include the donation of a full brigade and a comprehensive training package for Estonia, Latvia and Lithuania as part of a larger international effort.

The PfP, thus, became a tool not only for increasing interoperability and building capabilities in order to prepare participants for membership in NATO, but also a tool to further aims and objectives related to a wider strategic interest. This was an important driving fac-

---

[6]The Foreign Affairs Committee report 1993/94:UU18, Security Policy Issues, Swedish Parliament. www.riksdagen.se

[7]Ibid.

tor in the development of the PfP in the years to come, resulting in an enhanced partnership and the Euro Atlantic Partnership Council being established at the Summit in Sintra in 1997.[8]

Building on the Example of PfP—The Mediterranean Dialogue (MD), The Istanbul Cooperation Initiative (ICI) and Partnerships Across the Globe

In the fall of 1994, NATO initiated an enhanced dialogue with partner nations in the Mediterranean region. NATO based its decision on the conviction that security in Europe is closely linked to security and stability in the Mediterranean. Apart from contributing to regional security and stability, the MD was aimed at improving mutual understanding to avoid misconceptions about NATO and its policies. The practical dimension of the MD is based on the same objective as that of the PfP, i.e. "to contribute towards regional security and stability through stronger practical cooperation, including by enhancing the existing political dialogue, achieving interoperability, developing defense reform and contributing to the fight against terrorism."[9]

At its summit in Istanbul in 2004, NATO offered countries of the broader Middle East region an opportunity to engage in practical bilateral security cooperation. Having focused initially on the political dimension and cooperation within peace support operations, the ICI has gradually developed its practical dimension.[10]

In preparing for the 2006 summit in Riga, a proposal was put forward to "launch a program reaching out to global partners, those democratic nations who are interested and capable of working together and addressing security challenges." The goal was to develop an enhanced partnership with a core group of countries that are not in NATO, but want to develop a greater practical relationship with the Alliance. The focus was "to be on practical cooperation such as military and political exchanges between NATO and the new global partners."[11]

---

[8]Final Communiqué, Ministerial Meeting of the North Atlantic Council in Sintra, Portugal, 29 May 1997.

[9]Ibid.

[10]The Istanbul Declaration—Our security in a new era, Issued by the Heads of State and Government participating in the meeting of the North Atlantic Council in Istanbul, 28 June 2004, www.nato.int

[11]Kurt Volker and Dan Fata, statements at Hearing on The United States and NATO: Transformation and the Riga Summit before the subcommittee on Europe and Emerging threats

At the summit, it was decided that NATO should increase the operational relevance of relations with non-NATO countries, make consultations with PfP Partners more focused, for example by making full use of the different formats of NATO's interactions with partners, and enabling the Alliance to call ad-hoc meetings with those who contribute or are potential contributors, considering their interest in specific regions where NATO is engaged.[12]

NATO's cooperation with its partners across the globe has mainly been based on cooperation in NATO-led peace support operations such as in the Balkans, in Afghanistan and in Libya. The level of ambition varies greatly between global partners with some focusing on the political dialogue and others having a more comprehensive approach with a stronger emphasis on practical cooperation. The decision was, however, significant with respect to the importance it attached to inviting potential contributors to consultations on the planning of operations.

From Outreach and Dialogue to an Essential Core Task

After some 15 years of cooperating with partners in building capabilities, developing interoperability, conducting peace support operations and engaging in political dialogue, NATO's partnerships had become an essential part of its modus operandi and of addressing the challenges of its security environment.

The nature of NATO's relationship with its partners varies with on a case-to-case basis. Depending on the active choices of each partner, their engagement ranges from pursuing a political dialogue or giving political support for a specific activity to being fully engaged in NATO-led operations and working actively to develop capabilities and interoperability with the Alliance. While NATO's partnership activities have greatly benefited its partners from the outset, partners have been able to contribute more to NATO's various activities with time.

At the November 2010 summit in Lisbon, a new strategic concept for the Alliance was adopted. In it, NATO concluded that the "promotion of Euro-Atlantic security is best assured through a wide network

---

of the Committee on International Relations, House of Representatives, U.S. Congress, May 3, 2006

[12]Riga Summit Declaration, Issued by the Heads of State and Government participating in the meeting of the North Atlantic Council in Riga on 29 November 2006, www.nato.int

of partner relationships with countries and organizations around the globe. These partnerships make a concrete and valued contribution to the success of NATO's fundamental tasks."[13]

Cooperative security is mentioned as one of three "essential core tasks" and NATO states that it "will engage actively to enhance international security, through partnership with relevant countries and other international organisations."[14]

In April 2011, NATO's Foreign Ministers, following up on the Lisbon Summit, decided on a new Partnership Policy. The policy includes all the strategic objectives and cooperation areas of the existing partnerships, while respecting the specific nature of the different partnerships. It reiterates NATO's intention to allow partners contributing to NATO-led operations to take part in shaping decisions related to those operations. It also states that all NATO partners with an Individual Partnership and Cooperation Programme should have equal access to all activities offered by NATO. The decision meant that the number of activities accessible to partners in the MD, the ICI and to partners across the globe increased substantially.

NATO's 2012 Chicago Summit declaration stated: "With Operation Unified Protector-the Libyan Operation (OUP), NATO set new standards of consultation and practical cooperation with partner countries who contributed to our operation."[15] NATO also noted that "Partnerships play a crucial role in the promotion of international peace and security,"[16] and summing up the experiences from two decades of activities, it concluded that "for twenty years, our partnerships have facilitated and provided frameworks for political dialogue and practical regional cooperation in the fields of security and defense, contributed to advancing our common values, allowed us to share expertise and experience, and made a significant contribution to the success of many of our operations and missions."[17]

---

[13]Active Engagement, Modern Defense, Strategic Concept for the Defense and Security of the Members of the North Atlantic Treaty Organisation adopted by Heads of State and Government in Lisbon, 19 November 2010, www.nato.int

[14]Ibid.

[15]Chicago Summit Declaration, Issued by the Heads of State and Government participating in the meeting of the North Atlantic Council in Chicago on 20 May 2012, www.nato.int

[16]Ibid.

[17]Ibid.

NATO's Partnerships Today

A Larger NATO and Fewer Partners

In the years since the Partnership for Peace was established, NATO has gone through a number of enlargement rounds. While this has transformed the Alliance, it has also transformed the PfP. From a partnership mainly with nations preparing to join the Alliance, it has now transformed into a partnership mainly with partners who identify themselves as partners and that look at the partnership with this perspective. Rather than developing interoperability in order to prove themselves as prospective members, active partners are to a larger degree interested in developing interoperability in order to be able to contribute to NATO-led operations. The need for NATO to engage in support for security and democratic development of PfP partners is also relatively less than before.

At the same time, because a large number of partners with a very high level of ambition for their partnership have become members, the diversity among the remaining partners has increased. As the more ambitious of the remaining partners continue to develop their already modern armed forces, they have less and less in common with those that pursue more limited reform agendas. As for NATO's cooperation with partners outside of the PfP, heterogeneity is similarly as obvious.

Contributing Partners that Make a Difference

Since NATO decided to go "out of area" and take the responsibility to lead the Implementation Force (IFOR) in Bosnia, partners have contributed to NATO-led operations. Sometimes that has meant taking a political stand, providing contributions of a mainly symbolic value and sometimes it has meant providing sizable forces of acceptable quality.

Occasionally, however, contributions have been of great importance to the conduct of an operation. This has perhaps been most evident in the case of International Security Assistance Force (ISAF), where partner nations have made substantial contributions, running their own Provincial Reconstruction Teams (PRT) or providing advanced capabilities such as Intelligence, Surveillance and Reconnaissance (ISR) assets and Special Forces. The Swedish contribution to OUP with reconnaissance aircraft is another such example. These more advanced contributions are primarily made by a small group of partners that do not necessarily belong to the same partnership format.

The ability of these partners to provide advanced contributions to NATO's efforts are directly dependent on their level of interoperability and their experiences in working and exercising with NATO forces. Their needs include taking part of relevant documentation regarding standards, taking part in development of capabilities, be it within Smart Defense or participation in advanced exercises as well as participating in the decision-making related to the operations to which they contribute.

A Partner's Perspective—Building Security Together with Others

Since Sweden joined the PfP, it has gradually increased its cooperation and its commitment to the combined efforts with other partners and the Alliance. From a participation that was limited to practical activities, but politically important in the early years, the need for development of interoperability stemming from practical experiences in the field in the Balkans has grown to a determined policy to contribute to the development of the PfP to meet the needs identified.

This was also fuelled by the experiences from working together with members and partners in providing support to the Baltic states. In seeing PfP's potential, Sweden became one of the strongest driving forces in its development.

Sweden's capability development now takes place to a large and growing extent within the PfP. NATO standards, the Planning and Review Process (PARP), PfP exercises and training within the PfP have all become necessary and natural parts in developing Sweden's military capabilities. Leaving a paradigm of self-sufficiency, Sweden has come to pursue building security together with others. It is now looking primarily at an international context when developing its capabilities and contributing to peace support operations.[18] Sweden's cooperation with NATO is "Smart Defense" in the making.

---

[18]The Defense Committee report on Defense, 2008/09:FöU10, Swedish Parliament, www.riksdagen.se

Cooperative Security and True Partnership—A Europe Whole and Free

The closer relations between NATO's more committed partners and the Alliance itself have occasionally been questioned. Why should NATO work so closely with partners who do not share the burden of collective defense? Why should NATO let partners influence decisions the members make? The two questions are often coupled to a more direct one: If you want closer cooperation, then why don't you join?

These questions hint at an underlying view that all partners cooperate with NATO in order to prepare themselves for membership. This view was, of course, to a substantial degree correct some 15 years ago. Developments since then have, as has been shown earlier, made it clear that a number of partners have chosen to engage in close cooperation with NATO for other reasons. Through this cooperation, they have been better positioned to contribute to peace and security, as well as work related to capacity building, than would otherwise have been the case.

As has also been shown, it has been to NATO's distinct advantage that these partners have contributed. The Implementation Force (IFOR), the Stabilization Force (SFOR), the Kosovo Force (KFOR), ISAF and OUP are all good examples of that.

NATO and Partners share an interest in working for peace and security in the world. In working together, they achieve a synergetic effect greater than the sum of the parts. This is the message from the summit in Lisbon and in the Strategic Concept: if NATO is to undertake an endeavor, it is better off working together with its partners.

The words from the 1994 Summit Declaration in Brussels that "Our own security is inseparably linked to that of all other states in Europe" and NATO's "conviction that stability and security in the Euro-Atlantic area can be achieved only through cooperation and common action" as expressed in the PfP Framework Document serve as reminders that while NATO members' security might be a collective undertaking within the Alliance, the security of Europe is an interest that NATO shares with its European partners. As envisioned in the PfP Framework Document, it is in all of our interest to "… forge a real partnership—a Partnership for Peace."

Forging a Real Partnership with a Clear Purpose

Striking the Balance—A Strong Alliance and an Effective Partnership

There needs to be a clear separation between NATO members and non-members. Among allies, there is a strong bond of solidarity ultimately expressed in Article 5 of the North Atlantic Treaty. But more than that, there is a readiness and commitment to bear the burden of upholding the capabilities needed to guarantee the validity of Article 5, to accept the responsibility of doing one's part as part of a greater whole.

Needless to say, non-allies have not made these commitments. They might bear the burden of maintaining modern armed forces at some level of readiness, but they do so according to their own best judgement, not accepting the peer pressure and scrutiny that the allies have accepted. They might decide to contribute to NATO-led operations, but they have not given any guarantees to come to the aid of allies under attack. Neither have they, of course, accepted any such guarantees.

This means that a partnership between, on the one hand, NATO, and on the other hand, partner countries, needs to reflect these basic facts. A partner cannot take for granted that NATO would come to its support in a military conflict. Nor can a partner be part of the decision-making within the Alliance.

At the same time, it is reasonable that partners would have the possibility to put forward their views before NATO takes decisions on matters that are of significant concern to them. As was decided by NATO at the Lisbon Summit in 2010 and incorporated into guidelines in 2011,[19] partners should be part of the decision-shaping processes in operations to which they contribute. If partners put their soldiers in harm's way to support NATO, the Alliance should do what it can to keep them informed and seek their views on decisions affecting them in this regard. As in the case of ongoing operations, it should also be in NATO's interest to include partners that have repeatedly and substantially contributed to its operations when shaping its decisions concerning the development of the capabilities needed to contribute. This, after all, is what partnership is about.

---

[19]Political Military Framework for Partner Involvement in NATO-led Operations, Meeting of NATO Foreign Ministers in Berlin, 15 April 2011, www.nato.int

Therefore, partners' contributions to NATO activities should not be necessary for NATO's ability to conduct the activity. Partner's contributions to NATO forces, such as the NATO Response Force (NRF), or to NATO exercises should be seen as enhancing the effect or effectiveness of NATO's efforts, but not be allowed to fill the need that the Alliance has for contributions from its members. Partners' contributions should continue to be regarded as add-ons to a functioning and fully resourced activity.

Given the growing number of partners to the Alliance and the global nature of NATO's partnerships, NATO should make sure that partners that are ready to commit to highly developed cooperation and ready to contribute to more complex military operations, regardless of their geographical location, are given the opportunity to pursue this objective. The significance of distances in military conflict and military operations is less than it used to be and the interests of partners in this regard are less bound by geographical location.

The decision to create a Partnership Cooperation Menu open to all partners should, therefore, be followed by the creation of cooperative arrangements that disregard the geographical divisions between different partnerships.

NATO's Continuously Changing Challenges

NATO's challenges continue to change. At the time of PfP's creation, NATO faced a large number of newly independent states in need of support to secure stable and democratic societies. Focus was put on giving support accordingly towards democratic control of armed forces, capacity building and political dialogue. Soon these needs were complemented with new ones resulting from the need to work with partners in securing peace in former Yugoslavia and preparing partners for membership in the Alliance. New aspects came to the fore, including language training, interoperability and exercises. As the complexity of NATO's operations grew, so did the demands related to preparing partner nations for contributing to these operations. ISAF and OUP represented an increase in complexity of military activities compared to that of earlier operations.

At the same time, PfP transformed into a vehicle for partners to develop their own capabilities for conventional warfare. In the case of

Sweden, previous limitations for participation in exercises under Article 5 were done away with, and such exercises are now seen by Sweden as a natural part of the international exercise program that can be used to enhance its national defense capabilities.

As the operations in the Balkans and in Afghanistan wind down and as military technology continues to develop against the background of Russian occupation of part of Ukraine, and as a result of the continued shift in economic and military weight towards Asia and the Pacific, NATO's challenges continue to change.[20] This, in turn, is changing the nature of NATO's partnerships.

A Partnership for the Challenges of Today and Tomorrow

NATO's partnerships should continue to be based on the principles of open-endedness, self-differentiation and transparency. Open-endedness has provided NATO with the possibility to cooperate with an increasing number of partners. The principle of self-differentiation lets partners choose their level of ambition, making sure that there is a possibility for a partner country to gradually evolve, building its capabilities and ability to contribute to ever more complex activities. The principle of transparency serves the important purpose of confidence building, making sure that NATO's and partners' activities are not misinterpreted or perceived as threatening.

At the same time, it is clear that NATO needs to find ways to develop cooperation with those partners that are willing and able to commit more to common activities. It follows from the principle of self-differentiation that one form of cooperation will not fit all partners. While some partners might be satisfied with having a political dialogue with NATO, others might wish to contribute to the most advanced of NATO's activities, be it within operations, within capability development or in other activities.[21]

---

[20]The evolving challenges of NATO and its partners have been described in e.g. Franklin Kramer, *Transatlantic Nations and Global Security: Pivoting and Partnerships*, Atlantic Council, March 2012

[21]Proposals on developing NATO's partnerships to meet the evolving challenges have been described in e.g. Franklin Kramer, *NATO Global Partnerships: Strategic Opportunities and Imperatives in a Globalized World*, Atlantic Council, March 2013

ISAF has allowed for NATO's partners across the globe to be more engaged in contributing to the efforts of the Alliance, and in so doing, cooperation between partners in different partnership formats has increased. It has become obvious that the more committed and able partners are not grouped in some specific corner of the world, and that geography is not a proper criterion when determining which partners have common interests and levels of commitment. Against this background and ahead of the Chicago summit, voices were raised arguing for the establishment of a "Pacific Peace Partnership" between NATO and partners within PfP and partners in the Asia/Pacific regions.[22]

After more than a decade of operations in Afghanistan, NATO's focus is changing. More emphasis is again placed on the security of Europe and on capabilities related to high intensity operations.

Sweden is going through a similar process. It is clear that operations out of area will play a lesser role in the foreseeable future. More focus will be put on preparing for operations in support of stability in its own region in northern Europe. Sweden's security policy dictates that it is prepared to conduct military operations, together with others, in support of security and stability in its region. These operations do not necessarily have to be connected to the defense of Sweden itself. It might, in fact, be related to the defense of a NATO member. If such operations are to be conducted with NATO, it is imperative that the forces Sweden contributes are highly interoperable, to a much greater extent than has been needed in peace support operations within ISAF, KFOR or even OUP. Sweden, thus, needs to be able to conduct operations together with NATO and a group of its most capable partners at the absolutely highest end of the conflict spectrum and to be able to prepare for such operations. Today's partnership is not adequate to facilitate such a capability.

At the same time, Sweden's capability development, in terms of defense materiel projects, will to an increasing extent be conducted in global partnerships. Swedish activities related to capability development will, therefore, also take place in cooperation with these part-

---

[22]R. Nicholas Burns, Damon M. Wilson and Jeff Lightfoot, *Anchoring the Alliance*, Atlantic Council, May 2012.

ners, some of which are countries envisaged to be part of the proposed Pacific Peace Partnership.

The highest levels of interoperability, making partners able to take part in the most complex of operations, require access to the most advanced exercises and the most advanced training, i.e., information and documentation that NATO might not readily want to make available to any partner country. A partnership with those more committed needs to, therefore, be based on a high level of trust and confidence between NATO and the partner country concerned.

Years of joint NATO-led operations, of building security together through Security Sector Reform (SSR) activities as well as conducting joint exercises contribute to building such trust. A close and frank political dialogue on issues of mutual interest would be an important addition to this.

A Proposal for a New Partnership Structure

NATO's partnership structure should consist of three levels. At a first basic level partners and NATO engage in political dialogue and improving mutual understanding in order to avoid misconceptions about NATO and its policies. This should constitute the entry point for new partners.

The second level should consist of opening NATO to partners who wish to develop their capabilities and their interoperability, in order to be able to contribute to peace support operations, to other activities or to prepare themselves for membership, which would in principle be similar to today's PfP.

The third level of partnership should be to open to those that have demonstrated willingness and ability to contribute to NATO's efforts that goes beyond what has so far been the norm in the PfP.

Earlier this year, Sweden and Finland put forward a proposal for a developed partnership that would allow those partners more committed to cooperating with NATO to take further steps in developing their abilities to contribute to the cooperation. Building on the thoughts presented above, the proposal described what a third, new level of partnership could contain and what could be the criteria

NATO might wish to apply in accepting such a partner. These criteria might include a partner's military capability, its degree of military interoperability, its history of participation in military operations and exercises led by the Alliance, as well as its participation in programs such as the Planning and Review Process (PARP), the Operational Capabilities Concept Evaluation and Feedback (OCC E&F) and forces such as the NRF.

Having taken a decision on a partner's eligibility, based on the criteria of its choosing, NATO could then extend to this partner the possibility to take part in a package of activities that would give it the opportunity to even further develop its ability to contribute to future cooperative endeavours. Sweden and Finland suggested that this package might include:

- A structured and regular substance-driven political dialogue, taking place on all levels including Minister's level and covering all relevant matters related to operational connectivity, capability development, capacity building as well as prevention and thematic issues of political significance;
- Earlier involvement in policy discussions on operational activities;
- Extensive involvement in Smart Defense and all parts of the Connected Forces Initiative (CFI);
- Participation in planning and decision shaping related to exercises, including within the NRF;
- Continued good use of PARP and OCC.

This third level of partnership should not be viewed as a substitute for membership, nor is it aimed at replacing the need for membership action plans. It is a tool to promote partners' work towards becoming more able to contribute to addressing the challenges facing them and NATO.

Looking Ahead

NATO's partnerships have been established to engage non-allies in a closer dialogue and cooperation with NATO in accordance with the needs identified and relevant to the specific group of partners concerned. For the Partnership for Peace, the focus has, as we have seen, shifted over time to address the issues at hand as the security environment and the challenges for NATO and partners have changed. We are currently in the middle of such a transformation, ending the challenges of military operations in Afghanistan and the Balkans and entering into an era of a resurgent Russian aggression and military capability, of an increasing weight of the Asia-Pacific in international affairs and of the continued evolution in military affairs. NATO's partnerships must change accordingly. Partners that are prepared to continue to contribute to security, to capability development and to the securing of democracy in Europe and globally should be supported in their pursuit. It lies in their interest, but above all, it lies in the interest of NATO.

Chapter 6

NATO Enlargement and Enhanced Partnership: The Nordic Case

Hans Binnendijk, Debra L. Cagan, and Andras Simonyi

In a very short span of time, the geostrategic situation in Europe has changed dramatically. President Putin has presented a systemic, long-term challenge for the NATO Alliance. What this means for the Baltic-Nordic region can be understood in the context of overall Russian strategy, which is to regain as much control as possible over Russian-speaking areas in its neighborhood and to present an alternative governance model to liberal democracy. In light of continuing and clearly tailored and differentiated Russian actions in the Nordics and Baltics, and the more sophisticated, but less obvious efforts in the Czech Republic, Slovakia, Hungary and Bulgaria, we are left with this conclusion: Putin's Russia will continue to attempt to destabilize the Baltic states through open provocations and covert actions. The Nordic-Baltic region is steadfast in its resolve to hang on to the western, liberal, value-based model, and this is a special threat to Putin's ideal Russia. It is in this context that we call for bolder steps for the full integration of Sweden and Finland into the Alliance.

The recently concluded NATO Summit has taken steps in the right direction with the new partnership arrangements for Sweden, Finland, Australia, Georgia, and Jordan. And new NATO Memorandums for Host Nation Support with Sweden and Finland are critical steps forward. That is a good start. But they do not go far enough. We argue here for immediate implementation of these new Understandings, with fundamental and tangible actions so that there can be no mistake that Sweden and Finland are entering a new era with NATO.

This chapter will focus on Finland and Sweden and explore both the case for membership and ways to enhance their partnership with NATO until a political consensus emerges in those countries for membership.

Almost A Member, But Not Quite

Sweden and Finland have begun the process of entering into a new kind of relationship with NATO, a new level of partnership which would enhance abilities and contributions for NATO, Sweden and Finland. Both Nordic nations have effectively used the Partnership for Peace to integrate militarily with the Alliance. That process of enhancing the network of military ties with the Alliance took another major step with the conclusion of Host Nation Support Memorandums of Understanding (MOUs) Umbrella Agreements with NATO. But contrary to press reports, these MOUs do not extend NATO's security guarantees known as Article 5 commitments to Sweden and Finland. They only make such a commitment operationally easier to accomplish.

These MOUs are the latest elements in a web of military arrangements that draws these two Nordic countries closer to the Alliance. Sweden has a similar MoU with NATO. In January 2014, Sweden and Finland signed an agreement drawing their two militaries closer together and there is discussion of a bilateral defense treaty between the two. Both nations have participated in NATO operations in Afghanistan and in joint military exercises, including with the NATO Response Force (NRF). Both have developed closer military ties to other Nordic and Baltic nations who are members of the Alliance. But these thickening military and operational ties have not been matched by corresponding ties with the Alliance on the political side. The pull towards non-alignment has remained strong in both countries, although the debate on the need for change is heating up, as a result of the dynamics of the security environment and the transatlantic relationship as a whole.

For Finland, non-alignment was less of a choice and more of a necessity. It was forced upon Finland as part of the post-war architecture by the Soviet Union as the price for national survival. For Sweden, non-alignment held great attraction during the Cold War. It viewed itself as a bridge between east and west; a kind of moral voice that only a neutral power could have and use. While Sweden had very close and deep cooperation with the West, especially with the United States, it still portrayed itself and had a national ethos of firm neutrality.

This ethos of non-alignment persists to this day in Sweden, but is now more often portrayed as the moral voice espousing active support for humanitarian assistance, disaster relief and development and support for those most in need. But views evolve over time and Sweden's joining of the European Union (EU), hugely controversial at the time, has been part of that evolution. Sweden and Finland are already part of the transatlantic community that shares democratic values and ideals and rejects nationalistic fervor, military encroachment and blatant intolerance. These same values stand in stark contrast to their eastern neighbor.

Public opinion in both countries has become more favorably inclined towards NATO membership since Russia's annexation of Crimea and support for membership in both countries has risen. That support could increase to a thin majority if their national leadership would embrace and work actively for membership. The new Prime Minister of Finland, Alexander Stubb, has been a vocal proponent of joining NATO and wants to begin a debate in Finland about membership. Three Russian airspace violations in the span of a single week in summer of 2014 have only added to this debate.

In Sweden, the Chief of the Defense staff began the debate anew by declaring that if attacked by Russia, it could defend itself alone for only a week. Then Russian bombers approached Sweden in an exercise in March 2013 and demonstrated that the Swedish Air Force was unable to respond. Russia also carried out exercises near the Swedish island of Gotland. Russia is building its military capability in the High North, which concerns both counties. Russia has also indicated that it would reopen military facilities for 150,000 personnel near the border with Finland. Then, came the annexation of Crimea. On March 18, Finnish Prime Minister Jyrki Katainen declared that while his nation was non-aligned, it was not neutral. And former Finnish President Martti Ahtisaari in April called for both countries to join the Alliance. The two nations are likely to consult closely to coordinate their policies.

While the drift is clearly in the direction of support for membership, there remains reluctance to take the final step. A referendum would be needed in both nations, and given their history of non-alignment, the outcome would be uncertain. If a referendum failed, the process might be set back by decades. And Russia has declared its firm opposition to membership for both countries, could use its energy exports in the region as a weapon to demonstrate that opposition and seek to influence the internal debate in both countries. So leadership in both countries is moving cautiously.

There are measures short of membership that would strengthen the position of Sweden and Finland, which would entail a stronger political partnership with NATO. Before we explore these measures, we first want to make the case for membership, which we believe would be preferable for both of these countries and for the Alliance.

The Case for NATO Membership

Sweden and Finland are currently betting that the thickening web of military relationships with NATO members will provide an adequate insurance policy against future Russian aggression. They are paying a premium for that insurance policy by integrating militarily with the Alliance and participating as Partners in NATO military operations. The question is: is that insurance policy adequate to cover the risks posed by a revanchist Russia? We think that the premium that these two Nordic States are paying is already about what it would be if they were NATO members and that they are not receiving an insurance policy equivalent to NATO membership. So they should join.

The starting point for this analysis is the nature of Russian policy today. One might argue that Russia is more dangerous today than the Soviet Union was during the Cold War. While the Soviet Union was considerably more powerful economically, ideologically and militarily than Russia is today, during the last decades of the Cold War, the Soviet Union was essentially a status quo power. The Brezhnev Doctrine was about preventing roll back, not gaining new territory. Vladimir Putin's Russia is about using coercion, intimidation and occasionally military power to regain some of what it considers to be a lost empire. Russia is a power in decline with a still potent conventional military capability and a powerful nuclear force. That makes Russia particularly dangerous to its neighbors. Russia will aim to destabilize the Nordic-Baltic region where it can.

The risk posed by Russia to its neighbors is one of hubris and over-reach. Putin has won what he considers to be a series of recent successes by taking steps just short of what might cause a major Western response. He has used these so-called successes to gain significant political strength at home. In the process, he has ignited Russian nationalism and expectations. History is full of examples of bold leaders who have overreached and blundered badly in the process. Putin poses that risk. Swedish and Finnish membership in the Alliance would be a clear deterrent signal that he has gone too far.

Sweden and Finland have had a ringside seat to observe recent Russian behavior. As NATO moved ahead with enlargement, bringing the Baltic countries into the Alliance, Russia was actively violating its side of the bargain in Ukraine and Armenia where it "negotiated" multi-decade agreements to keep Russian forces in those countries. In Transnistria, Russia claimed that its troops could not leave because the rail lines were blocked by those begging them to stay. When threats and cajoling proved ineffective, Russia invaded Georgia and occupied territory in South Ossetia and Abkhazia. When the West let that one go without major recrimination, Russia decided there was little downside to invading Ukraine and illegally occupying Crimea. When you are living next to that neighbor, non-alignment might look a lot less appealing.

NATO's response to Russian occupation of parts of Georgia and Ukraine should be particularly sobering to European non-aligned nations. It reinforced that fact that NATO "Partners" are not "Members" and their insurance policy against military attack has a very high deductible. Sweden and Finland may believe that they are different and that NATO would defend them because they were never part of the Soviet empire, because they are members of the European Union and because they are culturally fully part of Western Europe. That assessment may or may not be correct, but they may be betting their sovereignty on it.

In considering the costs and benefits of NATO membership, Sweden and Finland will calculate the risk that NATO membership might drag them into an unwanted conflict with Russia. This is, however, counterintuitive: their membership will likely deter any maverick action by Russia. The most likely scenarios to trigger NATO's Article 5 common defense commitment today are in northeast Europe, particularly the Baltic states. Should overt Russian aggression be launched there, the two Nordic non-aligned states would become involved in any event (they are also bound by the EU Solidarity Clause). That is inherent in their close political and military relationships with the Baltic states. Their leaders admit as much. So if they would defend their neighbors anyway, why not gain a clearer mutual agreement about common defense by joining the Alliance? There is also a nuclear element to these concerns: that they will be a part of a nuclear Alliance when they are decidedly anti-nuclear. But in reality, most NATO countries do not have nuclear weapons deployed on their territory. Russia does not share similar qualms and continues to play nuclear chess in Kaliningrad. Nations can be NATO members and still maintain a strong national identity and bilateral relationships.

Another strong argument for NATO membership is that today Sweden and Finland follow NATO's lead on multiple issues including military operations, but they have no vote. To borrow a phrase from the American Revolution, there is "taxation without representation." By joining the Alliance, they would develop a strong say in its future decision making.

Efforts to strengthen military interoperability between NATO and these partners, a nudging up against the Article 5 line without quite embracing it, reflect the reality that strict non-alignment in the 21st century is a far less attractive choice than it was even a decade ago. Indeed, non-alignment in the context of the geographical neighborhood in which Sweden and Finland reside may be far more difficult today that at any time in the last 25 years. Citizens of these two countries have overwhelmingly supported many NATO missions, and Sweden's support of the Libyan operation exceeded that of many NATO Allies. Indeed, partnering with NATO has not been very controversial. There has never been a more compelling and urgent reason for Sweden and Finland to join NATO as there is now. From the perspective of Sweden and Finland, Ukraine should serve as the ultimate wake-up call that almost being a member, regardless of a multitude of special arrangements, leaves you on the wrong side of the line of those countries who will be collectively defended.

For NATO, the Alliance is clearly better with Sweden and Finland as members. Already militarily integrated and interoperable from years of deployment experience and exercises, these countries have gone beyond that original concept of partners who are useful, but not necessary. In Afghanistan and Libya they were necessary. Sweden and Finland add logical geographic space to the Alliance, which enhances NATO's credibility with its Baltic members. These Nordic countries also add considerable experience in humanitarian assistance and in other operations where military force is not an option. Not every operation NATO engages in will be kinetic. Finally, from both the NATO perspective and that of Sweden and Finland, global challenges mean global partnerships and both of these countries and NATO will benefit in the decades ahead from their continued integration and interoperability with countries like Australia, New Zealand and others who will remain active partners of the Alliance.

Therefore, NATO could declare that it would welcome Sweden and Finland for membership the moment they declare their willingness.

Just Shy of Membership: An Enhanced Partnership

If the time is not yet right politically in Sweden and Finland for them to join the Alliance formally, new steps need to be taken now to give substance to the new Umbrella Understandings. These tangible arrangements would provide greater political cohesion and consultation to complement their growing military interoperability. NATO with Sweden and Finland must be unified in a commitment to creating a new type of NATO partnership to ensure that these countries can be closer and more integral than ever before.

NATO must focus on partnerships as a tangible way to strengthen the Alliance, and as an instrument of strategic importance that can enhance defense planning and capability development, and critically in this current environment, contribute to collective defense and territorial integrity. For the Alliance to move forward, it will need to develop big ideas with defined incremental steps, like making room for partner participation in the NATO Response Force (NRF), to ensure that partners who want to join NATO have a clear cut path to that goal, that partners who want to remain partners but continue to be an integral part of operations and transformation have their own path, and newer partners can have an enabling relationship with the Alliance for the equal sharing of knowledge and expertise.

As NATO moves beyond the paternalism of Partnership for Peace, it will need new focus and new ideas. NATO has long had conceptual ideas of partnership, but it was not until Afghanistan that a new and comprehensive approach to partnerships occurred. Born out of the crucible of daily conflict, NATO forged deeper security relationships with Sweden and Finland, cooperating on training, education, exercises, integration, intelligence sharing and joint development of critical technologies. Partnerships in Afghanistan were not defined solely by what NATO did or could do for its partners, but what its partners did and could do for NATO.

Inside NATO, the historical discussion about burden-sharing turned into one about risk-sharing, from a discussion of budgets to one of political will and from deploying military capabilities into effects achieved. For partners, their contributions to this out of area operation could be measured on par with NATO member contributions. The result was that some partners clearly were perceived to be more effective than some members of the Alliance. For their part, NATO's partners need to know that this Alliance is still committed to relationships and partnerships that can enhance the safety and security of every country involved. And most importantly, NATO's partners need to know that their sacrifices fighting alongside NATO in Afghanistan count for something. Partners that have made the supreme sacrifice to join NATO in Afghanistan and in other operations, who have endured the tragic costs of war without regard to NATO membership, deserve a new kind of relationship. The world and especially NATO's partners are watching to see how this Alliance, this guarantor of security for so many countries, reacts to this latest incursion right next door to NATO. They want to be certain that their sacrifices fighting alongside NATO in Afghanistan do not become distant memories.

How It Might Work

The Nordic-Baltic countries and the United States, as nations and collectively through NATO, are more operational, integrated and interoperable than at any time in history and are among the most militarily capable grouping of countries in the world. NATO, along with its partners Sweden and Finland, has become more resilient, flexible and agile. Because of its partners, NATO has been able to not only provide for collective defense at home, but face global challenges in Afghanistan, North Africa and elsewhere. Instead of viewing partners as a burden as some in NATO have alluded, NATO should instead view Sweden and Finland as part of the guarantor of security for a Europe whole and free, or put another way, you don't have to be a member of the club to share the same values and want the same outcomes. The worth of these Nordic partnerships should be measured not just by formal status, but by what they bring to the table.

While there is no better time than the present for Sweden and Finland to declare their intent to join NATO, there are a number of steps that the Alliance can take to hasten this momentous decision.

- Their partnership with the Alliance must reflect trust, confidence and a spirit of cooperation. These European partnerships should be viewed by NATO as a strategic mission for the Alliance; giving new life and new meaning to them is the best guarantee for long-term stability and a Europe whole and free.

- NATO must go beyond being merely a headline framework for partnerships and must devise and implement a new mechanism with specific tangible activities and consultations that are directly relevant to partners as well as to allies.

- This new mechanism must allow for allies and partners to cooperate on a new kind of equal footing. This new partnership approach for Sweden and Finland would build on years of experience and accommodate these two countries who are partners by choice.

NATO's commitment to a fundamental restructuring of the partnership mechanism can easily begin with Sweden and Finland. They are net contributors and have a military track record on par with many of the most capable members of the Alliance. They have substantial military capacity, are already militarily integrated, interoperable and have a long history of and exercises with NATO members, deploying and operating in Afghanistan on a level matched by some, but clearly not all NATO members.

- Using what we call the Opt-In model, NATO would establish a formal mechanism that would provide for a weekly routine consultation at the political, military and intelligence levels with Finland and Sweden, with the North Atlantic Council (NAC), the Military Committee, the International Staff and the International Military Staff.

- This would occur routinely on all levels, including ministerials and summits. These would not be simply plus-one models, but instead would become a practical and regular part of doing business at NATO headquarters, the Supreme Headquarters Allied Powers Europe (SHAPE) and at the Allied Command Transformation (ACT) in Norfolk.

- It would give both countries early involvement in policy discussions relevant to operations. It would give them a role in planning and decision shaping relating to exercises. It would give them full access to NATO Smart Defense programs and to the Connected Forces Initiative.

- Sweden and Finland could decide to Opt-Out of these consultations and operations, but NATO would put everything on the table. In other words, Sweden and Finland get to make the decision of how much or how little they choose to be engaged.

- The NRF would be used as a facilitator for continued interoperability and force integration, and Sweden and Finland would be given the opportunity to not only participate, but have a role in the planning involved in force rotations and related exercises and operations.

- Sweden and Finland would also be given the opportunity to Opt-In or Out of exercises, education, training and operations and could also propose or make recommendations for exercises, training and education and even for potential operations.

- Implementation of this approach could begin immediately.

While there is full support for military interoperability with partners in the Alliance, there may be some opposition to the degree of political integration with Enhanced Partners that we propose. Some believe that territorial defense is a matter for allies only, while others would prefer to see Sweden and Finland connect to European defense through the European Union. We believe that the case for eventual Swedish and Finish memberships in the Alliance is so strong that taking an Opt-In step like the one we propose trumps these other concerns.

Conclusion

Despite Russia's very active efforts to revise the narrative on NATO membership, it has only encouraged other countries to want to join this Alliance. Some members may prefer to see an end to the enlargement process, and by taking every possible "agitprop" measure to stir dissent in Europe and contribute to growing ultra-nationalism and isolationism, Russia is confident that it can ensure a smaller footprint for a future NATO. Meanwhile, NATO aspirants have been sitting anxiously on the sidelines waiting for that supposed open door to finally unlock. Some of these countries have done everything according to the rules, have implemented a succession of changes and have fully integrated their forces into NATO, including serving bravely in Afghanistan, and still find themselves on the outside looking in.

NATO still has an enormous opportunity to show that the door is still open and that partnerships really mean something. NATO can do this by fundamentally changing its relationship with Sweden and Finland not just with MOUs but with real substantive change, thus establishing a new path for other partners, and in the course of this make it very clear that if these two countries choose to step over that threshold, there will be a fast track to membership in place and NATO will welcome them as its newest members.

Chapter 7

Challenges to the Nordic-Baltic Region after Crimea: A Baltic View

Pauli Järvenpää

Russia's annexation of Crimea has changed the security debate paradigm in Northern Europe. In the region, as in the rest of Europe, there has been an agreement on a certain rules of behavior that are accepted and respected by all state actors. The principles of territorial integrity, inviolability of state borders and the abstention from the use of force against other states have been the fundamentals that the post-World War II Western state system is based on.

These principles have been enshrined, *inter alia*, in the United Nations Charter of 1945, in the Helsinki Final Act of 1975 and in the 1990 Commission on Security and Cooperation in Europe (CSCE) "Charter of Paris for a New Europe," in which all of the signatories, including the Soviet Union, solemnly promise to refrain from the use of force against each other and "fully recognize the freedom of States to choose their own security arrangements."[1]

Nordic and Baltic states are part and parcel of that security system. As small states in the system, they have all relied on a friendly Russia in an attempt to integrate in peaceful cooperation with its neighbors. Instead, they now see in Moscow a regime that has defined itself not only in opposition to the West and its values, but one that has gone on to annex a part of its neighbor and continue to interfere in its internal affairs.[2]

---

[1] P.6 of the document. Also, in the opening paragraph the signatories, the Heads of State and Government of the participating States of the Conference on Security and Cooperation in Europe (CSCE), declare that "The era of confrontation and division of Europe has ended. We declare that henceforth our relations will be founded on respect and cooperation." http://www.osce.org/mc.

[2] A wise and seasoned observer has recently stated that "I would argue that if we are to look for an analogous era, we can rather find it in a pre-Cold War period, in say 1946 or 1947, feeling around to figure out what we should do." President Toomas Hendrik Ilves at Wroclaw Global Forum, June 6, 2014. http:/www.president.ee/en/official-duties/speeches.

This chapter briefly addresses two aspects of the conundrum that Nordic and Baltic countries now find themselves in. Firstly, what does the fundamental change in the attitude and behavior of a major player in the system, the Russian Federation, mean for these small states? And, secondly, what might these countries do to mitigate the negative effects of the system change?

Russian Military Build-Up

A starting point is to note that security issues around the Nordic-Baltic region have in the last few years become highly militarized. Energy security, trade and commerce, investments and other more "soft" security issues continue to be important for the region, but they have been increasingly pushed back, and the political discourse has been more and more focused on the military capabilities that have a bearing in the region. There is perhaps no imminent danger of military force against the countries of this region, but it cannot be excluded entirely. In this context, Russia's steady improvement of its military capabilities has drawn much attention.[3]

Since 2004, when Estonia, Latvia and Lithuania joined the North Atlantic Treaty Organization (NATO), the question of whether these three states—squeezed into a relatively narrow sliver of land between the Baltic Sea and Russia—are defensible, has been at the heart of debate.[4] For a long time, the question remained unanswered. NATO was busy in Afghanistan, the United States was engaged first in Iraq and then in Afghanistan, and the conventional wisdom held that speaking about military threats in northern Europe was both impolite and outdated. After all, why continue to cling to a Cold War-era mindset when the only foreseeable military threat to the Nordic-

---

[3]For an excellent detailed study, see the publication coauthored by a well-known Finnish national security scholar and three former high-level Finnish military intelligence officers Stefan Forss, Lauri Kiianlinna, Pertti Inkinen and Heikki Hult, *The Development of Russian Military Policy and Finland*, National Defense University, Department of Strategic and Defense Studies, Series 2: Research Reports no.49, Helsinki, 2013.

[4]A particularly useful study is Bo Ljung, Tomas Malmlöf, Karlis Neretnieks and Mike Winnerstieg (eds.), *The Security and Defensibility of the Baltic States. A Comprehensive Analysis of a Security Complex in the Making*, October 2012, FOI, Stockholm.

Baltic region was the cooperation with the Western Alliance in the NATO-Russia Council?

Russian behavior in and around Ukraine has now brought new relevance to that question. Russia's audacity has taken most observers by surprise. Yet, there have been signs over the past decade that should have been detected. These signs are related to Russia's build-up of military capabilities and the way it trained and exercised them.

Firstly, in order to use its forces more efficiently, Russia adopted a new military command structure of "power ministries" forces—not only the military ones. The most relevant new command to the Nordic-Baltic region is the Western Military District, whose headquarters are stationed in Saint Petersburg. It combines the forces of the former Leningrad and Moscow military districts, the Northern and Baltic Fleets, the First Air Force and Air Defense Command, as well as the Russian forces based in Kaliningrad.[5]

Secondly, former heavy divisions were restructured into lighter and more flexible brigades. The long-term goal is for all ground force formations to eventually become fully-manned, permanently ready units. General conscription will not be abandoned, but the high-readiness forces will mainly consist of professional soldiers. That, for its part, will make it possible for Russia to carry out fast, well-coordinated and joint military operations. All in all, with new military equipment introduced to the units, combined with the availability of the high-readiness units, Russian military capabilities have improved by leaps and bounds.

Thirdly, these improvements were reflected in Russian military exercises, especially in those that were carried out in the western parts of Russia. For example, in September 2013, a Russian-led military exercise *Zapad-2013* took place in the Russian Western Military District and in Belarus. This was a combined joint forces exercise, which geographically covered the western parts of Russia, western Belarus, the enclave of Kaliningrad and the Baltic Sea. According to the Russian official notification to the Organization for Security and Co-operation (OSCE) notification regime, *Zapad-2013* was an exercise that brought together 12,900 troops in Belarus, of which 2,500 troops

---

[5]For more details, see Forss, Kiianlinna, Inkinen and Hult, op.cit.

were Russian. In Kaliningrad, the exercise was to include 9,400 troops, 200 of which from Belarus.[6]

In reality, however, *Zapad-2013* was a much larger exercise than declared to the OSCE. If all units are included —not only the ground forces units—the number of different troops involved adds up to more than the declared 22,000 soldiers, with a more accurate estimation being 70,000 troops. These troops included, for example, various staff, logistics units and railroad troops. If one counts the simultaneously-run Ministry of the Interior troop mobilization exercises as being a part of *Zapad-2013*, the total figure becomes as high as 90,000 troops.[7]

During 2013, in addition to the regular, pre-planned and pre-notified exercises, there were also several military-district-wide, unannounced readiness exercises ("snap combat exercises") in all four Russian military districts. It is important to note that the same troops that participated in *Zapad-2013's* exercises—according to Russia's own source, roughly 150,000 of them—were put on high alert in such a snap combat exercise in February 2014, in the midst of the Ukrainian crisis.

Why is all of this relevant to the security of the Nordic and Baltic countries? Firstly, as is the case with military exercises in general, Russian exercises are important because they reveal where, against whom and with what capabilities Russia is prepared to use its military forces. Secondly, *Zapad-2013* is most relevant in today's security context, as the same troops involved in it were put on a high alert in a snap combat exercise while events in Ukraine were unfolding. And, finally, as *Zapad-2013* demonstrated, Russian capabilities as well as moves in Crimea and in eastern Ukraine highlighted Putin's political will to use these capabilities.

These actions also affected Finland, a militarily non-aligned country, by way of the highly publicized and televised appearance of President Vladimir Putin with his Defense Minister Sergei Shoigu and an entourage of generals observing a massive live-fire demonstration of

---

[6]The information the Russian authorities provided in their OSCE notification is summed up by Colonel General Alexander N. Postnikov, Deputy Chief of the General Staff of the Armed Forces of the Russian Federation to the 732nd Meeting of the Forum for Security Cooperation, October 30, 2013, OSCE, Vienna.

[7]Interviews of several countries' intelligence officers by the author of this article.

Russian power at the Kirilovski training site on the Karelian Isthmus west of Saint Petersburg (Kirilovski is in fact a former pre-World War II Finnish artillery training site called Perkjärvi), while Russian troops infiltrated Crimea.[8]

Of course, there were even earlier signs that should have provided ample warning, but they were largely ignored: examples are the Russian military actions against Georgia in August 2008 and the *Zapad* and *Ladoga* exercises in 2009, in which the Russians simulated military operations against the Baltic States and Poland, with the attacks culminating in a nuclear strike against Warsaw. There was also a show of force against Sweden on Good Friday in April 2013, where the Russian bombers, flanked by their fighter escorts, simulated thrusts against the non-aligned country, going as far as feigning nuclear missile releases against targets in the Stockholm area.[9]

Military Responses to Russian Actions

What measures have the Nordic and Baltic countries taken, then, in order to respond to Russia's bold and unprecedented actions?

The North Atlantic Treaty Organization (NATO) operation *Steadfast Jazz 2013*, conducted on the territories of the three Baltic States and Poland on November 2-9, 2013 should be examined in the context of the Russian *Zapad* exercises. Its overall aim was to allow NATO troops to train for a full spectrum of potential missions, including humanitarian missions, cyber defense and anti-missile defense, as well as high-intensity combat. The specific task was to test the Alliance's ability to defend the territories of Poland and the Baltic states, in the framework of the NATO contingency plan called *Eagle Guardian*.[10]

It should be recalled that there was much behind-the-scenes maneuvering before the *Eagle Guardian* came to be approved by NATO's Military Council in January 2010 as a contingency plan to

[8]"Putin seurasi harjoitusta Kannaksella," *Helsingin Sanomat*, 3.3.2014, http://www.hs.fi/ulkomaat.

[9]Mikael Holmström, "Ryskt flyg övade anfall mot Sverige," *Svenska Dagbladet*, April 22, 2014.

[10]Vladimir Socor, "NATO Holds Article Five Exercise in the Baltic Region," November 12, 2013, http://www.jamestown .org/blog.

defend the Baltic States. Many NATO governments, among them the German government in particular, were concerned that such a plan, if publicly disclosed, would damage the West's relations with Russia. However, Poland and the Baltic States' vigorous efforts to approve the plans bore fruit, which helped alleviate Baltic States' anxiety about the military situation vis-à-vis Russia.[11]

Steadfast Jazz 2013 consisted of approximately 6,000 troops, of which roughly half participated in live exercises in combat formations; the remainder worked in the various exercise headquarters. One sub-command headquarters was located in the Ādaži Base near Riga. By nationality, about 3,000 soldiers participating in the exercise were Polish, 1,000 came from France (which held command of the land component of the NATO Response Force—NRF—in 2014), and the rest of the troops originated from nearly all of the 28 NATO members states. Baltic States provided contingents of 200-300 soldiers each. Non-NATO partner nations Ukraine, Sweden and Finland participated with small groups of staff officers each.[12]

An interesting part of *Steadfast Jazz* was *Baltic Host*, which tested Baltic states' capability to provide the necessary support for incoming NATO troops. After all, not only are ports and airfields instrumental in transporting troops safely to their destinations, but they are also significant for a range of logistics infrastructure, from feeding the troops to moving them into their defensive positions to resupplying them with ammunition, which are vital to the success of any defense strategy.

Much of this is "back to basics" for NATO. With NATO's presence in Afghanistan drastically reduced post-2014, it is difficult to predict where the Alliance assets could be used "out of area." Therefore, there will be a need to strike a balance between expeditionary capabilities and NATO's somewhat neglected capability for collective defense. Also, testing the Alliance's ability to defend the territories of its more exposed members is a sound and necessary check on the concept of Connected Forces Initiative (CFI), which together with Smart

---

[11]An excellent overview of how the *Eagle Guardian* contingency defense plan was finally approved is offered by Mark Kramer in "Russia, the Baltic Region, and the Challenge for NATO," PONARS Eurasia Policy Memo No.267, July 2013, Harvard University.

[12]http://www.aco.nato.int/steadfast-jazz.aspx

Defense is designed to become a main vehicle for the Alliance's future transformation.

"As the International Security Assistant Force (ISAF) mission winds down, NATO's challenge is to maintain the cohesiveness and compatibility it has achieved through the years," said Commander Joint Force Command Brunssum, General Hans-Lothar Domröse, during *Steadfast Jazz*.[13] Also, in the words of General Philip Breedlove, Supreme Allied Commander Europe (SACEUR) and Commander United States European Command (USEUCOM), the Alliance is now, as a result of working together in Afghanistan, "at the pinnacle of our interconnectedness."[14] That level can be maintained only through frequent and demanding exercises.

Interestingly, *Steadfast Jazz* marked only the first time since 2006 that NATO exercised all command and control levels (strategic, operational and tactical) together with all four components of the NATO Response Force (land, maritime, air and special forces). Whatever the reasons for previous omissions, it is clear that NRF is the "tip of the spear" in NATO's ability to respond to emerging crises, which is why realistic and demanding exercises like *Steadfast Jazz 2013* are essential.

For the militarily non-aligned countries Finland and Sweden, NATO exercises are also valuable, since it helps these countries develop and test their level of interoperability with the Alliance. In a manner typical for these two countries, there are now moves under way to quietly, but steadily improve national defenses through international cooperation. One avenue of cooperation has been the arrangement for Nordic Defense Cooperation (NORDEFCO), where two Nordic NATO countries, Norway and Denmark, are also active. Furthermore, a bilateral action plan on improving defense cooperation between Sweden and Finland was signed in early May 2014, and the final conclusions will be published in January 2015.[15]

On May 15, a majority of the Swedish Defense Review Board, an official parliamentary group with all eight parties represented, agreed

---

[13]http://sj13.nato.int/jazz-ends-on-a-high-note.aspx

[14]http://www.defense.gov/news/newsarticle.aspx?id=121014

[15]For an analysis, see Pauli Järvenpää, "Swedish-Finnish Defense Cooperation: How to Make It count?," www.icds.ee/blogs, May 10, 2014.

on an increase of future defense spending, including the purchase of major new weapons systems of submarines and fighter aircrafts. Meanwhile, a rising parliamentary consensus in Finland wants to allot more resources to defense after the parliamentary elections in April 2015.

In both countries, the fresh positive look on defense spending can be interpreted as a reaction to the aggressive exercise patterns of the Russian forces near the Swedish and Finnish borders, as well as Russian actions in Crimea and beyond.[16]

Raising the Deterrence Threshold: Baltic Countries' Responses

Robust NATO exercises in the Baltic Sea region illustrate Alliance solidarity and promote practical military-to-military cooperation. What else could be done to expand reassurance measures?

The argument here is that to raise the threshold of deterrence, much could be done relatively quickly and at rather little additional cost.[17] Here are a few specific suggestions of what the Alliance could do in the Baltic states, and also what the Baltic states could do themselves.

First, the Alliance, spearheaded by the United States, reacted in a timely fashion to augment its presence in the Baltic states. For example, in early March 2014, the United States deployed an additional six *F15Cs* to augment the four F-15Cs already in Lithuania, honoring a NATO peacetime commitment to offer a quick reaction interceptor aircraft to ensure the air-policing mission over Estonia, Latvia and Lithuania. At the same time, the United States deployed twelve *F16s* and three *C130J* aircrafts to Poland to participate in U.S.-Poland aviation detachment training. Furthermore, in April 2014, approximately 600 U.S. Special Forces personnel were deployed to the Baltic states and Poland to take part in training and exercises. Also, NATO will update its defense plans concerning the Baltic states and Poland and develop a readiness plan that includes a review of joint exercises,

---

[16]See, for example, Mats Johansson and Pauli Järvenpää, "Suomen ja Ruotsin sotilaallisesta yhteistyöstä," Helsingin Sanomat , June 4, 2014.

[17]Some of these arguments were presented in my ICDS blog on March 20, 2014, "On Deterrence and Defense: The Case of Estonia," http://blog.icds.ee/article/pauli-jaervenpaeae/on-deterrence-and-defense-the-case-of-estonia.

threat assessments, intelligence-sharing arrangements, early-warnings procedures and crisis response planning.[18] U.S. efforts included a 1 billion dollar European Reassurance Initiative, which will be spent on increasing training and exercises, as well as on rotational presence of U.S. troops in Europe, particularly on the territory of the newer NATO allies.[19]

These measures contribute towards reassuring Baltic States of the Alliance's concrete and robust support. In addition, the Alliance should seriously consider establishing a permanent military presence in each of the Baltic States. No large formations of troops need to necessarily be deployed. However, the stationed troops should provide an exhaustive mixture of various key military specialties. The units should, for example, include experts on logistics, to be used in training and exercising those Baltic units that would provide host-nation support (HNS) for incoming Allied troops. That would be of crucial importance. There should also be specialists in intelligence gathering and analysis, as well as experts in electronic and cyber counter-measures. Finally, the units should have specialists on air-to-ground fire support, anti-tank weaponry and anti-aircraft defense. These specialists should be used to train Baltic militaries to call for Allied fire support or to be engaged in early anti-tank and anti-aircraft defense, if hostile forces ever violated the Baltic borders.

These permanent Allied contingents would not need to be large in numbers: a battalion-sized unit would suffice for each Baltic State. For political purposes, they should be multi-national, displaying a wide commitment within the Alliance. Such units would act not simply as a classic trip-wire, but would also provide visible reassurance of the Allied commitment to uphold the collective security pledge of Article 5 of the North Atlantic Treaty.

---

[18]For further details of support to the Baltic States and Poland by the United States and NATO, see Fact Sheet: U.S. Efforts in Support of NATO Allies and Partners, March 26, 2014, http://www.whitehouse.gov/the-press-office/2014/03/26/fact-sheet-us-efforts-support-of-NATO-allies-and-partners and Fact Sheet: European Reassurance Initiative and Other U.S. Efforts in Support of NATO Allies and Partners, June 3, 2014, http://www.whitehouse.gov/the-press-office/2014/06/03/fact-sheet-european-reassurance-initiative-and-other-us-efforts-in-support -of-NATO-allies-and-partners.

[19]Ibid.

One cannot stress enough the need for these units to be multi-national. What the Baltic States probably want most is U.S. presence in their countries, but it would also be a politically powerful signal to any aggressor if the units contained meaningful numbers of soldiers from other major European NATO countries. German troops are a particular case, and a special effort should be made to include them in these formations.

Second, NATO should take another look at the concept of pre-stocking military equipment, fuel, lubricants and ammunition. It worked well during the Cold War for countries like Norway and Turkey, so why wouldn't it work now for the Baltic States? Foreign trips would be paired with their kit for exercises in those areas they would be operating in, and pre-positioning would have a deterrent value of its own, as it would obviously help to bring the Allied troops faster into the operations areas. In each of the Baltic countries, the need for pre-stocking would be for a brigade-sized land forces unit, in addition to pre-stocking materiel for the incoming air force and naval units.

Third, NATO should regularly update its defense plans for the Baltic States. These plans should be exercised and fine-tuned annually. Such exercises should regularly bring Allied troops to the Baltic countries, especially troops from NATO's larger allies. U.S., British and German troops, as well as troops from France, would be an explicit sign of Allied commitment.

Finally, larger Allied countries could bolster Baltic states' national defense quickly through donations of excess equipment or through favorable conditions to purchase such equipment.[20] The acquisitions would help these states develop the capabilities for the type of military contingencies they will most likely face, given the lessons of Russia's invasions of Georgia and Crimea and given Russia's *Zapad* exercises.

For the Baltic states, these lessons indicate that it would be a good idea to create a high number of small units —no more than a platoon or a company—equipped with modern, but simple-to-use and powerful anti-tank, anti-air and intelligence-related equipment, trained and

---

[20]The recent purchase of Estonia of the Javelin anti-tank missile system from the United States is a prime example of a small state buying into more than just a good missile system. See Martin Hurt, "Two Birds, One Stone," www.icds.ee/blogs, June 16, 2014.

deployed throughout these states by voluntary defense organizations (such as *Kaitseliit* in Estonia) to defend key assets which sustain the vital functions of society—airports, ports, transportation nodes, power stations and military facilities—whose vulnerability is high. And their vulnerability is high precisely because professional militaries are so small in all these states. Voluntary defense organizations, provided that their units are well-trained and adequately exercised, would be able to fill the gaps. They could also handle the "little green men," whom the Russians used first in Crimea and then in parts of eastern Ukraine. Improvements should be focused on rapid responses: events in Crimea show that it took very little time for the Russian forces to occupy strategic sites in Crimea. Therefore, rapid response defense units for the Baltic States should be prioritized.[21]

All this could be done relatively quickly and inexpensively. Also, it is important to note that these measures are purely defensive, and if carried out, would not escalate the military situation. Over time, such measures would need to be integrated into a comprehensive security strategy for all three Baltic countries.[22]

If adopted, these measures would make it exceedingly difficult to occupy Baltic states without a high cost to the potential attacker and would also win precious time for the Alliance to come to the rescue if push comes to shove.

Conclusions

As we contemplate the lessons identified for the Nordic and Baltic countries from the Russian use of military threats and actions in Crimea, it is useful to recall the classic adage that diplomatic power is the shadow cast by military power. The clear increase in Russian military capabilities, both through more flexible troop structures and

---

[21]See, Martin Hurt, "Lessons Identified in Crimea," www.icds.ee/publications, April 17, 2014.

[22]On the concept of comprehensive security, see Tomas Jermalavicius, Piret Pernik and Martin Hurt, with Henrik Breitenbauch and Pauli Järvenpää, *Comprehensive Security and Integrated Defense: Challenges of Implementing Whole-of-Government and Whole-of-Society Approaches*, February 2014, ICDS Report, Tallinn, Estonia.

through adoption of high-tech improvements in their weapons systems, casts a growing shadow over the Nordic-Baltic region.

In light of the preceding discussion, the following observations and recommendations are highlighted here:

1. Geopolitics is not dead. With its words and deeds, the Russian government has demonstrated that it is intent on carving out a dominant sphere of influence for Russia; its appeal to Russian-speakers in the neighboring countries poses a challenge to the small Baltic states with sizable Russian-speaking minorities.

2. While there is probably not an imminent threat to small Nordic-Baltic states' national sovereignty, Russian government attitude—backed by a public approval rate of more than 80% in the opinion polls—cannot be ignored. NATO's defense capabilities still remain unmatched and the Allied commitment to collective defense is solid. However, it is of utmost importance that the Allied capabilities will be available in time and place of relevance.

3. As Crimea and Georgia have demonstrated, Allied governments need to be prepared to deal with strategic surprises and disruptive shocks. To mitigate their consequences, Allied governments and partner nations should have the highest possible situational awareness. This, in turn, would require that certain Russian developments and activities—especially the military exercises—are continuously monitored and assessed, and that the results will be shared among the participating countries.

4. Early responses by regional Nordic-Baltic national forces would be critical. Therefore, all measures strengthening intelligence-gathering and assessment capabilities would be urgent. A special feature of Russian actions has been the "hybrid" use of force: mixing of "soft" and "hard" measures, spiced with cyber-attacks and strategic information wars over the hearts and minds of the population. To counter these actions, strategic communications, planned and delivered by the Allied and partner countries together, would be highly relevant.

5. As the regional security environment is multifaceted and evolving, regular monitoring and assessment is warranted. NATO's contingency plans for the collective defense of the Baltic States and Poland should be periodically re-assessed and regularly tested in robust and complex exercises. That would guarantee the coherence and effectiveness of potential crisis response and collective defense operations in the region.

6. In order to respond adequately to hybrid threats, Baltic states should design and execute complex comprehensive security or total defense plans that would involve these countries' civilian and military authorities to work together and integrate their separate efforts into a common disaster response plan.

7. For a rapid Allied response to unforeseen and quickly unfolding events, Host Nation Support (HNS) arrangements should be firmly in place in the Baltic states. To the extent possible, NATO infrastructure funds should be used to build up the needed facilities. In each country, local manpower should be recruited, trained and exercised.

8. To reassure Baltic states, a sustained, non-sporadic presence of U.S. troops in the region would be highly desirable. No large troop formations would be necessary, but it would be useful to have military specialists, with skills in, *inter alia*, intelligence, electronic and cyber counter-measures, air-to-ground fire support, anti-tank and anti-air defense systems and the HNS. That would not only reassure these States of the United States' support, but it would also raise the threshold of deterrence. These troops should also be engaged in regular exercises with regional forces.

9. In general, besides the United States, Europe's main allies should have a presence, temporary or more permanent, in each of the Baltic states. German troops are a particular case, and a special effort should be made to include them, but also the presence of French, Italian, Spanish and British troops would be desirable.

10. Pre-stocking of military equipment, fuel and lubricants, as well as different kinds of ammunition would also raise the deterrence threshold. It would bring the Allied troops faster

into their operations areas. The need for pre-stocking would most probably be for a brigade-sized unit in each of the Baltic states, in addition to pre-stocking materiel for the air force and naval units.

11. There are also measures that could be adopted by the Baltic states themselves. One such measure would be to create a high number of small local units equipped with modern, but simple-to-use weaponry by voluntary defense organizations. These units would, if needed, defend the vital functions of society (airports, ports, transportation nodes, power stations, military facilities, etc.). Provided these units are well trained and adequately exercised, they would offer a shield, which would win valuable time for the more conventional defense to get organized in the form of national forces or Allied reinforcements.

Chapter 8

Challenges to the Nordic-Baltic Region after Crimea As Seen from Washington

Heather A. Conley and Caroline Rohloff

On March 18, 2014, Europe's security architecture, crafted at the end of the Second World War and refined by the Helsinki Final Act, came to an abrupt end as Russian President Vladimir Putin formally annexed Crimea. The transatlantic community has not yet fully acknowledged the formal end of their former policy approach toward Russia and seems unable or perhaps unwilling to begin to outline a new security approach. The principal challenge to the transatlantic community and specifically to the Nordic-Baltic region will be to formally recognize the end of a nearly 70-year period of relative stability in Europe, to create a baseline understanding of the current and future threat posed by Russia over the next ten years and to begin to formulate a new European security architecture which directly engages and includes, for the first time, former Soviet and Warsaw Pact countries.

When observing recent events in Crimea and Eastern Ukraine, the transatlantic community was shocked by both the speed and completeness of this dramatic geopolitical shift. Yet why were Europe and the United States caught so unaware? Did European and American leaders not hear Putin in 2005 repudiate the post-Cold War settlement by suggesting that the collapse of the Soviet Union was the "greatest geopolitical catastrophe of the 20th Century"? Did they not hear Putin's 2007 speech at the Munich Security Conference, in which he declared that "Russia should play an increasingly active role in world affairs" and that Russia "has practically always used the privilege to carry out an independent foreign policy"? Didn't leaders see Russia's military build-up, including the deployment of nearly 3,000 "peacekeepers" in Abkhazia and 8,000 soldiers along the Georgian border in July and August 2008 in advance of Russia's rapid (though problematic) military mobilization and intervention in Abkhazia and South Ossetia? Did they not protest sufficiently about Russia's current occupation of these two territories through several thousand "authorized Russian peacekeepers" and "human rights defenders" as well as formal recognition of the "independence" or Russia's blatant violation of the 2008 cease fire agreement (which it signed)? Where was the strong transatlantic reaction to Russia's suspension of implementation of the Treaty on Conventional Armed Forces in Europe (CFE) in 2007 and where was the common NATO assessment of Russia's military modernization program (particularly readiness in the Western and Southern Military District and strategic Northern Fleet)? What has the repeated testing of Nordic-Baltic air sovereignty, such as the unauthorized March 29, 2013 incursion into Swedish airspace and large-scale Russian military exercises told us?

What this tells us is that nothing should have surprised the transatlantic community about Russian behavior towards Ukraine. However, after nearly a decade of clear policy messaging and use of force by Moscow, what has been demonstrated by the West has been an extraordinary display of transatlantic political and economic distraction as well as denial reminiscent of the late 1930s.

This chapter will provide a reflection on the current and future threats emanating from the Russian regime, which has and will continue to challenge the Nordic-Baltic region; it will outline the interactions and security engagement between the United States and the Nordic-Baltic region; and it will offer new thinking on NATO's and the United States' security role in the Nordic-Baltic region.

A Fundamental Shift or a Return to the Status Quo: A Transatlantic Threat Assessment

Since the end of the Cold War, Europe, and specifically NATO, has never developed a common perception of threats to its security. For southern Europe, the threat emanates from North Africa, the Sahel and the Middle East largely in the form of immigration and terrorism. For eastern Europe, the threat derives from Russia. For western Europe, there is little sense of threat at all, with the exception of threats from within the country itself. From the view of the United States, the threat is global in nature arising both from restive regional powers and non-state actors, which seek to control failing states, thereby creating regional and global instability.

As events in Ukraine have unfolded, the lack of a common European threat assessment continues to plague, if not outright debilitate, Europe's ability to appropriately respond to the annexation of Crimea as well as the asymmetrical warfare in eastern Ukraine and information campaign waged by Moscow. The crisis in Ukraine has also raised questions about America's future security role and presence in Europe. Without a common understanding of the security threat posed by Russia, the transatlantic community will be unable to develop a unified security response toward Russia.

To achieve some semblance of commonality, there are two questions that Europe and the United States must answer together: (1) what are Russia's (specifically Russian President Vladimir Putin's) long-term intentions toward the West and what is the nature of the Russian regime? And, (2) what will Europe's new security approach in the Nordic-Baltic region look like in response to these intentions? Uniquely, the Nordic-Baltic region may be able to articulate early responses to both questions, thereby offering a future guide to enhanced European collective defense.

When devising policy, it is important to understand patterns of behavior as well as the intentions of the key actor, here specifically President Putin, and the role they will play in shaping policy. As Vladimir Putin is *the* sole decision-maker in Russia, understanding what animates Putin is critical.

Patterns of Russian Behavior in the Region

The saying goes that with hindsight, vision is 20/20. In many ways, reviewing a series of Russian actions and behavior toward the Nordic-Baltic region and on regional security issues in general provides a clear and compelling narrative about Russia's likely future actions toward the region. In the future, Russia will sorely test Nordic-Baltic air and naval sovereignty, will increase its diplomatic, information and economic activities in the region to undercut those governments that counter Russia's historical narrative and will enhance its interactions with the ethnic Russian communities in Estonia and Latvia so as to weaken the governance and institutional structures of these two countries.

2007 Estonian Bronze Night Incident. In many ways, events in Estonia in April 2007 were the first overt display of Russian aggression toward a NATO and European Union member as a result of a different interpretation of history. The Estonian Parliament voted to relocate a monument, known as the Bronze Soldier, that honored Soviet soldiers for the "liberation and the defeat of Nazism" in World War II from an intersection in Estonia's capital to a near-by military cemetery. The movement of the monument caused a night of rioting in the capital between Estonia's ethnic Russian population and the Estonian population. Russian Foreign Minister Sergei Lavrov accused the Estonian government of having a "blasphemous attitude towards the memory of those who struggled against fascism." Another senior Russian official declared this was an attempt by Estonia toward the "legalization of neo-Nazism." Following the riots, Estonia experienced massive cyber-attacks, which NATO termed as an "operational security issue" and which continued for several weeks following historically significant days (Russia's victory in Europe Day—May 9) and following a speech in which Putin strongly criticized Estonia. Furthermore, the Estonian embassy in Moscow was besieged for a week and a Russian trade embargo against Estonia was implemented.

Russian Suspension of the CFE Treaty. On July 14, 2007, Russia announced that it would suspend compliance with the original 1990 Treaty on Conventional Armed Forces in Europe (CFE) due to "extraordinary circumstances ... which affect the security of the Russian Federation and require immediate measures." Russia's decision to suspend implementation of the CFE Treaty was based on a number of issues, including: the limited ratification of the 1999 adaptation agreement (only Russia, Ukraine, Belarus and Kazakhstan ratified it); the belief that the original treaty was only relevant in the immediate dissolution of the Soviet Union and that Russia has been disadvantaged by NATO's "Open Door Policy" and expansion into eastern Europe; and the expansion of U.S. military capabilities vis-à-vis an expanded NATO while Russia has been forced to limit their weaponization abilities. In addition to these dissenting views, Russia refused to act upon the "Istanbul obligations" under the renegotiated 1999 treaty, which required Russia to remove its troops from Georgia and Moldova. Moreover, in late 2007, Russia announced that it would no longer provide treaty-related information or permit inspections of its treaty-limited equipment (TLE) and would no longer limit its number of conventional weapons. Four years after Russia declared a moratorium on the CFE Treaty, the United States and NATO allies announced they would also cease performing the treaty obligations vis-à-vis Russia. The United States and NATO member states will no longer exchange information with Russia, provide notification of military activities to Russia or accept Russian-requested onsite inspections.

While it is difficult to pinpoint exactly how Russia's suspended compliance of the CFE Treaty impacted their mobilization efforts, there was wide speculation in 2007 that the required "immediate measures" would consist of troop buildups in border areas, particularly in the Caucasus, new pressures on Ukraine to maintain the Russian Black Sea Fleet in the Crimea beyond the 2017 withdrawal deadline and a refusal to leave Moldova. These speculations were not completely unfounded as Russia has maintained a "peacekeeping contingent" in Abkhazia, a unit in Transniestria to guard the estimated 20,000 tons of ammunition and equipment, and the agreement to maintain its Black Sea Fleet in Crimea was extended until 2042. Moreover, there has been some speculation that if the CFE Treaty had not been discarded, it could have provided an "off-ramp" to de-escalate the current crisis in Ukraine. Under the auspices of the treaty, Russia would have been required to notify in detail all treaty partners, including Ukraine and NATO members, of Russia's deployments along the Ukrainian border. However, without the obligations of the CFE Treaty, "Russia is free to engage in aggressive deployments and cat-and-mouse withdrawals and redeployments with no transparency or accountability."[1]

2008 Georgian-Russian Conflict. Prior to the August 2008 Georgian-Russian conflict, Russia, as a status quo power, upheld the principle of non-intervention in regards to other states' internal conflicts. However, Russia's military intervention in Georgia constituted a paradigm shift as Moscow not only demonstrated its right to violate the territorial integrity of a neighboring country to defend its interests (which was to prevent Georgia from entering NATO), but also recognized Abkhazia and South Ossetia as independent countries (only three

---

[1]Elisabeth Brocking, "Remember the CFE Treaty?" *The National Interest*, April 8, 2014, http://nationalinterest.org/commentary/remember-the-cfe-treaty-10203.

other states have recognized these territories). Prior to Russia's intervention, Russian passports were distributed to citizens living in Abkhazia and South Ossetia; Russia maintained 8,000 troops along the Georgian border after completing the Caucasus Frontier 2008 exercise; it shot down a Georgian unarmed aerial vehicle; and it established nearly 3,000 "peacekeepers" in Abkhazia and South Ossetia to conduct armed operations against Georgian troops if necessary. In Georgia in 2008, and then again in Crimea in 2014, Russia justified its intervention in these conflicts with the argument that Russian legislation permits the president to deploy troops to defend the honor and rights of Russian citizens.

Zapad Exercises and Russian Military Modernization. The years subsequent to the 2008 Georgian conflict have also revealed Russia's desire to modernize and strengthen its military forces, an effort which the Nordic-Baltic region has keenly observed. Between 2008 and 2013, the Russian government increased military spending by a third—in 2013 alone, the military budget rose by 26%—and drastically worked to reform both the armed forces and the defense industry.[2] Modernization efforts have been particularly focused on the Western Military District and the Northern Fleet. On September 8, 2009, Russia and Belarus staged *Zapad* 2009, a large-scale military exercise involving approximately 12,500 service personnel and up to 200 items of military equipment and hardware. The exercise rehearsed the interoperability within the framework of the Belarusian-Russian integrated air defense system.[3] While representatives from Latvia, Lithuania, Poland and Ukraine were invited to observe the *Zapad* 2009 exercises, many of the western observers perceived the exercise as a "regressive step: the exercise scenario concentrated on repelling a NATO-led attack on Belarus."[4] Of particular concern to western observers and Poland in

[2]Richard Weitz and Vera Zimmerman, "Modernization Leaves Russia's Military Improved but Limited", World Politics Review, April 15, 2014, http://www.worldpoliticsreview.com/articles/13705/modernization-leaves-russia-s-military-improved-but-limited#close; http://www.economist.com/news/international/21589900-atlantic-alliance-wants-new-role-after-afghanistan-time-being-it-looking.

[3]"Russia, Belarus start Zapad 2009 military exercise", Ria Novosti, August 9, 2009, http://en.ria.ru/military_news/20090908/156054418.html.

[4]Roger McDermott, "Zapad 2009 Rehearses Countering a NATO Attack on Belarus", The Jamestown Foundation, September 30, 2009, http://www.jamestown.org/single/?no_cache=1&tx_ttnews%5Btt_news%5D=35558#.U4eTnPldV8E.

particular was Russia's simulated nuclear strike on Warsaw as part of the exercises. The tactical nuclear element of these exercises was acutely noted in the Nordic-Baltic region and specifically represented a challenge to the U.S. nuclear security umbrella.

Four years later, from September 20-26, 2013, Russia and Belarus conducted the second round of *Zapad* exercises. Similar to *Zapad* 2009, exercises again envisioned joint forces repulsing an attack on Belarus; however, the 2013 training scenario was couched in an anti-terrorism narrative. Nordic, Baltic and Polish observers all registered concern regarding these exercises because they incorporated both anti-terrorist operations and urban warfare with an emphasis on special forces into a larger scenario that encompassed classic large-scale conventional theater operations.[5] Unlike the *Zapad* 2009 exercises, a simultaneous series of military exercises occurred stretching from the Russian Arctic to Voronezh and involved all branches of Russia's armed and special forces culminating in a combined mobilization of over 100,000 Russian military forces, including the mobilization of reservists in Leningrad and Nizhny Novgorod oblasts, as well as involvement from the energy, transport and interior ministries. In many ways, *Zapad* 2013 demonstrated Russia's considerable improvement in its armed forces' capabilities and the government's approach to mobilize, transport and deploy such large numbers of military personnel. In some ways, *Zapad* 2013 was a precursor to the annexation of Crimea. In the snap exercises executed by Moscow in March and April 2014, over 150,000 forces in the Western and Southern Military Districts were mobilized. These efforts are in stark contrast to NATO, which held its first collective defense exercise, the 2013 *Steadfast Jazz* exercise, in over a decade in Central Europe and the Baltics, which consisted of 6,000 NATO troops.

In March 2014, Russia conducted a large-scale military exercise of its Air Defense Troops in the Western Military District, which included 3,500 specialists and more than 1,000 pieces of military and special hardware. Russia has significantly increased the testing of the

[5]Stephen Blank, "What Do the Zapad 2013 Exercises Reveal?", The Jamestown Foundation, October 4, 2013, http://www.jamestown.org/regions/europe/single/?tx_ttnews%5Bpointer%5D=3&tx_ttnews%5Btt_news%5D=41449&tx_ttnews%5BbackPid%5D=668&cHash=3589f13e30f4c94e30e2de1d885de88e#.U445SfldXzg.

region's air sovereignty and intelligence and reconnaissance capabilities, as well as a testing of NATO's air response and reaction time. For the Nordic-Baltic region, this period has been reminiscent of the Cold War. In 2011, Russia resumed long-range flights of strategic bombers over the Nordic-Baltic region. Then, on March 29, 2013, two Russian Tu-22M3 Backfire heavy bombers, capable of carrying cruise missiles and nuclear weapons, with an escort of four Su-27 Flanker fighter jets, entered Swedish airspace without authorization. Swedish aircrafts were unable to respond in time and had to rely on Danish F-16s based in Lithuania to scramble and identify the unauthorized aircraft. A month later, on April 20, a Russian spy plane reportedly flew through the international airspace strip between Sweden's main Baltic islands of Oland and Gotland. This particular flyover happened to coincide with a large military training exercise Sweden was hosting with Finland, the United States and the Baltic states.

On May 21, 2014, Finland accused Russia of violating its airspace after two Russian-owned planes were suspected of flying over the Gulf of Finland without authorization, to which Finland responded by scrambling its own fighter jets. Since the annexation of Crimea, Russia has increasingly demonstrated its military readiness to include snap military exercises and air incursions into Finnish, U.S. and Canadian airspace. In May 2014, U.S. General Herbert Carlisle reported that there had been long-range Russian air patrols to the coast of California, as well as a circumnavigation of the U.S. Pacific territory of Guam. A U.S. F-15 fighter jet was scrambled to intercept the Russian strategic bomber near Guam. During the week of June 30 alone, Latvia experienced four Russian air incursions in a two-hour period requiring NATO jets to scramble in response. In addition to testing the region's air sovereignty, Russia has increased its naval presence in the Baltic Sea region, including a deployment in early June of 24 warships and vessels for military drills in the westernmost Kaliningrad region. On June 20, Navy Commander-in-Chief Admiral Viktor Chirkov announced that the Russian Navy would supply more than 50 combat and logistic vessels before the end of 2014. The unprecedented testing of Nordic-Baltic and North American air sovereignty will likely be "the new normal" for the foreseeable future.

Although there is intense regional focus on the Baltic Sea region, another region of great policy interest that will impact the security of the broader Nordic-Baltic region is the Arctic. Having placed policy focus on enhancing Russia's civilian and military presence in the Arctic, President Putin declared in March 2014, "Next is the further development of the combat personnel of our armed forces, including in the Arctic region." In December 2013, Russia reopened its base in the Novosibirsk archipelago and is currently renovating an additional six to seven airbases across the Russian Arctic. In spring 2014, Russia also announced its plan to reopen its military base in Alakurtti, close to the Finnish border. In addition to reopening many of its Arctic military bases, Russia has also been testing and modernizing its strategic nuclear capabilities. Russia currently has three completed Borei-class ballistic missile submarines, with an additional two to be in service by the end of 2014 and another three to be completed by 2020. On May 8, 2014, Russia demonstrated its nuclear capabilities when its Northern Fleet carried out a simulated nuclear attack in the Barents Sea involving submarines, bombers and land-based missiles.

Russian Movements in Kaliningrad. In early June 2014, Russia began a joint exercise of the Baltic Fleet, the Russian Airborne Troops and the Russian Air Force in the Kaliningrad Region. During the exercise, Russian Aerospace Defense Forces practiced placing S-300 air-defense missile systems, which have a 125-mile range, in combat readiness and locking on targets at different heights. These drills came in response to NATO's international exercises in the region, Saber Strike 2014 and BALTOPS 2014. Due to Kaliningrad's strategic borders with Poland in the south, Lithuania in the north and east and the Baltic Sea in the west, it is highly likely that Russia may perceive Kaliningrad as a "nuclear chess game." Moreover, since 2003, Lithuania and Russia have facilitated a bilateral transit procedure to Kaliningrad, increasing the strategic significance of the region. According to the transit agreement, Russian citizens traveling to the Russian region of Kaliningrad from mainland Russia via Lithuania are only required to produce transit documents instead of visas.

President Putin's March 18th Speech to the Federal Council. The totality of Russian military activities in the Nordic-Baltic region, beginning in 2007 with its cyber-attack against Estonia due to a different interpretation of Soviet influence to today's unprecedented level of activity in Ukraine, denotes an intensifying pattern of aggressive behavior by Russia in the region that must be immediately addressed. Yet, potentially more dramatic is Russia's political justification of its intervention in neighboring states as well as its increasingly authoritarian posture domestically.

As early as 1999, Russia articulated its "State Policy toward Compatriots Living Abroad," which covered Russian citizens living abroad, former Soviet Union citizens, Russian and former Soviet immigrants, descendants of compatriots and foreign citizens who admire Russian culture and language, thus creating a "Russkii Mir" or Russian world, in essence a virtual Russian supra-state populated with "compatriots."[6] Known as the Compatriot Policy, it focuses on former Soviet countries to include Latvia and Estonia with a particular emphasis on "the fight against the falsifiers of history", which means Russia will actively fight against any alternative view of the Soviet Union's role in the Great Patriotic War or World War II.[7] In 2010, Moscow provided substantial funding to Russian non-governmental organizations, Russian media outlets and cultural and language initiatives in these former countries.

The evolution of Russia's Compatriot Policy is important to understand in light of President Putin's speech on March 18 to the Russian Federal Council. Russia will defend and protect Russian speakers beyond its borders and those in Russia who oppose this policy are "national traitors." The role of history has also taken an outsized and aggressive role in Russia's policy toward its neighbors in the region as stated in both Russia's 2009 National Security Strategy and the 2013 Foreign Policy Concept, which states that Russia will "strongly counteract [...] attempts to rewrite history by using it to build confrontation and to provoke revanchism in global politics and to revise the outcomes of World War II." During his now famous March 18 speech, Putin made numerous historical references such as "Time and time again attempts were made to deprive Russians of their historical memory, even of their language and to subject them to forced assimilation. Nationalists, neo-Nazis, russophobes, anti-Semites executed this coup [...] these ideological heirs to Bandera, Hitler's accomplice during WWII." As of April 2014, it is a criminal offense in Russia to "rehabilitate Nazism."

[6]Heather A. Conley, *Russian Soft Power in the 21st Century: An Examination of Russian Compatriot Policy in Estonia*, Center for Strategic and International Studies, August 2011, p. 12.
[7]Ibid., p. 4.

A Transatlantic Security Response

With a clear pattern of threatening behavior and destabilizing neighboring countries implemented in the name of protecting Russian compatriots abroad, how should the transatlantic community respond?

Prior to the annexation of Crimea, NATO provided enhanced protection to European allies through the European Phased Adaptive Approach (EPAA) missile defense architecture, a system designed to protect against short- and medium-range ballistic missiles potentially from Iran, with missile defense interceptors based in Poland and Romania. As part of enhanced force protection for Poland, in May 2010, the United States sent a battery of surface-to-air Patriot-type missiles to the Polish military base Morag, the first such deployment on Polish soil. In addition to the Patriot missile battery, the United States also stationed about 100 to 150 troops in Germany to both service the battery in Poland and to train Polish soldiers to operate it. Because Patriot missiles are designed to intercept incoming surface-to-surface missiles and considering Morag is 40 miles from Kaliningrad, the United States has sent a strong signal of solidarity with, and protection of Poland.

NATO has also increased its exercise and training activities in the region—although quite belatedly. On November 2, 2013, over 6,000 NATO troops conducted large-scale exercises in Poland and the Baltic states as part of Operation Steadfast Jazz. These exercises came just weeks before the EU's Eastern Partnership Summit in Vilnius and were part of NATO's efforts to launch the NATO Response Force (NRF). The Steadfast Jazz exercises were the first time that NATO established a major military presence along Russia's border since Central European and the Baltic states joined NATO. These exercises signify a long-overdue focus on practicing collective defense after 13 years of out-of-area operations, as well as the need to signal strategic reassurance to the Baltic states and Poland amid increased Russian military spending and regional exercise activity. Operation Steadfast Jazz, however, revealed significant imbalances within the Alliance. France, as the lead NRF country, sent the largest contingent of 1,200 troops and Poland contributed 1,040 service personnel, while the United States and Germany only sent 160 and 55 troops, respectively. The very limited U.S. contingent was indicative both of Washington's reduced defense budget as well as of its assessment of low tensions in the region.

This picture has dramatically changed following the annexation of Crimea. The United States has deployed 600 military personnel to the Baltics and has reinforced its military presence in Poland by an additional 150 troops. The United States has also contributed ten aircraft to enhance Baltic air policing and has increased its participation in regional NATO exercises. On June 9, 2014, NATO exercise Saber Strike began at the Adazi training area in Latvia. The training operations sought to improve joint operational capability and interoperability, particularly integrating U.S. close air support with partner nation ground forces.[8] The 2014 BALTOPS exercise included the participation of naval forces from 14 countries and aimed to enhance maritime capabilities and interoperability and to support regional stability. America's enhanced military presence in Central Europe will be financially supported by the recently announced 1 billion dollar European Reassurance Initiative. The initiative will increase joint U.S.-European operations and training exercises; deploy detachments of U.S. planners to augment allied capabilities; increase responsiveness of U.S. forces to reinforce NATO initiatives; and will build the partner capacity of states such as Georgia, Moldova and Ukraine.

NATO's Multi-National Corps-North East (MNC-NE) based in Szczecin, Poland will also be considerably strengthened with additional forces from Denmark and Germany. On June 25, 2014, representatives from MNC-NE met to discuss the most urgent issues concerning the future of the Corps, including the need to upgrade the Corps readiness and how to improve its training program. The strengthening of MNC-NE in addition to a persistent, rotating NATO presence in the Baltics could be the beginning of a significant strengthening of NATO's presence in the Nordic-Baltic region. Finally, Finland recently signed a Memorandum of Understanding with NATO indicating Finland's readiness to receive assistance from allied forces and to maintain their military assets, such as ships and aircraft.[9]

---

[8]"NATO Joins Exercise Saber Strike 2014 in the Baltics", NATO Allied Command Operations, June 10, 2014, http://www.aco.nato.int/nato-joins-exercise-saber-strike-2014-in-the-baltics.aspx.

[9]"Finland to sign off on NATO assistance deal", Yle, April 22, 2014, http://yle.fi/uutiset/finland_to_sign_off_on_nato_assistance_deal/7201393.

The United States has also actively engaged with the five Nordic and three Baltic Defense Ministers to better coordinate their regional activities. U.S. Secretary of Defense Chuck Hagel attended a meeting with his Nordic and Baltic counterparts on June 3, in which they discussed a number of common security concerns as well as their desire for continued cooperation and the future implementation of the European Reassurance Initiative. As the five Nordic countries deepen and strengthen their defense and security cooperation through Northern Defense Cooperation (NORDEFCO), the United States has been an engaged partner with NORDEFCO. The NORDEFCO framework has enabled countries with common political and economic cultures as well as a common threat assessment to cooperate on security and defense issues. Today, NORDEFCO members conduct weekly cross border air force exercises. Bilaterally, the United States continues to strengthen its bilateral activities with Norway, including via the U.S.-Norway Cold Response Exercise, which rehearses high-intensity operations in winter conditions. In the March 2014 Cold Response Exercise, more than 1,200 partners and allies from 15 NATO countries met to conduct operations and training in the Arctic Circle, with the largest group of participants coming from the United States, Canada, France, the Netherlands, Great Britain and Sweden. Even on Arctic security issues, the U.S.-European Command has held the Arctic Security Forces Roundtable (ASFR) to discuss overall trends in the Arctic, such as search and rescue and shipping regulations, with the five Nordic countries.

Despite the plethora of NATO and U.S. security activities, enhanced physical presence and military engagement in the Nordic-Baltic region, the overall U.S. defense and security policy toward the region tends to be ad-hoc. The current U.S. policy is tactical and reactive to events rather than strategic, and a long-term and clear-eyed strategy about potential Russian destabilizing actions in the region is necessary.

A New U.S. and NATO Approach to the Nordic-Baltic Region

The annexation of Crimea has given NATO an opportunity to return to its core task of collective defense after 13 years of out-of-area operations in Afghanistan—but with a modern, 21st century approach to deterrence. This opportunity is tempered, however, by drastically-reduced European, and for the first time American, defense budgets. In June of this year, NATO Defense Ministers discussed the issue of collective defense and in particular, reviewed the measures needed to enhance collective defense in Europe. NATO Secretary General Rasmussen noted that NATO needed to "make NATO fitter, faster and more flexible"[10] by developing a Readiness Action Plan, which will include measures such as pre-positioning supplies and equipment in NATO member states as well as increasing NATO's reaction time to possible threats in response to Russia's mobilization efforts.

Another deliverable will be the roll-out of the Framework Nation Concept (FNC), originally a German initiative that has developed into a NATO concept, and in which MNC-NE could become a model of enhanced regional NATO command to the East. The FNC currently seeks to systematically address Europe's capability problem and efforts are being made to develop the FNC into flexible exercise and training programs. It is likely that the NRF will, at long last, be a focused operational effort with its earliest application to NATO's eastern border. These deliverables would send a clear message of a persistent NATO presence on its eastern flank. Another important NATO message will be continued focus on missile defense. The first phase of the EPAA has been successfully implemented and the next two phases are still on schedule. Although the fourth and final phase of this missile defense concept was cancelled in March 2013, a June 2013 bill in Congress proposed an amendment to the 2014 defense authorization bill and encourages hastening the implementation of the third phase, which places ground inceptors in Poland by 2018.[11] It is an encouraging sign that Poland and the Baltic states are increasing their defense spending in coming years, and Warsaw has stated that it will be purchasing additional missile defense capabilities by the end of 2014. Washington welcomes this development as it will strongly encourage additional finan-

---

[10]"NATO Defense Ministers discuss collective defense, Summit priorities", NATO press release, June 3, 2014, http://www.nato.int/cps/en/natolive/news_110608.htm?selectedLocale=en.

[11]Rachel Oswald, "U.S. Official Defends Spending on NATO Missile Shield, Under GOP Attack," Global Security Newswire, June 25, 2013, http://www.nti.org/gsn/article/us-official-defends-spending-nato-missile-shield-under-gop-attack/.

cial contributions from its NATO partners to support the costs of its missile defense system.

There are two missing strategic pieces: the first question is related to Sweden and Finland's future relationship with NATO. As strong NATO partners in the Partnership for Peace Program, Finland and Sweden have maintained strong operational ties with NATO in out-of-area operations, but have not engaged in collective defense activities. However, the annexation of Crimea has completely changed the strategic landscape for both countries, and the political elites in Sweden and Finland are undertaking assessments about their future security and defense requirements and how best to enhance their territorial defense in the near term. The Baltic states view non-NATO Sweden and Finland as a strategic vulnerability in their region just as Sweden and Finland in the early 1990s viewed the Baltic states as their strategic vulnerability and worked closely with Estonia, Latvia and Lithuania to strengthen their security cooperation. Politically, Sweden and Finland are not prepared to take a pro-active decision to join NATO. However, NATO as well as Sweden and Finland, must carefully detail and articulate what their current and future partnership will mean in the collective defense realm. Collective defense is reserved for members of NATO, not partners. Strategic ambiguity about how or whether NATO would come to the aid of Sweden and Finland (as it did in the case of Sweden in April 2013) is unwise. Whether Finland or Sweden joins NATO or not, it is clear that Finland and Sweden must increase their respective military spending and defense capabilities.

The last and perhaps most important missing element is a NATO threat assessment and intelligence estimate on Russian intentions in its immediate neighborhood, as well as its strategic objectives. This assessment should closely examine Russia's military position in the Nordic-Baltic region as well as the consequences of a more robust and persistent NATO presence in the Baltic states and a closer relationship between NATO, Sweden and Finland. This assessment must also consider the extensive Russian political, economic and societal influence in NATO member states that may limit independent action and threaten governmental stability. With an agreed and common view on the regional patterns of Russia's behavior and its future intentions, NATO will be able to develop a strategic and unified response to Russia that will simultaneously demonstrate strength and unity while maintaining transparency with Russia and exploring future avenues for dialogue. This assessment would build on NATO's 2010 Strategic Concept and ideally would be initiated immediately following the September NATO Summit by inviting a select group of senior foreign and defense policy officials to develop this assessment. NATO's response—be that a re-examination of the tenets of the 1997 NATO-Russia Founding Act, ending or delaying the sale of NATO weapons systems, NATO's future nuclear posture or enhancing NATO's collective readiness—can be in part guided by this assessment.

The experience of the Nordic-Baltic region with Russia over the past seven years is an instructive guide to discern patterns of Russian action, and it is the region which has most swiftly enhanced and deepened its future security posture nationally, regionally (through NORDEFCO) and multi-nationally (through NATO). Rather than a reactive, ad hoc approach to regional security, Washington, together with the Nordic-Baltic region, should develop a more robust and long-term strategic approach toward enhanced security in the region. Rather than view the Baltic states in particular as the "canary in the mine" to warn NATO of pending danger, this region must be the vigilant watchman at post.

Chapter 9

Energy Security in the Baltic-Nordic Region

Andris Razāns

Twenty-five years ago news channels from the other side of the Berlin Wall broadcasted mesmerizing images of Lithuanians, Latvians and Estonians forming a human chain approximately 400 miles long, stretching from Vilnius to Riga and from Riga to Tallinn. These events took place in the USSR two months before the Germans broke through the concrete wall dividing one nation in Berlin. The Iron Curtain was an ugly, barbaric attempt to isolate European nations on the basis of false ideological pretext.

For the three occupied Baltic states, it was a truly unifying moment that undoubtedly accelerated the restoration of their independence two years later. But the Baltic Chain, aside from its strong symbolism, was something more. It relayed the very clear and simple message that the future well-being and prosperity of the Baltic states would very much be determined by a level of mutual and regional integration.

The Baltic Sea Region as it is known today, with its deep pattern of integration, is a relatively recent phenomenon. Of course, because of shared geography and history, nations of the region have always enjoyed a high level of economic interdependence and have benefited from cultural exchange. But the current level of integration among Baltic and Nordic states, a group that I would call the North European Eight (distinct in meaning from the term Nordic), is a relatively recent development and has historically not been necessarily self-evident.

The tragic consequences of World War II and the Cold War that followed deprived Baltic-Nordic states from exploring the mutually beneficial opportunities of integration. The irony of the Cold War divide in the Baltic Sea region was that it was a primary source for more formal Nordic cooperation and integration. A paradigm of Nordic cooperation through integration provided the necessary security platform for Finland during a phase known as Finlandization.

The breaking up of the Soviet Union and the restoration of sovereign and independent Baltic States almost a quarter century ago provided the North European Eight with a chance to build relations among the members of this club of eight on the basis of shared values, interests and geography. Still, one might point to a different type of relationship among individual members of this group based on their formal relationships with the European Union (EU) and the North Atlantic Treaty Organization (NATO), but one thing is obvious: Baltic and Nordic States have opted for genuine regional integration as an indispensable element of regional stability, security and well-being. These days, it is almost impossible to find an area where the North European Eight have not established some form of cooperation—starting from protection of the environment of the Baltic Sea region all the way to banking, education and security in its broader sense. These relationships have been developing parallel to the Baltic states' accession to the EU and NATO. There is no doubt that the scope and depth of integration of the North European Eight has reached an unprecedented level of any period in our history. It is a genuine success story of the Baltic Sea region's contemporary history.

But all success stories have their own weaknesses: an area where Baltic-Nordic States have not been as successful in finding mutually appealing reasons to integrate is the energy sector. This is a sector that in many ways will determine how prosperous and secure we are in the Baltic Sea region. Paradoxically, by European standards, the Baltic-Nordic region holds some significant sources of energy. Norway is one of the major global energy players with its hydrocarbon resources. The region possesses vast hydro energy resources, nuclear energy, extraordinary renewable energy resources and a technological edge. Besides, the region is known internationally for its innovative high standard energy saving technologies. Unfortunately, half a century of Cold War geopolitical reality projected completely different dynamics in the development of the regional energy pattern. Under Soviet occupation, the Baltic States had their energy sectors fully integrated into the Soviet energy grids with Russia, which supplied 100% of oil and natural gas. As an illustration of this situation one can observe the status of the huge underground natural gas storage facility in Inchukalns, Latvia: it was developed in Soviet times, with a storage capacity of up to three billion cubic meters of natural gas. Because it was a part of the energy infrastructure in the Soviet era, the facility still stores and provides natural gas for the Russian Federation as well.

Immediately after restoration of independence, conditions on the ground were not favorable for the Baltic States to deal with the energy isolation problem. Markets were small and relatively distant, which did not help to attract other investors in the new energy infrastructure so greatly needed in order to move away from the Baltic energy sector's isolation. In the 1990s, European Union membership was still a distant possibility. Attempts to leave isolation behind for the Baltic states at that time would mean possible energy price hikes. That would be negatively regarded by both local big energy consuming industries and household owners.

Baltic state membership in the EU from 2004 changed this situation, providing access to much needed EU financial assistance that became such a necessary source of financing for strategically important regional energy infrastructure projects. This development unlocked a virtuous circle providing a chance for the Baltic states (including Finland) to connect to the European energy market. It provided a way out of the energy sector's isolation. In this regard, the 2006 and 2009 Russian-Ukrainian gas crisis was a chilling reminder of vulnerability for those European states that had a single source of energy.

In October, 2008, the European Commission set up a High Level Group after the agreement of the EU member states of the Baltic Sea Region. A year later, this group put together the Baltic Energy Market Interconnection Plan (BEMIP)—a very concrete and comprehensive action plan on interconnections and market improvement in the Baltic Sea region. For the Baltic states, this plan includes two underwater electricity cables between the Baltic region and the Scandinavian Peninsula. One cable is referred to as NordBalt (between Sweden, Lithuania and Latvia) and the other one is called Estlink 2 (between Finland and Estonia). This plan also comprises concrete steps to strengthen the internal Latvian transmission grid.

Besides these very important projects that will provide interconnectivity between the Baltic and Nordic electricity grids, concrete steps are being taken to achieve full electricity market integration between Nordic and Baltic power markets through Nord Pool Spot power exchanges by 2015.

BEMIP includes a number of concrete infrastructure projects that, when implemented, will significantly contribute to the formation of a Baltic natural gas market and will ensure its integration into the European natural gas market. Among others, there are two natural gas pipeline projects: Gas Interconnection Poland—Lithuania (GIPL), connecting Poland and Lithuania, and the Baltic Connector, stretching from Estonia to Finland. In addition, BEMIP comprises projects to upgrade and develop the intra-Baltic natural gas networks. The plan provides for the development of a regional Liquefied Natural Gas (LNG) terminal on the shores of the Gulf of Finland, the exact location of which is still to be agreed upon. It is very important that in the Lithuanian case, EU financing is available in support of projects to upgrade Lithuanian natural gas infrastructure in connection with the LNG terminal.

Based on these facts, one can conclude that in the field of energy, EU membership of the Baltic and three out of the five Nordic States has contributed to putting an end to the Baltic States and Finland's energy isolation. The European Commission recommends the Baltic LNG regional terminal to be built either in Finland or in Estonia. Irrespective of the terminal's location, the energy security of the Baltic region will greatly benefit from it. Emerging Baltic regional energy infrastructure projects in combination with implementation of the EU Third Energy package requirements make the future for Baltic state energy look bright. By integrating into the Baltic-Nordic electricity market, the Baltic states can break out from their seemingly eternal energy island status within the EU. The same is going to happen within the natural gas sector, where the Baltic states and Finland are on their way to integration within a wider EU natural gas market.

In order to make this happen, there are still some missing elements that would facilitate this development:

1. I mentioned the Third Energy Package. It is a crucial element to connect Baltic energy sectors with the rest of Europe. There is no doubt that this set of EU energy legislation will be implemented in accordance with the EU time table (in Latvia's case, starting in 2017). It means that in principle every supplier of natural gas to the Baltic region should be able to gain access to the immense storage. The existing storage facil-

ity is not the only place in Latvia where one could have storage capabilities for big volume natural gas imports. Due to its very unique geological composition, Latvia could, in the middle-term perspective, play a very important role in storing natural gas for customers in the Baltic Sea region and in broader Europe. This might be Latvia's unique role within the EU energy market.

2. There is a clear role that the LNG terminal in Klipeda could play regionally as soon as 2015. It is of crucial importance that Finland and Estonia sort out their interests and agree on the venue for the Baltic Sea regional LNG terminal in way that allows the project to receive EU financing as soon as possible. Here Latvia has always stood for maintaining regional unity and, therefore my country believes it would be in the mutual interest of Finland, Estonia, Lithuania and Latvia if we proceed with the responsible implementation of the European Commission's recommendation. We should step outside the box of narrow national interests and think more broadly. If four states act together and responsibly prioritize the common interest, they shall succeed.

3. It is impossible to end the isolation of the Baltic region's natural gas sector and to increase the region's energy security if there is no close strategic relationship between Finland, Estonia, Latvia and Lithuania, on one side, and Poland on the other. Poland has a unique role to play here. Poland will provide the flow of natural gas of alternative origin to consumers of the Baltic States and Finland through a GIPL interconnector. Connected to Latvia's natural gas storage facility and further to regional LNG terminal in Finland/Estonia, the interconnection will, in principle, provide natural gas flow in the westbound direction as well. The gains for regional energy security and the formation of a real regional natural gas market are obvious.

4. One of the missing elements within the regional relationship between the Baltic and Nordic states has been a lack of interest and ability to work together strategically on energy issues. That, I think, is the primary reason as to why it has taken so long for this otherwise very cohesive group within the Baltic

Sea region to create something of meaning for everybody within the energy sector. But a good thing is that today things are changing. It is of paramount importance for the North European Eight to look strategically and together for the best solutions for the energy security deficit. This will do both—increase our common energy security and add natural gas suppliers to the Baltic Sea region.

5. It is important that the United States as the biggest energy resources producer in the world understands its unique strategic role and open natural gas exports to Europe. Without a doubt, that would be a game changer that will not only be beneficial for the Unites States and its energy companies and European customers, but it would also boost the transatlantic relationship in the form of a genuine transatlantic energy partnership.

After two decades of unprecedented Nordic-Baltic cooperation, we have finally reached a stage when the group of North European Eight can step into a new level of mutual integration. A common Nordic-Baltic energy market would become a reality. The EU's energy policy and availability of both new energy suppliers and modern energy technologies are facilitating this development. However, to get there, we must take important steps together. And often we should do it in close partnership with the United States. Therefore, the opening of American natural gas exports to Europe stands importantly among our common interest.

Chapter 10

Bringing Nordic Energy Security
to the Baltic States

Keith Smith

Energy security has been a constant subject of discussion in the Nordic-Baltic region since the collapse of the Soviet Union. Only in a few parts of Europe has it had more of an impact on sovereignty and governance issues than in Lithuania, Latvia and Estonia. With the Russian military takeover of Crimea and Moscow's direct interference in east and south Ukraine, the importance of loosening Moscow's grip on pipelines and oil and gas markets in the Baltic states has moved close to the top of the political agenda in the region. Although Russia has used its hydrocarbon exports as a coercive political instrument since 1990, President Putin's willingness to order the invasion of neighboring Ukraine in 2014 has demonstrated that he will resort to extreme measures to restore Moscow's dominance over the former Soviet Republics. This is an especially critical threat to countries like Estonia and Latvia which contain a significant population of ethnic Russians or "Russian speakers" and are highly dependent on Russian energy imports. The conflict in Ukraine points to the need to increase the pace of Nordic-Baltic and inter-Baltic cooperation in order to reduce energy dependency on Russia. The goal should be to eliminate energy insecurity as a tool, used repeatedly by Putin to advance his foreign policy objectives in the former Soviet space. It is time that we re-examine the energy situation in this vulnerable region and look for mechanisms to increase the effectiveness of measures being taken by national governments, regional cooperation bodies and the European Union (EU) that would improve energy security in the Nordic-Baltic region. Although regional energy cooperation has increased substantially since 2011, more can be done to align the energy policies and link the infrastructure of the entire region.

Nordic Sunshine

Political and economic relations between the Nordic and Baltic states have developed at a rapid, if uneven, pace since the collapse of the Soviet Union. The three Baltic countries have benefited politically and economically from their close ties to the mature democracies of Norway, Sweden, Denmark and Finland. Sweden has been particularly generous with providing Estonia, Latvia and Lithuania military equipment. Private investments from the Nordic countries have played a significant role in the regions' economic development, again with Swedish companies taking the lead. Perhaps equally important, the Nordics have also provided the three Baltic states with world-class role models. They personify the best in good governance, transparency and low corruption levels. Nordic investments played a key role in the ability of the Baltic states to weather the economic downturn in 2007-2009, thereby assisting the three newer democracies to aspire to provide their citizens with a "European standard of living."

There remains, however, a substantial gap between the Nordic and Baltic states in building economies that are able to fend off outside attempts to influence their policies through energy coercion. Norway is energy independent and a major exporter of gas and oil to the rest of Europe. Sweden is close to being energy independent by possessing an economy powered by a combination of nuclear, hydro and renewable energy. Denmark is also substantially energy secure. It is a pioneer in the use of wind and biomass and has easy access to Western-sourced oil and gas to supplement its own off-shore fields.[1] Although Finland is presently a substantial importer of Russian natural gas and oil, its nuclear plants and soon-to-be constructed Liquefied Natural Gas (LNG) import facility, will give it an additional degree of security from any arbitrary cut off of imports. Finland is also moving rapidly to construct additional power plants fueled by bio-mass.[2]

Therefore, none of the Nordic states (I have omitted Iceland) are in any danger of being affected by a cutoff of oil through Russia's Baltic

---

[1]Nordic Energy Research, "Denmark," http://www.nordicenergy.org/thenordicway/country/denmark/.

[2]Nordic Energy Research, "Finland," http://www.nordicenergy.org/thenordicway/country/finland/.

Pipeline System that exports its product via the Port of Primorsk, or of the large natural gas pipelines that transit Ukraine or the Baltic Sea. If the political situation in Europe were to become more threatening as a result of Russia's invasion of Ukraine, the linked power grids and energy import facilities in the Nordic countries would permit them to work around any supply disruption. In the Nord Pool Spot, the Nordics have had an integrated electricity market of the Nordic countries for almost twenty years. This model was used by the EU when it conceived the Baltic Energy Ring and the more recent Baltic Energy Market and Interconnection Plan (BEMIP). It should be noted that Estonia is now participating fully in the Nord Pool Spot.[3]

Clouds over the Baltics

Lithuania, Latvia and Estonia will however, remain in a much more insecure situation than the Nordic states for the next decade. This insecurity will be even more worrisome if Cold War instability were to return to European-Russian relations. All three Baltic countries rely on Soviet-era pipelines for their natural gas, as well as for oil imports from West Siberian fields. Most of their energy infrastructure, constructed during the Soviet period, was designed to put them under Moscow's control. They continue to import 100% of their natural gas from Russia.[4] The gas companies in each state are effectively dominated by the Kremlin-controlled Gazprom with the help of E.ON, a German company with close ties to Russia. Almost all Baltic oil imports arrive directly or indirectly from Russia.[5] Up to now, Baltic membership in the EU has not yet brought significant energy security to the three countries, although the situation should improve in two or three years' time.

---

[3] *The Nordic Electricity Exchange and The Nordic Model for a Liberalized Electricity Market*, Denmark, Nord Pool Spot, 2009.

[4] Keith C. Smith, *Managing the Challenge of Russian Energy Policies*, (Washington, D.C.: Center for Strategic and International Studies (CSIS), November 2010), http://csis.org/files/publication/101123_Smith_ManagingChallenge_Web.pdf.

[5] "Paying the piper," *The Economist*, January 4, 2014, http://www.economist.com/news/business/21592639-european-efforts-reduce-russian-state-owned-companys-sway-over-gas-prices-have-been.

Often lost in the discussion of Baltic energy insecurity is their need to import almost all of their oil from Russia. All three countries have reduced the per capita use of oil products for energy generation and heating. At the same time, the rapid increase in the number of cars and trucks has undercut some of the efficiencies attained in district heating and power generation. Baltic dependency on Russian imports will not diminish as a result of EU-funded infrastructure projects.

EU membership had until recently brought greater energy insecurity to the Baltic states, particularly to Lithuania and Estonia. Due to pressure from environmental and anti-nuclear power lobbies within the EU, the Baltic states were required to agree to restrictions on domestic energy production as a condition to become members of the EU. For example, the EU required Lithuania to close both of its existing nuclear power plants by 2009, even though significant safety upgrades had already been carried out to the Ignalina II reactor by the U.S. and Sweden. Several foreign nuclear safety experts believed that the plant could operate safely for at least ten more years.[6] Lithuania thereby quickly lost 70% of its domestic electricity production and was forced to become even more reliant on Russian natural gas and electricity imports.[7] The EU refused to pay for a replacement nuclear plant. In order to meet strict EU emission standards, Estonia will have to reduce its generation of electricity. This can be done through the use of domestically produced oil shale but a more efficient plant will not be available for use until 2016. Though Estonia is using power imported to Estonia via the Estlink lines from Finland, it still may not be sufficient to cover current domestic production from oil shale. This may increase Estonian demand for expensive Russian oil and gas.[8]

---

[6]U.S. nuclear physicist working on nuclear safety, conversation with the author, March, 2000.

[7]Matthew Day, "Lithuania power crisis looms as nuclear plant shuts," *Telegraph*, December 29, 2009, http://www.telegraph.co.uk/news/worldnews/europe/lithuania/6904781/Lithuania-power-crisis-looms-as-nuclear-plant-shuts.html.

[8]Raul Mälk, "Estonia and Energy Security," Estonain Ministry of Foreign Affairs, 2006, http://web-static.vm.ee/static/failid/085/Raul_Malk.pdf.

A Pattern of Energy Disruptions

Since the breakup of the Soviet Union, Estonia, Latvia and Lithuania have long been the main targets of Russia's use of politically-motivated energy disruptions. During EU membership negotiations for the Baltic states, EU officials failed to take this into account. The first energy cut-offs occurred as early as 1990, when elements in the Russian government tried to prevent the Baltic states from breaking free from Moscow's control. Fortunately, support from Sweden and Finland convinced Moscow that this was a losing strategy. Soon thereafter, however, in late 1992, energy was cut off from Estonia and Latvia in the dead of winter in an attempt to dissuade those two countries from expelling the large Russian military officer corps from their two countries. Only strong political pressure from the United States and Germany (and officer housing in Russia paid for by the United States) convinced the Kremlin to reopen the gas and oil taps.[9]

During the Soviet and post-Soviet periods, the giant Druzhba oil pipeline carried crude from West Siberian fields to Central Europe. Over 20 million tons of crude oil transited the Druzhba line to the Ventspils port in Latvia and to the Mazeikai Refinery in Lithuania. Even after the Kremlin formally recognized the independence of the three Baltic states, the Russian government clearly intended to retain control of the entire pipeline, oil ports and the refineries. As one Russian official told this author in 1998, "the pipelines, ports, and refineries were built by us (Russia) and they should still belong to us."[10] Not surprisingly, the governments of Latvia and Lithuania had a different view.

In 1996 and 1997, the Lithuanian government announced that it was seeking a Western company to buy the Druzhba pipeline in Lithuania, the Refinery at Mazeikiai and the oil port of Butinge. While the Lithuanians were shopping for a Western suitor, Moscow made it clear that it wanted the entire oil infrastructure to be given without charge to a Russian company in exchange for continued shipments of crude oil. Russia had no intention of modernizing the refinery or port facility in order to meet EU standards. Instead Moscow

---

[9]Keith C. Smith, "*Russian Energy Politics in the Baltics, Poland, and Ukraine: A New Stealth Imperialism?*" Washington, D.C., CSIS, 2004.

[10]Russian Official to the author, 1998.

planned to shut the plant when Russian refineries in the St. Petersburg region came on line. When it appeared that a Western company would buy and run the Lithuanian facilities, crude supplies were cut nine times between the years 1998-2000 in an attempt to sabotage negotiations. In an unusual move, Moscow replaced its ambassador in Vilnius with a KGB veteran who had long been the agency's liaison with Russian energy companies.

A public relations campaign directed against the foreign firm and financed by the Russian Embassy then ensued.[11] Nevertheless, it failed to stop the agreement from going through. In 2003, Transneft, the monopoly exporter of Russian crude, notified Latvia that no more oil would make its way to Ventspils, as a result of Riga's refusal to turn the port over to Russian control.[12] About the same time, a mysterious fire resulted in extensive damage to Lithuania's Mazeikiai refinery. Transneft then notified the Lithuanians that due to a break in the Druzhba pipeline, crude could not be sent to Mazeikiai. At the time, Moscow claimed that the disruption would be temporary. Russian authorities refused to allow Lithuanians to inspect the line, and also turned down an offer from the EU to help bring the pipeline back into service. Several months later, Transneft announced that no shipments from Russia would be sent to either Lithuania or Latvia via the Druzhba line in the future. That remains the situation today. Fortunately, the natural gas pipeline supplying the Russian enclave of Kaliningrad transits Lithuania, thereby preventing a gas supply disruption. However, this is due to change when a planned pipeline connection is constructed from the Nord Stream line to Kaliningrad.

Price Control or Control through Prices

The three Baltic states, Poland and Ukraine pay higher prices for Russian natural gas than do countries in western Europe. One can easily note that the prices charged to individual countries by Gazprom are in direct relation to the state of that country's political relations

---

[11]Keith C. Smith, *"Russian Energy Politics in the Baltics, Poland, and Ukraine: A New Stealth Imperialism?"*

[12]Michael Lelyveld, "Russia: Moscow Seeks Takeover Of Latvian Oil Port," *Radio Free Europe Radio Liberty*, February 12, 2003, http://www.rferl.org/content/article/1102205.html.

with Russia. According to Gazprom, gas export prices are indexed to world market prices for crude oil. If that were the case, the import price for Russian gas would be the same throughout the EU, with some small adjustment for transit costs. This is obviously not the case, since Germany and Belgium pay significantly less than do the countries mentioned above. Ukraine is currently importing Russian gas from Germany at a lower price. When Ukraine refused to accept Russia's takeover of Crimea, Gazprom announced that the price of Russian gas to Ukraine would double from 268 dollars to 485 dollars a thousand cubic meter (TCM) on April 1, 2014.[13]

Lithuania pays the highest price of any EU member for Russian gas. In part, this is in retaliation for Lithuanian determination to fully implement the EU's Third Energy Package, which prohibits importers of gas and electricity from being the distributors in the same country. If the Third Energy Package were implemented fully, it would reduce Russia's hold over Lithuania's domestic energy market and reduce Gazprom's political influence in the country. When Lithuania attempted to put the EU directive into effect, Russia took the case to international arbitration. Unfortunately, Lithuania was awarded only a small decrease in price, with Gazprom reserving the right to return to arbitration if they were dissatisfied with Lithuania's policies regarding further unbundling of supply from distribution. Stronger support by the EU might have resulted in a much lower price. By the end of 2014, however, a floating import facility at Klaipedia Port will be in operation in Lithuania, and it should allow the country to bring in enough non-Russian gas to counter a cut off and/or provide Lithuania a stronger bargaining position with Gazprom over future prices.[14] Completion of a new gas interconnector to the other Baltic states would allow some imports through Klaipedia to reach Latvia. Unfortunately, the Baltic states have been painfully slow at integrating their energy markets or in constructing modern pipeline systems.

---

[13]Gleb Garanich, "Ukraine suspends gas payments to Russia until talks conclude," *Reuters*, April 12, 2014, http://www.reuters.com/article/2014/04/12/us-ukraine-crisis-gas-naftogaz-idUSBREA3B05E20140412.

[14]"President: Gas terminal will serve to strengthen Lithuania's energy independence," Lithuania Tribune, February 19, 2014, http://www.lithuaniatribune.com/63619/president-gas-terminal-will-serve-to-strengthen-lithuanias-energy-independence-201463619/.

The high prices paid by the Baltic countries slow their ability to close the economic gap with the older EU member states. Such ties to an imperial minded neighbor weigh on both their economic and political structures. The situation will only slowly improve as the EU implements its energy integration plans. The policies of post-Crimea Russia clearly point to the special vulnerabilities confronting the Baltic states. They are now faced with the urgent need to increase defense spending while at the same time earmarking scarce resources to construct an energy infrastructure with the needed redundancy to deal with unexpected difficulties.

The EU Helps at Last

Prior to the Russian cut off of natural gas to Ukraine in 2009, EU leaders demonstrated little concern for the needs of the "energy islands" of the Baltic states. Western Europe appeared unaware of the exposure of the central Europeans to Russian energy coercion and of the repeated disruptions in the supply of oil and gas. The lack of urgency was in part due to the fact that the 2004 cut off of Russian gas to Ukraine (or the earlier ones to the Baltic states) did not directly affect supplies to western Europe. Also, the crisis in 2004 was shorter lasting than that of 2009. With most of Europe impacted by the 2009 Russian-Ukrainian energy disputes, the EU Commission began to pay more attention to issues of energy security.[15] In addition, the Baltic states benefited from the 2010 reorganization in the EU's Directorate General for Energy and the appointment of a new and more dynamic Directorate. The EU became more focused on the energy supply vulnerabilities of member states, and particularly those that depended almost totally on Russian imports for their oil and natural gas.

Prior to the EU reorganization, Finland and Estonia had already commissioned the construction of a High Voltage Direct Current (HVDC) undersea electricity line between their two countries. The Estlink I began operations in 2007 and was eventually connected to the electricity grids of Lithuania and Latvia. A second HVDC line from Finland to Estonia (Estlink II) was financed by the EU and was

---

[15]Paul Taylor, "Ukraine gas crisis spurs EU energy policy," Reuters, January 13, 2009, http://blogs.reuters.com/great-debate/2009/01/13/ukraine-gas-crisis-spurs-eu-energy-policy/.

declared operational in March of 2014.[16] When fully connected to the power grids of Latvia and Estonia, the two lines from Finland will allow the Baltic states a greater degree of electricity independence from existing power lines from the East, and will provide additional security from arbitrary disruptions from Russia's electricity grid.

An existing HVDC link between Germany and Sweden has been in operation for over ten years.[17] A power line between Sweden and Poland was commissioned in 2000, but has had several technical problems that have had to be overcome. The NordBalt HVDC line between Lithuania and Sweden is now under construction and should become operational in 2015. This link was held up for almost two years while Latvia and Lithuania vied to be the location for the connector with Sweden. All of the electricity projects under way since 2011 are part of the EU's Baltic Energy Market's Integration Plan and are funded as EU Projects of Common Interest.[18]

On the natural gas front, the EU is financing the Baltic Connector, which will be a two way gas line between Finland and Estonia on completion. The line will eventually (2016-2018) unite the region's gas interconnectors with Latvia's large underground gas storage facility at Incukains. The Baltic Connector will also eventually draw natural gas from EU supported LNG import facilities to be built on the Finnish southern coast and the northern coast of Estonia.[19] There is still some uncertainty if more than one of the plants will be constructed on the Gulf of Finland. The source of LNG for all three plants is still to be determined, but the projects will provide flexibility in choosing the sources of supply. The Finnish-Estonian gas line is projected to be linked to the floating LNG facility now under construction at the Port of Klaipeda on the Lithuanian coast. The

[16]"Laying of EstLink 2 submarine cable has started," *Estlink2*, October 15, 2012, http://estlink2. elering.ee/news-2/?article=15955.

[17]"Who, when and where," *Baltic Cable*, http://www.balticcable.com/about.html.

[18]"Progress Report June 2012," *Baltic Energy Market Interconnection Plan*, June 2012, http://ec.europa.eu/energy/infrastructure/doc/20121016_4rd_bemip_progress_report_final.pdf.

[19]"Balticconnector: Baltic Seabed Exploration Works Start Amid Disputes," *Natural Gas Europe*, December 18, 2013, http://www.naturalgaseurope.com/balticconnector-dispute-location-contractors-seabed-exploration.

Klaipeda LNG port is due to become operational sometime in 2015, with an initial capacity of 3.5 billion cubic meters (BCM).[20]

Inter-Baltic cooperation on energy issues has not always been productive. Projects such as the electricity connector to Sweden were delayed by national rivalry. Lithuania has been unable to secure Latvian financial support for a replacement for the Ignalina II nuclear power plant, and Lithuania has signaled its reluctance to rely on natural gas storage facilities in Latvia. Latvia's Parliament also has failed to ratify a sea border agreement reached in 1999 with Lithuania. In the mid-1990s, a Western energy company conducted seismic work in the off-shore area and had concluded that there was commercial prospects for hydrocarbon development. The company left the region when the two countries could not reach a sea-border agreement.[21] Plans to develop natural gas in western Lithuania got underway in 2013, but the Butkavicius Government failed to publicly support the exploration activities using hydraulic fracturing. Although only one company had responded to the government's offer, public opposition to hydraulic fracturing appeared to unnerve the Government. Some of the opposition appeared to have been supported by officials in the Kaliningrad Oblast and from European Green Parties. In the end, the foreign firm concluded that Lithuania was not a good place to invest in natural gas development, at least for time being.

Corruption and Transparency

The Baltic states have at times been plagued by a lack of transparency in energy transactions, particularly when dealing with Russian energy companies. These firms, most of which are state-owned or state-controlled are generally under the direction of individuals who worked with civilian or military intelligence organs in the former Soviet Union. As we saw in Lithuania in 1998, Moscow is not constrained as much as Western countries in using intelligence personnel and their normal

---

[20]Vladimir Socor, "Baltic LNG Terminals Conditioned by Gas Sector Reform," *Eurasia Daily Monitor* Volume: 9 Issue: 128, July 6, http://www.jamestown.org/single/?no_cache=1&tx_ttnews%5Btt_news%5D=39591.

[21]Nick Coleman, "Oil exploration tender process to begin," *The Baltic Times*, November 30, 2000, http://www.baltictimes.com/news/articles/3466/

sources and methods when pursuing a strategy of employing energy exports for coercive reasons. It should be noted that until recently, Itera, the Russian natural gas company active in Latvia, was led by a former top official in Russia's military intelligence agency (GRU). Russian energy companies have developed a substantial list of supporters within the business communities in the Baltic states, many having personal connections dating back to the 1980s. Therefore, it is vitally important that the Baltic states adopt and enforce commercial policies that result in transparent negotiations, when working with Russian export companies and their affiliates abroad. Some Western firms are financially dependent on their business with Russia and are willing to assist their Russian counterparts in non-transparency business dealings in third countries. For this reason, Baltic governments contemplating the privatization of their energy infrastructure must carefully carry out due diligence when considering any foreign investor.

Since enormous sums of money trade hands in the energy export and import business, the temptation to use corruption as a business instrument, particularly, but not exclusively, by Russian firms, is well documented. It should also be noted that the Russian owned Nord Stream and South Stream pipeline companies are led, at least officially, by non-Russians, and particularly by former officials from Germany, Finland and Austria. The Nord Stream pipeline was conceived as a method of bypassing the Baltic states and Poland, and the South Stream to bypass Ukraine, even though cheaper and more practical routes were available in both instances. The pipelines were designed to achieve political objectives rather than for profitability. While both pipelines provide additional routes for natural gas to Europe, they do not carry non-Russian gas and only add to Russia's dominant competitive position in the gas markets of Europe. They also add to the energy isolation of the newer members of the European Union, such as the Baltic states, Poland, Bulgaria, Romania and Hungary.

The Nordic Advantage

Although the three Baltic states and Poland are historically tied to Russian gas and oil imports, these countries have the advantage of being close neighbors and friends with the highly wealthy and democratically-governed Nordic states. Finland, Sweden, Denmark and

Norway are among the best examples of open and transparent democracies and each has achieved a high degree of economic growth and security. The four countries have the capacity to assist the more vulnerable Baltic states reach Northern European standards of governance and economic performance. The Nordic region contains oil and gas resources, off-shore exploration technology, advanced wind and biomass technology, some of the world's highest best technology for combined cycle power units, and energy efficiency standards for large housing and industrial units.

A significant amount of EU assistance to Baltic energy security has already been provided through the construction of electricity interconnectors. Additional help has been pledged for the construction of a Baltic gas connector. Nevertheless the Nordic countries have the resources and technology to provide substantial additional energy security technologies, particularly in the areas of efficiency and the use of alternative fuels. The Baltic region is rich in wood products that could be combined with the latest technology from Denmark and Finland to reduce further their dependency on Russian imports. Up to now, Norwegian policy has focused on assistance to the poorest in the world, with a concentration on Africa. With the more aggressive Russian foreign policy now in play, Oslo would help its own security interests and those of the entire region by including more financial assistance to the economically fragile Baltic republics.

The four Nordic countries are also active participants in international financial institutions, including the European Bank for Reconstruction and Development (EBRD), the World Bank and International Monetary Fund (IMF). They are in a position to steer additional aid to the Baltic states for nuclear and renewable projects. Within the EU, the Nordics can use their influence to push the organization to take faster steps to develop a common energy import market, so that the exposed Baltic states would have greater bargaining power when negotiating with Russia's state firms. The past few years have brought a greater degree of energy cooperation between the Nordic and the Baltic states and a significant step up of EU assistance in the construction of two directional interconnectors.

Since 2012, there has been greater Nordic-Baltic energy coordination through the Nordic-Baltic Eight (including Iceland). Sweden and

Finland have already demonstrated an interest in providing concrete help to the Baltic states. Up to now, Norway and Denmark have focused less attention than Sweden and Finland on the three Baltic states. The security of the entire region will be enhanced by the development of more successful and secure democracies along Russia's western border.

Recommendations for Nordic Assistance

The coordinated mobilization of the Nordic experience, combined with the EU's planning and financial resources, could, with the right policies, rapidly reduce Russia's ability to use energy coercion as a means of influencing the region's security policies. Russia's military thrust into Ukraine has demonstrated that the Baltic states, the EU's member states that contain the largest minorities of ethnic Russians, may be more exposed than before to energy and cyber disruptions, and other types of coercion from Moscow. Some specific suggestions are:

- Norway and Denmark should use their experience with offshore oil and gas exploration and development to assist the Baltic states explore with the latest seismic technology the seabed off of the Baltic states for commercially profitable hydrocarbons.
- The Nordic countries, particularly Sweden, Denmark and Finland should fund and administer a robust program for wind and bio-mass production in the three Baltic states.
- The Finnish government should take the lead in assisting Lithuania to carry out a new analysis regarding the commercial viability of constructing a new nuclear power plant in Lithuania.
- Baltic states should speed up integration of their energy sectors, including electricity, natural gas, renewables and efficiency standards.
- The Baltic states must move faster to resolve existing disputes over energy issues. For example, the sea-border dispute between Latvia and Lithuania should be resolved very quickly in order to attract foreign energy investors to the region. The

Nordic countries should pressure Latvia to sign the existing agreement with Lithuania, or otherwise submit the issue to Nordic arbitration.

- The Nordics can assist in providing a greater degree of security by constructing additional gas and oil storage, bringing more energy supply redundancy for the three Baltic states.

- Nordic North Atlantic Treaty Organization (NATO) and EU members should focus more attention on military defenses in the Baltics and the Nordic states should re-examine whether they can use their robust economies and rich energy experience to provide even greater help to Latvia, Lithuania and Estonia.

- Although Sweden and Finland are not members of NATO, they could provide additional resources (human and financial) to the Cybersecurity Center in Tallinn and the Energy Security Center in Vilnius. The fragile power grids, refineries and pipeline pumping stations in the Baltic states should be made more secure so as to be able to sustain operations in the event of another cyber-attack from the East.

- Norway, with its energy exports and massive foreign reserves could use some of its oil and gas resources to provide competition to the Russian monopoly import role. Furnishing a small amount of discounted oil and LNG might incentivize Russian companies to reduce their energy bullying and agree to more reasonable prices.

Chapter 11

U.S.-Nordic Global Security Cooperation

Erik Brattberg

President Barack Obama's visit to Stockholm in September 2013 was symbolic of the importance the United States is currently attaching to the Nordic region. The United States views Nordic states as strong advocates of shared global values such as peace, democracy, human rights and free market economics across the globe. Nordic countries' recent contributions to various international efforts to promote peace and stability—in places ranging from Afghanistan to sub-Saharan Africa—have also been noted in Washington. These efforts are especially pertinent in light of declining defense budgets on both sides of the Atlantic, combined with a diminishing U.S. appetite to provide for security in Europe's neighborhood. Nordic countries are good examples of small states "punching above their weight" and provide a model for other countries in Europe. In light of President Obama's recent trip to the region, it is now high time to further strengthen the U.S.-Nordic cooperation on global security issues. This agenda should, in particular, include political support for countries in eastern Europe, cooperation on issues in the Arctic region and civilian crisis management issues.

Nordic Contributions to Global Security

Political Contributions

Nordic countries have a long tradition of supporting international organizations. Today, they remain the major per capita contributors to the United Nations (UN) and its agencies as well as other international and aid organizations. Several Nordic countries also maintain distinct national roles on the international stage. Recent examples include Norway's role in supporting the peace process in the Middle East during the 1990s, and in mediating in Sri Lanka, Finnish President Marti Ahtisaari's role resolving conflicts in places like Indonesia and Kosovo, and Sweden's former Prime Minister (and subsequent Foreign Minister) Carl Bildt's role in mediating between the warring parties in the Balkans during the 1990s.

In addition to these activities, Nordic countries have played an important role in the promotion of peace and security in Europe since the end of the Cold War. Nordic countries were formative in backing the U.S. agenda for a Europe "whole and free". They have been instrumental in supporting economic and political transitions in former Soviet states. In particular, they were quick to extend an open arm to the three Baltic states (Estonia, Latvia and Lithuania) following the collapse of the Soviet Union. The Nordic countries were strong supporters of Baltic independence after the subsequent end of Soviet occupation: they provided their Baltic neighbors with significant political and financial support in the 1990s, including allowing visa-free travel within the Baltic Sea area. The Nordic Council allowed for new forms of cooperation with Baltic political structures. The Nordic states also worked closely with the United States, through its 1997 Northern Europe Initiative (NEI), to support the reintegration of the Baltic states into the Euro-Atlantic community—a process that culminated with them joining the European Union (EU) and the North Atlantic Treaty Organization (NATO) in 2004. The successful transformation of the Baltic states into fully fledged democracies and free market economies is remarkable. Today, the five Nordic states and the three Baltic states cooperate closely under the Nordic-Baltic Eight (NB8) label on issues ranging from the economy, energy security, and implementation of the EU strategy for the Baltic Sea region.

Humanitarian Assistance and Development

Another area related to global security and stability where the Nordic countries are major contributors is humanitarian assistance and development. According to the Organization for Economic Cooperation and Development's Development Assistance Committee (OECD-DAC), Norway, Finland, Denmark and Sweden all ranked among the world's highest donors per capita. In terms of official development assistance (ODA), the four Nordic countries and Estonia's ODA reached 15.8 billion dollars in 2010, roughly equaling that of the United Kingdom (UK) and more than either France or Germany.[1] International disaster response is another area of growing significance where the Nordics have an impressive track record. During the 2010 earthquake in Haiti, the four Nordic countries pledged more than France, Germany and the UK combined.[2] Also during the 2004 Asian tsunami, Nordic countries were among the top donors.[3] During the 2014 typhoon in the Philippines, Norway was a major contributor, offering 41.6 million dollars in cash and 100 tons of food and medical supplies.

Peacekeeping and Crisis Management

The Nordic countries have been committed to a long tradition of supporting UN 'blue helmet' peacekeeping operations. Though their active military contributions are significantly smaller today than in the past, several ongoing UN peacekeeping missions still have Nordic participation.[4] In recent years, the Nordic countries have carried out far-reaching defense reforms at home, making their armed forces more expeditionary in nature. This has allowed for active contributions to out-of-area peace operations in places like Africa, the Balkans and Central Asia.

Furthermore, Nordic states actively support the EU's Common Security and Defense Policy (CSDP), contributing to its military and civilian missions. Even non-EU member Norway has sent personnel to EU missions and contributed to the Nordic Battle Group, which is considered to be one of Europe's most prepared crisis response forces. The fact that the Nordics have contributed to both NATO and EU missions also illustrates that the region has come a long way in bridging the organizational divide that still characterizes European security

---

[1] OCED Development Cooperation Report, 2010. Estonia, Latvia, Lithuania are not included in the OECD DAC statistics (although Estonia becomes a member in 2010).

[2] This is based on data from UN Office for the Coordination of Humanitarian Affairs (OCHA), presented in the Guardian, available online at: http://www.guardian.co.uk/news/ data-blog/2010/jan/14/haiti-quake-aid-pledges-country-donations

[3] Congressional Research Report "Indian Ocean Earthquake and Tsunami: Humanitarian Assistance and Relief Operations", January, 2005, available online at: http://www.fas.org/ sgp/crs/row/RL32715.pdf

[4] Data gathered from website of UN Department of Peacekeeping Operations (DPKO): http://www.un.org/en/peacekeeping/operations/current.shtml

affairs, something that may, thus, serve as a model for others to follow. Denmark and Norway, both members of NATO, are known within the Alliance to frequently "punch above their weight". Norway, for example, is one of the few NATO members that maintain a spending of more than 2% of gross domestic product (GDP) on defense. Sweden and Finland, which formally remain outside the Alliance, are, nevertheless, close partners and have actively contributed to NATO missions and trainings.

In addition to hard security, the Nordic nations, particularly Denmark, Finland and Sweden, have also come a long way in the effort to develop civilian crisis management tools, such as police, judiciary and customs reforms and capacity building, to be used in post-conflict zones.[5] Nordic countries have played an important role in supporting security sector reform (SSR) in post-conflict zones. Nordic states have also supported many of Organization for Security and Co-operation in Europe (OSCE) missions in Europe's neighborhood.

Below we will look at some specific examples of Nordic military contributions during the past two decades.

The Balkan crisis marked a watershed moment for many of the Nordic states. Having previously mostly supported UN peacekeeping operations, they would now become more active supporters of peace enforcement missions, often orchestrated by NATO.[6] Nordic states actively contributed to crisis management in the Balkans. In particular, since 1995, they contributed to the NATO-led peacekeeping force in Bosnia-Herzegovina and to the UN-operation of the United Nations Protection Force (UNPROFOR). Denmark and Norway contributed to NATO's air campaign in Kosovo in 1998-1999. All four Nordic countries have made troop contributions to the Kosovo Force (KFOR) in Kosovo.

In Afghanistan, the Nordic countries have made sizable contributions to the International Security Assistance Force (ISAF) mission. Though their individual contributions may seem modest compared to the U.S. and British forces, taken together the Nordic countries make

---

[5]For an evaluation of European Union civilian crisis management capabilities, see http://www.ecfr.eu/page/-/documents/08e8648caa55523ceb_g2m6yhyrv.pdf

[6]Peter Viggo Jakobsen, *Nordic Approaches to Peace Operations: A New Model in the Making.*

up one of the largest troop contributors to the ISAF force since its establishment at the end of 2001. Though troop levels have varied considerably throughout the duration of the mission, in October, 2011, the combined figure of around 1,800 troops surpassed those of countries such as Australia and Spain and equaling Turkey.[7] Furthermore, the Nordic contributions look even more impressive when accounting for population size. In 2008, Denmark topped the troops per capita list and Norway was number three. Around the same time, Denmark was also number one when it came to troop fatalities per capita.[8] In Afghanistan, Nordic countries have also made contributions to the European Union's European Police Office (EUPOL) mission, providing a third of total European Union contributions as of July, 2011.[9] Several Nordic countries have signaled their intent to maintain troops in Afghanistan after the end of the ISAF mission at the end of 2014, to train and advise Afghan forces as a part of Resolute Support Mission (RSM). When it comes to providing development support to Afghanistan, Nordic countries again score highly. For example, Sweden has declared willingness to provide long-term support to Kabul between 2015, and 2024, totaling over 1.2 billion dollars, thus making Afghanistan the biggest single recipient of Swedish development support.[10] In addition to development assistance, Sweden has also contributed to humanitarian assistance and support to multilateral organizations active in the country.

During the recent NATO-led air campaign in Libya in 2011, Nordic countries again punched above their weight: with Denmark and Norway each providing six F-16M fighter jets and Sweden eight Jas 29 Gripen planes to the mission.[11] The combined contributions of Denmark, Estonia, Finland and Sweden to the humanitarian effort in Libya amounted to 25 million euros as of February, 2012.[12] As of

---

[7]http://www.isaf.nato.int/images/stories/File/Placemats/9%20September%202011%20ISAF%20Placemat(1).pdf

[8]http://blog.foreignpolicy.com/posts/2008/04/02/mighty_denmark_pulls_its_weight_in_afghanistan

[9]http://www.csdpmap.eu/mission-personnel

[10]http://www.regeringen.se/sb/d/7331/a/228066

[11]Sweden only did aerial surveillance whereas Denmark and Norway took part in offensive operations. The Baltic States did not participate in the Libya campaign.

[12]EU Directorate General (DG) Humanitarian Aid and Civil Protection Department (ECHO), available online at: http://ec.europa.eu/echo/files/aid/countries/libya_factsheet.pdf

March, 2011, Norway was among the five largest donors to the crisis in Libya.[13] Interesting to note is also that Nordic countries had high public support for this humanitarian mission.

Finally, when it comes to patrolling the coast of Somalia, Denmark and Norway participated in NATO's Operation Ocean Shield while Norway, Finland and Sweden all participated in the EU Naval Force (NAVFOR) Atalanta mission—Sweden with four vessels and Finland and Norway with one each.

Strengthening the U.S.-Nordic Global Security Agenda

Taking into account the range of global security issues still at hand, and the broader need for renewed transatlantic political energy, there are good reasons for the United States to consider further developing its dialogue and partnership with the Nordic region. With a history of stability and prosperity, shared values, norms and a commitment to pragmatic cooperation, the region is an attractive partner to the United States. The region has a long track record of working together with the United States in promoting global peace and security around the world. This often-overlooked insight should provide impetus for an even stronger U.S. engagement with the Nordic region. It is also viewed as a credible stakeholder in many parts of the world where Nordic organizations have been delivering development assistance for decades.

Naturally, such a strengthened partnership should complement, rather than substitute, the broader transatlantic dialogue. With a new perspective on U.S.-Nordic cooperation, possibilities may emerge to break new ground and lead the way in a number of security-related areas for the benefit of the broader transatlantic community. In this way, the U.S.-Nordic format presents an opportunity that should not be missed. But what should the increased U.S.-Nordic cooperation framework on global security issues look like? The U.S.-Nordic Security Dialogue, agreed on during President Obama's Stockholm visit, needs an agenda for implementation.

---

[13]Integrated Regional Information Networks (IRIN) News "In Brief: Donors pledge $65m for Libyan humanitarian crisis", available online at: http://www.irinnews.org/Report/92121/In-Brief-Donors-pledge-65m-for-Libyan-humanitarian-crisis

Some potential areas of what such an agenda might contain are discussed here:

First, the experience of the Nordic countries in supporting economic and political transitions in the Baltic states in the 1990s, brings many valuable lessons that could be applied elsewhere today—particularly in eastern Europe. Countries such as Ukraine, Moldova and Georgia are still in need of domestic reforms in areas such as governance, rule of law and the creation of stronger political institutions. Events in Ukraine highlight the need for these types of activities. Nordic countries could make important contributions in this regard—efforts which often times would also benefit from close cooperation with the United States.

Second, the Arctic is another area where the Nordic countries can make vital contributions. The strategic importance of the High North has been increasingly recognized—as noted by recent U.S. strategic documents. However, the United States remains far from a strategic player in the region. It is currently looking for partners to cooperate with and here the Nordic countries could play an even bigger role than is the case today. Maritime security and safety is one potential avenue for enhanced U.S.-Nordic cooperation in the region.

Third, Nordic approaches to crisis management can bring added value in crisis situations. There is a growing realization that military solutions alone are insufficient in addressing complex crises and that civilian approaches and long-term efforts are needed to support and build local capacities. Here, the Nordic countries' expertise in civilian crisis management could make important contributions and help promote civil-military ties in conflict settings.

Chapter 12

Strengthening Nordic-Baltic Defense Capabilities: Open NORDEFCO to the Baltic States

Henrik Breitenbauch

The most straightforward way to strengthen Nordic-Baltic defense capabilities is for Sweden and Finland to join the North Atlantic Treaty Organization (NATO). By enlarging the Alliance with these two countries, defense cooperation among the Nordic-Baltic countries would become more straightforward in terms of both the upstream development of capabilities as well as in the downstream use of these capabilities. The Alliance itself would be strengthened and the security of all of the countries would be enhanced. Every other proposal than Sweden and Finland joining NATO will offer only more circumscribed means for less effect.

Barring such a development in the short to medium term a number of initiatives can, nonetheless, be imagined that would strengthen Nordic-Baltic defense capabilities from an aggregate perspective. These include:

- Open Nordic Defense Cooperation (NORDEFCO) to the Baltic states and create a Nordic-Baltic Defense Cooperation framework NORBALDEFCO. Consider how to involve Poland and Germany.
- Upstream focus: Defense planning, Professional Military Education (PME) cooperation, and training facilities.
- Downstream focus: Push training and exercises as "operations light" without stepping over Article 5, new capability for defense capacity building in third countries.

A further consideration or implementation of either or all of these proposals would yield both feasible and in different ways substantial contributions to Nordic-Baltic defense capabilities. While all of them will be useful, the first and most ambitious proposition is also the most effective.

This chapter contributes to the discussion of how to strengthen Nordic-Baltic defense capabilities.[1] The geopolitical starting point for the discussion has evolved quite a lot during the first six months of 2014 after Russia's behavior with regard to Ukraine. The Swedish government has proposed to increase the defense budget because of those geopolitical changes.[2] Even so, the analysis focuses on how to get more defense capability for the same money, by increasing the level of international cooperation.[3] As described below, the changing geopolitics outside the countries speak in favor of an increased sense of common fate among them and hence a push for more regional cooperation, even on—by international standards—sensitive areas. The paper, moreover, does not fully consider the European Union (EU) as a framework for cooperation. While the EU's Common Defense and Security Policy has enabled the EU to become a not negligible actor in international crisis management, it does not in reality have an important role to play in global security for its members. NATO is the only organization that can provide something akin to a security guarantee. Cooperation inside NATO, moreover, is where best practice on military and defense affairs is diffused and shared in general.

The chapter therefore begins by describing two important contexts for the issue of defense capability development in and among the Nordic-Baltic countries. These are respectively the geopolitics of the

---

[1]The author wishes to express his gratitude to the participants on the review seminar at Center for Transatlantic Relations, SAIS, Johns Hopkins held on June 19, 2014, as well as to the participants in the seminar on the future of NORDEFCO held at the Centre for Military Studies, University of Copenhagen on June 3, 2014 for valuable comments and analysis, in particular to Ann-Sofie Dahl and Pauli Järvenpää for insightful comments. Even so, the author bears full responsibility for the resulting analysis.

[2]Defense News, May 7, 2014, "Russia's Aggression Spurs Sweden to Boost Spending, Acquire New Capabilities," (http://www.defensenews.com/article/20140507/DEFREG01/305070038/ Russia-s-Aggression-Spurs-Sweden-Boost-Spending-Acquire-New-Capabilities), see also the earlier hike announcement in Defense News, October 15, 2013, (http://www.defensenews.com/ article/20131015/DEFREG01/310150017/Sweden-Plans-Defense-Spending-Boost).

[3]There is no particular reason why the Nordic-Baltic perspective as such or practical attempts at fostering more cooperation between these countries in and by themselves would increase defense budgets. Rather, such cooperation may either allow for a more effective use of existing budgets or enable less relative expenditure in an area of cooperation for the same effect leaving the residual funds for other defense expenditure.

Nordic-Baltic area and the regional trend in European defense cooperation. After that, the paper uses the current NORDEFCO framework as a basis for a fuller introduction and discussion of the above proposals and proposes concrete ways forward.

A Proto-Region: Geopolitics of the Nordic-Baltic Area

The Nordic-Baltic area consists in a group of states mostly around the Baltic Sea that share the challenge of Russia in their vicinity. Yet they share neither institutional affiliations in terms of alliances, nor—in spite of a substantial growth in political and economic relations between the Baltics and the Nordics since the end of the Cold War—a strong cultural affinity.[4] The Nordic-Baltic area consists in a group of states mostly around the Baltic Sea that on the one hand share the challenge of Russia in their vicinity, but on the other hand do not share institutional affiliations in terms of alliances. Together, they form not a proper region, but what might be called a proto-region.[5] In geopolitical terms, the Nordic-Baltic area is particular in that it is not really a region as classically understood: as a more or less self-containing unit with a higher degree of internal than external relations.[6] As the name suggests, the Nordic-Baltic group of countries is an amalgamate consisting in the traditional group of the Nordic countries as well as a selection of the countries with a Baltic coastline, the equally traditional "Baltic states," Estonia, Latvia and Lithuania.[7] Instead of

---

[4]For an early review of extending the Nordic to include the Baltic see Ole Wæver "Nordic Nostalgia: Northern Europe after the Cold War," *International Affairs*, 68(1), 1992, pp. 77-102.

[5]Following the terminology regarding regional security complexes (RSCs) in Barry Buzan and Ole Wæver *Regions and Powers* (Cambridge: Cambridge University Press, 2003). Note that Wæver and Buzan literally cuts through what we here call a proto-region by placing the Baltic countries under the post-Soviet great power RSC, while the rest of the states in question are categorized as belonging to the Western European Great Power RSC (350, 374, 414-416). The Baltic states "constitute the biggest problem" for the interrelationship between these two RSCs. The concept means that such RSCs are not defined by allegiance or membership. Instead, the "most common way of being tied together is the negative dynamics, i.e. by being each other's security problem" (430). Categorizations such as that and the one employed in this chapter are of course not naturally given, but deeply strategically significant categorizations.

[6]E.g. Buzan and Wæver 2003, pp. 40-65.

[7]As the Nordic-Baltic states are a geopolitically defined group of states connected by the Baltic Sea it might be asked how to delimit the group and whether for example Poland or

being defined from the inside out, the Nordic-Baltic "region" is defined by the relations of power surrounding the countries as expressed by the structure of national Alliance and other institutional affiliations. Strengthening defense capabilities among these states therefore means navigating this mismatch between the regional geopolitics and the institutional setup.

Importantly, all of the eight nations bar Sweden and Finland are members of NATO. All countries are members of the EU with the exception of Iceland (which withdrew its membership application in 2014) and Norway (which has an association agreement and is subject to the *acquis communautaire* without having a voice in its regulation). Denmark is a full member of the EU, but has opted out of four major dimensions, including the Common Defense and Security Policy and Denmark cannot, therefore, participate in any EU missions or defense planning.

Because of Russia's presence on the land-borders of most of these countries (except Iceland, Denmark and Sweden), the most important distinction with regard to geopolitics, however, is NATO membership. Both Sweden and Finland have, since the Cold War, shifted away from strict neutrality without for that matter actually joining NATO. Russia has been vocal in its reservations with regard to potential Swedish and Finnish membership.[8] Accordingly, the geopolitical logic of the shift away from neutrality and its limits is of central interest. The recent geopolitical changes around the proto-region have created the basis for a changed and increasingly shared outlook and sense of threat among the countries. Such an increase in shared threat perception is a valuable currency insofar as it makes the likelihood higher that nations will be willing to change established patterns of priority and coopera-tion and consider new, international solutions. In the end, the changed geopolitical situation in the immediate vicinity of these countries can make the proto-region more of a region in a proper sense, paving the

---

even Germany are not natural members as Baltic states? Both countries are moreover involved in NATO contingency plans for the three Baltic states. In practice, Great Britain has for a while pursued the so-called Northern Group with regard to cooperation in defense issues such as procurement. The Northern Group idea then proposes that also the United Kingdom could be included in this perspective.

[8]Defense News, June 16, 2014, "Russia Warns Sweden and Finland Against NATO Member-ship," (http://www.defensenews.com/article/20140612/DEFREG01/306120040/Russia-Warns-Sweden-Finland-Against-NATO-Membership).

way for more cooperation and the emergence of new, more formal frameworks corresponding to that region.

Inside NATO, the main strategic division until the events in Ukraine and as witnessed in the declarations at the 2012 NATO summit in Chicago, was between international activists, pushing for reform in order to enable participation in Out of Area operations such as mostly north-western European nations—and those, mostly eastern European countries with borders to Russia, that were most concerned with collective defense.[9] Both perspectives are clearly represented among the eight countries, but with somewhat unpredictable results. In fact, those who until now have been most and least concerned with Russian behavior, Denmark and the Baltics, have also been the most active contributors to the hard fighting in the International Security Assistance Force (ISAF). All of them have been so in order to cultivate strategic bilateral relationships with the United States and the United Kingdom. Even if all of the countries share the small state's natural preference for *multilateral* solutions, they are also acutely aware of the value of *bilateral* strategic relationships. For the NATO-members especially, Nordic and Nordic-Baltic defense cooperation always comes with the risk of being a distraction from this main game of international defense policy.

The geopolitics of the proto-region is in other words such that there are both centrifugal and centripetal forces pulling the countries closer together and further apart. The biggest joker is whether the Russian critiques will end up pushing Sweden and Finland towards a NATO membership. In fact, the question of whether the proto-region will become a proper region, and start exhibiting such characteristics including in defense cooperation, may well hinge on whether national threat perception is in fact converging. Regardless of material change underway in that respect, the proto-region stands out in the European, international context because of the already existing level of defense cooperation.

Because of the international interest in NORDEFCO—not least the interest paid in NATO and in the United States—the continued

---

[9]NATO "Chicago Summit Declaration," May 20, 2012, (http://www.nato.int/cps/en/ nato-live/official_texts_87593.htm).

development of such cooperation, also including beyond the existing framework of NORDEFCO is very much in the interest of the Nordic and Baltic countries. The next section therefore examines the regional trend in international, European defense cooperation.

NORDEFCO and the Regional Trend in Defense Cooperation

Capability development is an essential part of defense policy. Spurred by the financial crisis, capability development inside NATO has increasingly focused on regional cooperation as a means to more effective defense policy. In generic terms, there are two different models for regional cooperation, each emphasizing different parts of overall defense policy. In the framework nation approach—developed in part by Germany—the emphasis is on *upstream* cooperation. In this approach, one country—the framework nation—stands as a hub and other nations as spokes in a particular capability development project. Upstream here refers to capability development and procurement. The challenge in creating upstream coordination is thus one mostly of coordination of defense planning including synchronization and convergence of requirements.[10] As seen in the relatively modest progress made over the years in EU pooling and sharing as well as in NATO Smart Defense cooperation, even these challenges are hard to overcome.

A different approach focuses on *downstream* cooperation and is developed in part by the United Kingdom. Downstream here refers to the actual use of those military forces that result of the upstream defense development policies. In this perspective, the most important thing is to create better aggregate effects of available forces and the focus is therefore on cooperation on joint deployable forces and joint commands. In this context the Battle Group model has largely been following a regional logic, just as regular NATO contingency planning and headquarters distribution has been for a long time. More recently, an increase in bilateral defense cooperation agreements is a concrete example of how this approach is being applied as a sort of defense cooperation beyond NATO. This also takes a hub and spokes form.

---

[10]Henrik Breitenbauch, Gary Schaub and Flemming Pradhan-Blach, *Get it Together: Smart Defense Solutions to NATO's Compound Challenge of Multinational Procurement*, CMS Report, February 2013, (http://cms.polsci.ku.dk/publikationer/getittogether/Get_it_Together.pdf).

Most important, of course, is the agreements between the large European nations of France and the United Kingdom with the Lancaster House Treaties (2010). At the spokes level, these agreements were followed for example by Denmark, which has signed a Memorandum of Understanding with the United Kingdom (2012) and a Letter of Intent with France (2014). In this downstream perspective, continued and closer operative cooperation is a vehicle for maintaining interoperability as well as for enabling joint missions inside the NATO area or out of area.

Both upstream and downstream approaches hide the difficult question of specialization. In theory, the most effective way of spending the defense budgets across several nations would be to coordinate capability development in such a way that duplication is avoided. As Christian Mölling of the German Institute for International and Security Affairs (SWP) has spelled out, the alternative, especially among the smaller European nations, is a situation where each country has only one of each kind of defense capability, leaving in fact the continent with "bonsai armies."[11] Accordingly, nations should coordinate their defense policies to a much larger degree and specialize in specific capabilities according to the overall requirements.[12]

Against this argument stands the political reality of nations. Even governments of small European countries are likely to conceive of their armed forces as a whole that does not lend itself to international specialization for two reasons. First, even if some cases of specialization can be cited—such as Denmark forgoing its submarines in 2003 or the Baltic nations" lack of fighter aircraft—it is nevertheless generally the preference of governments to retain at least "one of each" of defense capabilities. This is exactly because this theoretically allows for continued and full national defense or at least a regeneration of such a capability in case the government should decide to do so.

Second, European armed forces and their employment in multinational military missions have increasingly become an important ele-

---

[11]Christian Mölling, "Europe without Defense," SWP Comments 38, November 2011, (http://www.swp-berlin.org/fileadmin/contents/products/comments/2011C38_mlg_ks.pdf)

[12]See e.g. the NATO Secretary General repeat the coda on preferring specialization by design to specialization by default: NATO "Monthly Press Briefing," March 5, 2012, (http://www.nato.int/cps/en/natolive/opinions_84865.htm)

ment in these nations" Alliance management and general security foreign policy. The move towards being security providers has meant that the perceived political utility of the military has increased in many European nations. In consequence, the optimal structure of the armed forces is exactly "one of each," or at least a somewhat or minimally capable contribution from each of the services plus special operations forces and support capabilities. This allows the government to decide on whether to contribute to any given international demand for such forces and thus to have the ability to decide. This political logic is the most important impediment to any dreams of further specialization in either a NATO or EU context. It also explains why such efforts are likely to be forever disappointed.

Since NATO launched its Smart Defense initiative, NORDEFCO has continuously been touted as a role model to follow for other subregional constellations.[13] According to the NORDEFCO Memorandum of Understanding, its purpose is to "strengthen the participating nations" national defense, explore common synergies and facilitate common solutions."[14] The goal of NORDEFCO on the military level is "pragmatic cooperation across the *entire range of defense structures* in order to achieve better cost-effectiveness and quality, and thereby creating enhanced operational capability for the nations."[15] To NATO, NORDEFCO is an example of Smart Defense where different sovereign countries come together to find common solutions to defense issues. NORDEFCO indeed does consist of a promising and innovative framework.

With regard to capability development, two planning documents published in the end of 2013 show the concrete progress and aims for NORDEFCO. In "Nordic Defense Cooperation 2020," the vision is

---

[13]Founding and other documents can be found at (http://www.nordefco.org/Docs) as well as at (http://www.nordefco.org/documents). See also *Terms of Reference* here on the Norwegian Ministry of Defense homepage: (http://www.regjeringen.no/nb/dep/fd/tema/forsvarspolitikk/ nordefco-terms-of-reference.html?id=589717).

[14]*Memorandum of Understanding between the Ministry of Defense of the Kingdom of Denmark and the Ministry of Defense of the Republic of Finland and the Ministry of Foreign Affairs of Iceland and the Ministry of Defense of the Kingdom of Norway and the Ministry of Defense of the Kingdom of Sweden on Nordic Defense Cooperation*, November 5, 2009, available at (http://www.nordefco.org/ files/Design/NORDEFCO%20MOU.pdf), p. 2.

[15]NORDEF MCC Action Plan 2014-17, p. 3, emphasis added.

that by that year the Nordic countries will have "deepened their defense cooperation with the aim to create systems similarity, including armaments, interoperability and shared solutions to identified gaps and shortfalls. Possibilities for pooling of capabilities will be actively sought... Joint Nordic Acquisition will be enabled by the establishment of common processes and routines. We have established an ongoing close dialogue with Nordic defense industry."[16] In the parallel Action Plan 2014-17 issued by the Nordic Military Coordination Committee two fairly aggressive ambitions stand out.

First, the ambition is to install intensive information sharing on defense planning and procurement plans in order to ultimately facilitate synchronization and harmonization of requirements and changes in procurement priorities. As the Action Plan states: "To achieve operational benefits and exploit the economical (sic) potential, transparency in capability long term planning and procurement plans, is essential. Nordic countries will compare national plans continuously within all areas of cooperation, but also conduct a mix of bottom-up and top-down processes to identify activities that could benefit from high level attention and priority." This corresponds to a high level of ambition with regard to internationalizing a rather sensitive area of national defense policy. Listed under military level objectives in the respective Cooperation Areas (COPA), this means that COPA CAPA (Capabilities) shall for example "continuously compare national capability development plans in order to present identified short, medium and long term co-development areas by the second MCC meeting in 2014."[17] For COPA ARMA (Armaments), the goal is even more extensive as it must "suggest armament procurement priority changes in respective nations" procurement plans in order to facilitate common acquisitions."[18]

Second, and to support this focus on synchronization and harmonization, the Action Plan also states that the national working group members "shall use their national positions to merge agreed on activities into national steering documents and thereby transfer them to the responsibilities of their line organizations."[19] This is so because in

---

[16]"Nordic Defense Cooperation 2020," p. 2.

[17]NORDEF MCC Action Plan 2014-17, p. 6.

[18]NORDEF MCC Action Plan 2014-17, p. 7.

order for the military level to actually produce results, it is "pertinent that Nordic activities are included in national plans, orders and budgets." In sum, the vision for establishing a rather far-reaching process of cooperation on capability development—one that by virtue of national "ambassadors" may be more effectual than NATO's Defense Planning Process—is strong. Making it come true is of course a matter of not only political, but also civilian and military administrative will.[20]

Even in spite of these promises, it should also be acknowledged that the strategic effect of NORDEFCO—in terms of percentages of defense budgets—is limited and it would be naïve to declare the Nordic defense cooperation an unmitigated success. Resistance among the other countries to procure Swedish defense materiel in the context of NORDEFCO has resulted in "strained relations."[21] The recent establishment of a "Cooperation Area Armaments" might result in more explicit engagements about defense industrial dimensions of the framework, but the uneven distribution of defense industries makes these matters very sensitive, for both willing producers and prospective buyers. In geopolitical terms, NORDEFCO has been particularly interesting for Sweden and Finland as the cooperation offered access to closer relationships with NATO members Norway and Denmark.[22] For Denmark in particular, NORDEFCO has been seen as more of a deviation as the really important defense relationships in a Danish perspective are those found "upwards" (the United States, United Kingdom and France are Denmark's "strategic military partners") rather than sideways such as in NORDEFCO. At issue, moreover, is NORDEFCO's possible role as a vehicle for military sales with Swedish defense industry in the lead, and the other Nordic countries as potential buyers. In general, arms exports are a challenging factor in building defense cooperation relationships. Arms sales and long-term cooperation on operational use and development can be a valuable contribution to cementing such relationships. In the NORDEFCO case it is notable that Norway, Finland and Denmark on different

---

[19]NORDEF MCC Action Plan 2014-17, p. 5.

[20]See Breitenbauch et al. 2013 on the domestic "iron triangle" hindering multinational defense procurement.

[21]Ann-Sofie Dahl "NORDEFCO and NATO: 'Smart Defense' in the North?," NATO Defense College, Research Paper No. 101, May 2014.

[22]Iceland is mostly irrelevant by not having a defense structure.

accounts have opted not to procure important defense materiel in Sweden.[23]

As already mentioned, none of these tensions are likely to diminish the utility of the NORDEFCO framework as a case for more regional cooperation in the rest of Europe. Increased Nordic-Baltic cooperation may therefore be seen as a high value item in the Nordic-Baltic countries" bilateral relationships with the United States. In principle, Nordic-Baltic cooperation has the potential to replace—at least some of—the military diplomatic function of force contributions to multinational missions such as ISAF, which was to cultivate strategic military relationships with the United States (and to a lesser degree, the United Kingdom). According to this logic, the Nordic-Baltic countries can keep being seen in a positive light by Washington by being the poster boy for cooperation that leads to reductions in duplications and smarter ways to spend the defense budgets.

Options for Strengthening Nordic-Baltic Defense Capabilities

NORDEFCO is the unavoidable starting point option for further developing defense cooperation in the Nordic-Baltic region. NATO discussions on regional defense cooperation emphasize NORDEFCO's status a role model framework. NORDEFCO already enables cooperation between the Nordic-Baltic countries. The framework is in continuous, ambitious development and it contains, moreover, provisions for cooperation with third parties, and in particular, explicitly mentions cooperation with the Baltic nations. It also functions on a flexible à la carte basis meaning the cooperation in any area is opt-in for participants and that any given constellation of participants are welcome to move forward as they see fit without the rest.

As a starting point for strengthening Nordic-Baltic defense capabilities, NORDEFCO can be used in two ways. First, NORDEFCO can simply be broadened to include the three Baltic states. Second, as NORDEFCO rules already allow for, the Baltic countries can get further involved in each of the existing Cooperation Areas. Distinguishing between the already mentioned upstream or downstream defense

---

[23]See e.g. Dahl 2014, pp. 6-7, 11.

policy domains, this section examines each of the resulting three possibilities in turn.

NORBALDEFCO: Simply Let In the Baltics

Given the prominent role and solidity of the NORDEFCO framework, the most obvious way to improve Nordic-Baltic Defense Capabilities would be to open NORDEFCO up to full Baltic membership, in effect changing the organization to Nordic-Baltic Defense Cooperation (NORBALDEFCO). Even in the case of Swedish and Finnish membership, this idea would still be an obvious way forward for the regions" countries. NORDEFCO would in this case become an example of a purely NATO-internal regional cooperation. By opening the framework up to the rest of the Baltic countries, the new NORBALDEFCO would be spearheading the efforts inside NATO to further regional defense cooperation.

The "Nordic Defense Cooperation 2020" vision document signed by the Nordic ministers of defense provides "basis for the political guidance of Nordic defense cooperation as we move towards 2020." It furthermore emphasizes "possibilities for deeper regional and multi-national cooperation" with other countries and organizations as a primary ambition. In particular, "close cooperation with Estonia, Latvia and Lithuania continues to be important." As for the practical modalities of such cooperation the vision document only hints at cooperation rather than full participation (or membership), in that Nordic cooperation is "open to other third parties in selected activities based on mutual interests, operational output and cost-effectiveness."[24] Given the flexibility of the framework and the light bureaucracy touch to its implementation, there is little practical in the way of opening up NORDEFCO to the Baltic states. In terms of size and character, their defense structures would not fundamentally change the possibilities for cooperation, not least because of the degree of interoperability gained in ISAF and through other NATO cooperation such as host nation support to air policing. The Nordic countries, moreover, have a rather long and internationally successful history of cooperation with the Baltic countries. The establishment of the Baltic Defense College

---

[24]*Nordic Defense Cooperation 2020*, Helsinki December 4, 2014.

is a major achievement in itself and one of the first good examples of Smart Defense.

A special consideration has to do with the rest of the Baltic countries (bar Russia), namely Poland and Germany. As reflected in NATO contingency planning, these countries have an already substantial role in Baltic security. In a EU context, Poland, Germany, Slovakia, Lithuania and Latvia have formed an EU Battle Group. Poland in particular has cultivated relationships with the Baltic states and may already be interested in furthering its relationship with NORDEFCO.[25] Opening up NORDEFCO to include cooperation with Poland, for starters, would have a bigger potential than the Baltics alone, because of the size of the Polish armed forces.

Several things stand in the way of NORBALDEFCO, even in a version restricted to the Baltics. Nordic countries" preference for purely Nordic cooperation stem not only from their longstanding cooperation within the Nordic Council framework, based on a shared cultural and historical heritage. It stems also from a preference for avoiding a position that could be perceived to antagonize Russia. In this case, the Baltic states" perception of and policy toward Russia has been rather incommensurate with Nordic, particularly Norwegian and Finnish policy preferences. In this perspective, the actual success in shaping the solid bureaucratic NORDEFCO regime is partially built on the calmness provided by an absence of acute threat. In addition, the lack of clear institutional affiliation among the Nordic members is in this way a contributing factor because it made clear the necessity of a stand-alone framework, which would work as an add-on to NATO and EU memberships.

Upstream: Defense Planning, Professional Military Education, Training Grounds

Should it be unrealistic to establish NORBALDEFCO, it is still the existing NORDEFCO framework including for cooperation with third parties and in particular, the three Baltic nations that will most likely serve as a medium for increased cooperation in the region. The

---

[25]Sliwa, Zdislaw and Marcin Górnikiewicz, "Security Cooperation between Poland and the Baltic Region," *Baltic Security and Defense Review*, 15(2), 2013, pp. 146-182, 169.

upstream option is at first sight less problematic than the downstream that deals with operations, including Article 5 operations for the NATO members.

Upstream here refers to anything that has to do with defense capability development in a broad sense. In NORDEFCO parlance this is defined as capability development and "force provision," which again is taken to imply "all activities (including at least procuring equipment, manning, supplying, maintaining, educating, training and exercising) needed to set up forces needed by the individual countries to fulfill the tasks of their armed forces, which may range from national defense readiness to deployment in international operations."[26] Currently, NORDEFCO activities are organized under five Cooperation Areas (COPAs). Four of these are upstream: Capabilities, Human Resources and Education, Training and Exercises, and Armaments. A fifth COPA, Operations, is addressed under downstream measures.

In particular, such piecemeal upstream or force provision cooperation could benefit from focusing on defense planning, PME, and training and exercise utility sharing.

Defense planning is the overlapping concern of COPA CAPA and COPA ARMA. In both cases, the COPA's management groups are to analyze national planning. In CAPA, the tasker is to identify "co-development areas" for the short, medium and long-term. In ARMA, the tasker calls for the Cooperation Area to "suggest armament procurement priority changes in respective nations procurement plans in order to facilitate common acquisitions."[27] As NATO members, the three Baltic states all have processes in place to interact internationally regarding their defense planning. There are no large administrative commitments involved in cooperating on this domain and the three states are likely able to participate fairly easily.

Defense planning is of course at the heart of national prioritization processes in defense and security policy and as such very sensitive areas. As defense planning involves procurement, moreover, it also touches upon the role of national defense industrial partners and involves all of those related issues. NORDEFCO, as mentioned,

---

[26]MCC 2014-17, p. 4.

[27]MCC 2014-17, pp. 6-7.

moreover carries with it the question mark of in particular Swedish defense materiel exports. Accordingly, a piecemeal promotion of defense planning cooperation involving the Baltics may see it fit to begin more in COPA CAPA than in Arma. It could focus on a few, particular flagship projects in order to build the necessary familiarity with and confidence in the processes and the overall framework. One idea could be to work from a roster of shared, related or overlapping tasks such as in e.g. maritime situational awareness and related information sharing and probe such lists of tasks for areas and concrete projects of potential shared development.[28]

Professional Military Education covers a wide area of activities (from specific, specialized to general course) and levels (from cadets to colonels) and scopes (from in residence to distance learning and from weeks to years). PME is a labor-intensive part of force provisioning and as such contains opportunity costs beyond the immediate expenses for courses and school institutions. PME is also at the heart of domestic capacity building in that a well-educated officer corps is the basic capital from which military capabilities are developed. Platforms and training are only one part of the equation. PME provides not only professional identity to the group of officers. It also provides them with the mental tools necessary for coping with change and complex environments. As fewer and fewer tasks of the armed forces especially of small countries are strictly national, and more and more of them involve international elements, both in everyday and out of area operations, military officers—and in particular from the major level upwards—increasingly need to be not only "combined and joint," they need also to be international. The Baltic states" founding of the Baltic Defense College (with the support of the Nordic countries) is a testimony to an early realization of this fact.

One way forward in this area would be to focus on developing an English language common curriculum, and to introduce both a partially synchronized module course structure for English language courses as well as exchange possibilities to increase mobility among

---

[28]In this way, this proposition, just like the rest, cuts across the upstream/downstream divide. That crossing makes sense because in the end it is what we do with the capabilities that matter. As stated below, the NATO context evidently makes for some rather tangible limits to how far such cooperation can be pushed.

the eight nations" five major level staff courses.[29] Lower level common courses for common purposes (captains" and cadets" courses) can also contain such English language and international elements, even if an ambitious agenda here is moving into more sensitive territory. Colonel level courses are an obvious area of development because of the international content in corresponding positions, but not one with a lot of volume. Any cooperation should include efforts to cooperate also on quality assurance. As most countries have moved far in terms of harmonizing their military PME systems with their civilian higher education systems following the Bologna Process, a promising avenue for such cooperation already exists. Mobility, best practice transfers and quality control among teacher-researchers moreover is a precondition for not only further professionalization of the field but also ultimately for national education to international standards.

Training grounds are expensive to establish and difficult to put to effective use year round. Nordic cooperation on training grounds is moving forward in the NORDEFCO context and welcoming the Baltic states into this cooperation would be relatively easy. There are some logistical issues related to getting to and from training grounds, but Nordic nations have solid maritime transport capacity that can be put to good use in this context. Shared international training, moreover, is a central motive in NATO's Connected Forces Initiative in order to preserve and continuously develop interoperability among NATO and partner forces. By focusing on enabling cooperation around training grounds, the groundwork is also laid for further training together and thus for interoperability among the nations" armed forces.

Sharing training grounds also opens up possibilities for identification of potential new capability development as well as cooperation on specialist training courses (common courses for specific purposes). Artillery training is one such obvious area of cooperation as it takes up a lot of space and comprises relatively small units with a very specialized expertise. Sharing training grounds, finally, will enable more English language proficiency as exercises and training as well as coordina-

---

[29]Gary, Schaub, Henrik Breitenbauch and Flemming Pradhan-Blach, *Invading Bologna: Prospects for Nordic Cooperation in Professional Military Education*, CMS Report, November 2013, (http://cms.polsci.ku.dk/publikationer/bologna/Nordic_PME_report_final.pdf).

tion and everyday activities will provide military units with many opportunities to navigate an English military language situation.

Downstream: Mix Operations and Exercises, Create Capacity Building Capability

Because of the geopolitics of the region, downstream cooperation that focuses on operations, including both inside the region's area as well as out of area operations, is more sensitive than upstream cooperation. Of course, these very same geopolitics may be a reason to move forward on such cooperation—and even push for Sweden and Finland to join NATO. In general, operational cooperation including preparations for such operational cooperation, however, is also more straightforward than upstream cooperation because it deals more with using than producing national assets. Multinational operational cooperation is more readily perceived as a situation to "show the flag," whereas capability development cooperation comes with a higher risk in that it will be seen as a zero sum game for national interests. Overall, there are at least three such ways in which the Nordic-Baltic countries can strengthen their downstream defense cooperation: operations; training and exercises; and by gradually developing and deploying a new capacity building capability.

Operations, training, and exercises are an area where the distinction between NATO members and partners is most clear. Institutional affiliations of the countries of the region—as it stands currently—pose a challenge for how far downstream operational cooperation can go. Article 5 considerations means that NATO is unlikely to blur the border between membership and non-membership. Recent events in Ukraine will only exacerbate this distinction when it comes to operations.

From a NATO perspective, it is more difficult to include partners in Article 5 related exercises than other types of exercises. This difficulty is compounded by the functional drift of exercises from training to assurance purposes. Through their high frequency and scope, exercises have begun to function as assurance operations within NATO. Even so, including Sweden and Finland in such exercises is one way of strengthening Nordic-Baltic defense cooperation. As such, there are ways to cooperate for the Nordic-Baltic countries on operations that push up against, without for that matter crossing, the Article 5 border.

Basically, the nations should treat training and exercises cooperation as "operations light," and push such cooperation as far as possible without making it part of NATO collective defense operations.[30]

As mentioned above, military officers need to be international as well as joint and combined. In the Nordic-Baltic area, this is particularly true. The long-standing Nordic and Baltic tradition for peacekeeping and peace support operations as well as for high-intensity NATO-led operations has also been a history of evolving operation cooperation. Cooperation on operational capabilities has a long history in the area, also crossing outside the area with the example of Poland and Germany's role in the EU Battle Group. If Sweden and Finland are being let into the NATO Response Force (NRF), then this will be the obvious area for enhancing also the regional cooperation.

NORDEFCO's Cooperation Area Operations comprises both operational capabilities and doctrine development and is tasked with developing "future common approaches to operations." Including the Baltic states in this work will not only ensure an even stronger a NATO standard orientation, but also take into account the particular Baltic operational experiences and visions, including for example, the cyber dimension. COPA Ops is moreover tasked with preparing to "coordinate the support to United Nations (UN) peace keeping operations when a common Nordic political decision so demands." The expectation is that a common Nordic approach at the political level is a real possibility. The Baltic countries can easily be included in United Nations peace operations planning if the political level, including their own, accepts this framework. A final task deals with the investigation of further optimization of combined logistics in operations. Given the shared experiences with extensive and complex deployment to Afghanistan, the Baltic states are good candidates for inclusion here too.

Capacity building in third countries has emerged as a major strategic challenge for the West. Because of their shared history in Baltic defense capacity building, extensive practical experience with, and investments in development policy, including in stabilization missions the Nordic-Baltic countries are an ideal cluster of nations for developing a capability for capacity building.

---

[30]This is already being done, cf. Dahl 2014, p. 10.

Seeing capacity building in third countries as a new defense capability properly speaking is not uncontroversial.[31] While platforms are essential, it does not necessarily follow that an incremental increase in expense is always best placed on platforms. What matters most is to identify ways to use the input smarter with regard to the intended output. The challenge of strengthening defense capabilities in an international perspective is thus also a matter of including other elements of existing state capabilities than platforms in a broad, strategic defense planning perspective. American and Western defense policy, moreover, has clearly moved upstream from a focus on post-conflict stabilization (like in Iraq and Afghanistan) to a more general conflict management or even conflict prevention perspective.[32] Working with and through partners with indirect engagement is an unavoidable long-term challenge for the West.

The Nordic and Baltic countries have invested a lot in both the complex stabilization missions of the last decade as well as in EU and United Nations missions before and after the turn of the millennium.[33] Whole-of-government approaches have become the order of the day in order to deal with such challenges that cut across the security-development frontier.[34] In the NORDEFCO 2020 vision, capacity building is emphasized as the second element for future investments. Capacity building will, in six years, be "an integrated part of Nordic contribu-

---

[31]Traditionally, the notion of defense capabilities concerns available and able operational military units. Numbers and qualities of platforms surely is a substantial part of that notion. However, it is important to understand with regard to what those defense capabilities are being developed and deployed. While input matters, the output of defense organizations should be the crucial yardstick with which not only to measure the quality of the process between input and output, but also a natural starting point for the design of defense policy effects.

[32]See e.g., Ministry of Foreign Affairs, Ministry of Justice, Ministry of Defense: *Denmark's Integrated Stabilisation Engagement in Fragile and Conflict-Affected Areas of the World*, November 2013, (http://amg.um.dk/en/~/media/amg/Documents/Policies%20and%20Strategies/Stability%20and%20Fragility/Stabiliseringspolitik_UK_web.pdf).

[33]Jakobsen, Peter Viggo *Nordic Approaches to Peace Operations: A New Model in the Making?* (London: Routledge 2006); Breitenbauch, Henrik "Samtænkning som læring og politisk kit. Udviklingen af Danmarks tilgang til stabiliseringsindsatser siden 2004," *Økonomi og Politik*, 2014, No. 1, pp. 33-48.

[34]Jemalavicius, Tomas et al. *Comprehensive Security and Integrated Defense: Challenges of implementing whole-of- government and whole-of-society approaches*, ICDS Report, February 2014, (http://icds.ee/fileadmin/failid/ICDS_Report-Comprehensive_Security_and_Integrated_Defense-10_February_2014.pdf).

tions to international engagements. The Nordic countries [will] have established a roster of specialists and military advisors to conduct capacity building and security sector reform tasks. The Nordic countries will be able to provide financial, material and advisory support."[35] While the Baltic states may have less experience with development policy than the Nordics, they may very well have a much more recent memory of the notoriously challenging situation it is to be subjected to capacity building from the outside and not least with regard to the shift from Soviet era-styled organizations to NATO standards. This, in particular, is a challenge with regard to Ukraine. Including the Baltic states in this project therefore makes a lot of sense.

A Way Forward for Strengthening Nordic-Baltic Defense Capabilities

The Nordic-Baltic countries are not really a region, but a proto-region that perhaps is coming closer to being a proper region because of the changing geopolitical conditions outside the area. Russian actions in Ukraine have increased threat perception in the region and pose a fundamental and troubling challenge to the way international security has been structured in Europe since the end of the Cold War. While most of the existing defense cooperation with a view of strengthening defense capabilities has been carried out within the internationally renowned framework of NORDEFCO, there is no reason why this framework could not be extended to the Baltic states.[36] A NORBALDEFCO would not only cement the prominent role of Sweden and Finland within NATO as premier partners, it would also formally continue the work begun with Baltic independence after the Cold War, and furthermore strengthen the NATO aspect of Nordic-Baltic security.

A less comprehensive solution—of pursuing piecemeal cooperation inside NORDEFCO as allowed by the existing framework—is also

---

[35]Vision 2020, p. 2.

[36]The argument here echoes in a somewhat hardened way the one made by Sven Sakkov in "Towards Nordic-Baltic Defense Cooperation. A View from Estonia," Ann-Sofie Dahl and Pauli Järvenpää (eds.) *Northern Security and Global Politics. Nordic-Baltic Strategic Influence in a Post-Unipolar World*, London: Routledge, 2014, pp. 155-169.

possible. In any case, as this paper has pointed out, at least six particular elements are worth considering when making the cooperation move forward. As the nations do consider the next steps, they would be well advised to see also the alliance political aspects of furthering cooperation in the region. In particular the partners, but also Denmark, Norway and the Baltic states, have had a relatively prominent status in the Alliance context and with regard to the United States in particular because of their important contributions to multinational operations over the last long decade such as in Afghanistan. These large operations are ending, however. The United States is likely to pursue input (defense budgets and burden sharing) as much as outputs (risk sharing with boots on the ground) in its future alliance management. Emphasizing the positive and to some extent path-breaking role of NORDEFCO in a Baltic context would be one way for nations of the region to replace contributions made in Afghanistan in terms of gaining positive attention. In this way too, there are particularly good reasons for including the Baltic states in the existing framework.

Chapter 13

Forward Resilience and Networked Capabilities: Finland's Softer Power Tools in the Wake of Ukraine

Mika Aaltola

After Ukraine, the geostrategic challenges to small, but highly open and connected states have become hotly debated in the Nordic–Baltic region. Instead of being self-reliant, smaller states have long faced the imperative of adapting to competitive interdependencies and supply insecurities.[1] Their own resource base is not large enough to supply all of their security capability needs. The gap between resources and needed security capabilities has been highlighted by their asymmetric interdependencies, which offer an increasingly illiberal Russia routes of influence and coercion. The changing global reality reinforces the need to turn to global networks and circulations.

Secure access to global flows of people, goods, resources, and data provide a key strategic interest for export-oriented small states. This deep adaptation, however, comes with vulnerabilities that are hard to capture with the older language of territorial defense and state security. Non-territorial resilience is increasingly the framework that is better able to capture the present security needs of modern societies.

This chapter examines how Finland, as a small state outside of the North Atlantic Treaty Organization (NATO) and with a long border with Russia, illustrates the puzzle of understanding and learning to combine traditional geopolitical strategies with emerging geo-economic tools.[2] What are Finland's specific set of resources and capabil-

---

[1]Forward resilience refers to a process of sharing societal resilience strategies with allies and partners and identify their own resiliency with that of others. Daniel Hamilton, ed., (2011), *Shoulder to Shoulder: Forging a Strategic U.S.-EU Partnership*. Washington, DC: Johns Hopkins University Center for Transatlantic Relations.

[2]On Finnish statecraft using agile combinations see Mika Aaltola (2011), "Agile small state agency: heuristic plays and flexible national identity markers in Finnish foreign policy." *Nationalities Papers* 39(2):257-276.

ity needs? What forms of softer power does it have and what hard power does it lack? How can different internal and networked capabilities be best utilized to immunize it from Russia's strategic interests? How can it enable its own resilience while supplying to others specific key necessary practices and expertise?

The co-existing and partially contradictory security paradigms—that is, defense, security, and resilience—create additional complexity for strategy planners. The general expectation since the end of the Cold War has been that European states are the vanguard of the move towards an increasingly interdependent world. Finnish and European Union (EU) strategies were formulated in the hope that economic integration would force all actors, Russia included, to homogenize their governance frameworks towards similar generic models of liberal interdependency. Ukraine seems to have shattered this expectation, as Russia is internally and externally moving away from the hoped-for path. It has a heavily export-oriented economy that is closely linked to the global flows of finance and natural resources. This contrarian move has shown how an actor can use asymmetric interdependencies in its favor. Russia's recent military build-up has reinforced these fears, with the result that the small states in the Nordic and Baltic regions are struggling to define their response.

Finland has developed itself as an open liberal actor with strong emphasis on societal security and an advanced economy. It has enjoyed considerable soft power as it is consistently ranked very high in measures and indicators of societal stability, education, and economic competitiveness. At the same time, it is very exposed to the new Russian geostrategy due to strong economic links with Russia and its 808-mile-long border with that country. Instead of being defined by the softer power of an open, but stable society, Finland risks being drawn into the position of "Finlandization", where the local regional influences and Russia risk can override the "softer" advances, and turn openness into vulnerability.

The Challenged Nordic–Baltic Region

It is difficult to find a Finnish national strategy document during the last 15 years that would *not* repeat the notion that the likelihood of conventional military conflict in Northern Europe is small and that this has to do with the ever-increasing interdependence in the region. Indeed, Finland has sought to connect to the global circulations of resources, data, people, and money, building on the notion that securing access to these flows and tighter interdependence is a crucial imperative for all levels of security and prosperity. In this, Finland has been, on many fronts, a success story. And it has derived much of its softer forms of power, influence, and respect from this successful transformation which has materialized in a flourishing export industry and high levels of investor confidence.

The tighter and more transnational economic competition has diffused political power among states and led to the emergence of new actors. Since the mid-2000s, Russia has centralized power away from private actors and companies to a cluster of companies that are either state-owned or close to the political elite. This development has many roots. One of them is the inability of Russia to find a viable model for its future in the liberal political and economic order. Many indicators show that Russia's competitiveness is based on its natural resources, which are further to the east and north, where their extraction is relatively expensive. Demographic change in Russia, with a decreasing population projection, shows the depth of the challenges that Russia faces in modernizing its economy in a way that will enable it to compete in the global markets. The now emerging blend of state capitalism, military build-up, geopolitical expansionism, and export dependency is a unique, but very risky, answer that came as no surprise to some of its Nordic–Baltic neighbors.

The path adopted by Russia has increased the already high insecurity felt in the Nordic–Baltic region. The need to build steady connections to the global flows is still an ongoing challenge for the small states. Most of the small states in the region have been relatively successful in building open state architectures and turning themselves into open platforms for private actors such as universities, start-ups, and multinational corporations. The economic crisis in the United States and the subsequent euro crisis demonstrate the need to maintain disruption-free links to global financial flows. At the same time, these economic crises indicated emerging new sources of instability and crisis. The events in the European periphery—as, for example, in Greece, Iceland, Ireland and Portugal—were read as danger signs in a world where power has already flown from smaller states to bigger ones and from states in general to new private actors. The Russian annexation of Crimea brought in worries about an anarchic reality the small states have been trying to avoid in the course of their development.

Volatility and insecurity take place in the context of the increased importance of the main arteries of global trade and interaction. In many ways, states are becoming re-contextualized as parts of the hub-and-spoke architecture of these flows, rather than as parts of their local geography. Russia's military actions in Ukraine served to remind them that this movement from the contours of geography to the typology of the global mobility infrastructure is still incomplete and that states may still be bound to the specifics of their geography to a relative degree.

On the one hand, there is much pressure to secure access to global flows. This means that the logistics of such flows have to function efficiently in both normal and unforeseen situations. The steady humming of the access points in different contingencies means that security of supply stands assured. The key term describing this optimal situation is resilience. In practice, the term means that the down-time of key systems in a situation of sudden disruption is as short as possible. They bounce back. There are different methods for achieving resilience. Governmental and private actors are innovating their own resiliencies. Some global standards are also emerging. One sign of the new security situation is the recent emphasis of NATO on the security of supply issues. This has made NATO a more relevant actor even in the absence of military conflict.

States in general, and highly-exposed small states in particular, have a high demand for security of supply providers since some of them, with highly specialized economies and capabilities, cannot provide for their own resilience. The system has to be secured because disruptions radiate globally. Small states in the Nordic–Baltic region have become increasingly reliant on the networked production of the security of supply capabilities.

In the wake of Ukraine, this security of supply is bound to take on a more defense-related hue and drive states in the region into those networks that can produce resilience. Resilience requirements alone are an important driver of closer integration of Finland with NATO.

Defense and security considerations provide other arguments for this process.

The key challenge facing the Nordic–Baltic states is to strategically manage the flows on which they are dependent and the access points through which they are connected to the wider world. Especially crucial for Finland are four specific areas where interdependence poses a strategic challenge:

- the asymmetric relationships with Russia;
- the emergence of the Arctic challenge and possibilities;
- the cohesion of the EU as an actor; and
- the unpredictability of the global economy.

The long border with Russia and the Arctic highlight Finnish dependencies on Russia. To understand these challenges, a geo-economic perspective is more appropriate than a geopolitical one. A central focus should be on how Finnish strategic vision takes into consideration the new geo-economic reality of competitive interdependency among states and how this contradicts, yet also intertwines with, more traditional geopolitical threats. Geo-economic sensitivity can offer a more comprehensive assessment of Finland's strategic vulnerabilities and opportunities.

Smaller States and Geo-Economic Resilience

Geo-economics tries to capture the dynamics of interdependent competition, which is increasingly economic in nature, and how it re-contextualizes traditional geopolitical considerations. Richard Youngs defines geo-economy as a set of practices that uses statecraft for economic ends, focuses on relative economic gain and power, is aware of who controls resources, does not separate state and business sectors and accepts the importance of economic over other forms of security.[3]

Success in interdependent economic competition is a key enabler of geostrategic capabilities. This makes resorting to the use of military

---

[3]Richard Youngs, 2011. "Geo-economic futures", in Ana Martiningui and Richard Youngs (eds.), *Challenges for European Foreign Policy in 2012: What Kind of Geo-Economic Europe?*. Madrid: FRIDE.

power trickier and less straightforward. Use of power in tandem with other strategic actions is made more difficult by its unintended and systemic consequences, as was made clear by the Russian experiment in Ukraine. There are clear signs that interdependencies offer cooptive potential to expansive states.

Even outside of Russia, there are portents of returning political rivalry.[4] The Chinese model blends authoritarianism, state capitalism, and cooption of interdependency. Unlike Russia, this model is based on successful modernization of the economy and deep economic integration into the liberal international order. The heaviest military build-up concentrates on the emerging illiberal states. The economic gains from the successes in the interdependent competition are invested in building military power. This combination of military might and economic competitiveness has caused concern and indicated that the win-win situations of global interdependence might be turned into no-win and zero-sum scenarios.[5]

The West has responded to these concerns by punishing bad behavior via financial sanctions. The Russian annexation of Crimea, for instance, was met with targeted or smart sanctions. This highlights the changed nature of geopolitical rivalry. Asymmetries in economic interdependencies and outright dependencies are increasingly used as resources in conflict and rivalry. This worrying development is bound to re-contextualize small states' defense, security, and resilience strategies in the future.

The new realities raise concerns about how Finland's relatively open state platform can best be sustained, since it is mainly reliant on Western supply and value chains, but also how it can best manage its interdependencies—especially those related to Russia. What are the best combinations of old and new to hedge against risks while continuing to prosper from access to major global arteries?

---

[4]Ian Bremmer, 2012. *Every Nation for Itself: Winners and Losers in a G-Zero World*. London: Penguin Books.

[5]For example, Thomas Wright, 2013, "Sifting Through Interdependence", *Washington Quarterly*, 36 (4): pp. 7-23.

Small states are usually seen as facing stronger adaptive pressures and crosscutting challenges to their security.[6] On the one hand, securing access to the global flows of production, capital, knowledge, and security seems to call for agile adaption. On the other hand, equal attention must be paid to resilience in the face of the potentially disruptive effects of interdependent competition. Indeed, agility and resilience are often repeated slogans when debating small state foreign policy.[7] But what do they actually mean under the current circumstances, how can the necessary capabilities be developed and how can such capacities enable the new spectrum of power needed to compensate for the lack of the traditional hard power?

The traditional realist and idealist perspectives usually adopted to guide research on small state foreign and security policy fail to appreciate the full breadth of the different sources of small state agency— for example, how small states may, in some cases, occupy "privileged" positions in the hub-and-spoke international economic structure. Such a privileged position as a hub for global flows and an economic gateway may, on the one hand, allow the small state to carve out sectors of influence for itself. The Finnish state's success in primary education highlights one such sector and the former success of Nokia highlights another. Indeed, small states should have narrow sectors in which they have something to offer. They should balance their military weakness by supplying others with specific capabilities in some key practices. This softer power balances harder power and compensates for the lack of it. The balancing highlights economic value chains and innovation economies as methods of making others dependent on them in some strategic fields. This means that others would have a stake in the continued security of Finland because it is able to supply them with some important know-how or technology.

---

[6]For relevant small state studies, see, for example, Regina Karp (2007), "The Conditionality of Security Integration: Identity and Alignment Choices in Finland and Sweden," in Olav Knudsen, ed., *Security Strategies, Power Disparity and Identity: The Baltic Sea Region*. London: Ashgate: pp. 45–72. M. Aaltola, J. Käpylä, H. Mikkola, and T. Behr (2014), *Towards the Geopolitics of Flows: Implications for Finland*. FIIA Report 40. Helsinki: The Finnish Institute of International Affairs.

[7]Amy Verdun (2013), "Small States and the Global Economic Crisis: An Assessment," *European Political Science* 12: pp. 276-293.

However, softer balancing by small states means that they become increasingly intertwined in the complexities of asymmetric interdependencies and dependencies. Larger actors, which are relatively more self-reliant—are more capable of creating their own field of influences in the global interdependent competition. Russia's use of its energy sector to extract concessions and bring indecision into the EU offers a case in point. It is hard for a small actor to balance soft power alone without trusting some other actors and networks. Finland uses the EU and NATO—through the partnership program—as trusted actors. The need to trust the actors that supply key resources and capabilities is important from the perspective of resilience security. The key attribute of the Western alliance is the presence of value- and identification-based trust. It is likely that an interest-based geo-economy may be in contradiction to this trust. This difference between value- and interest-based approaches should be made clear for small states that are sensitive to the pull of lucrative economic deals because of their economic vulnerabilities.

The Changing Meaning and Strategic Weight of Finnish Territory

One key effect of a geo-economy is its influence on the fixedness of territoriality. The Finnish territorial dimension has always been in a relative flux for external, but also internal, reasons—for example, people migrating to the Helsinki region and Finnish production being outsourced into Estonia. It can be claimed that functional territory is becoming the key factor in understanding the smallness of small states and the largeness of large ones. Thus, territory is seen as a function of secure access points to global flows. The integration into the global hub-and-spoke systems leads to remolding of territoriality and to creation of new territory, as, for example, in the case of connectedness to the cyber modality. Some of the existing territories are becoming weightier and some previously strategic locations are becoming lighter and less meaningful as *functional space*.

According to Mayer, three common templates give meaning to territory: state-based, empire-centric, and nomadic.[8] Firstly, the state-

---

[8]Charles Maier (2014), *Leviathan 2.0: Inventing Modern Statehood*. Cambridge: Harvard University Press.

centric Westphalian model is based on strictly delineated territory that is governed by a sovereign state. Overall, European territory, filled as it is by clearly demarcated states, is seen as stable and ordered by clearly set-out rules, norms, and institutions. For example, the rules and norms embodied by the Organization for Security and Cooperation in Europe (OSCE) are supposed to act as a guardian of the relative stability of state boundaries and political order.

Second, the old empire-based understanding of territory has not disappeared from Europe. The European international order includes many states born from the remnants of empires. The older imperial notions and traditions highlight much more flexible understanding of state boundaries. Empires are characterized by flexible and fluid outer perimeters. Often, the boundary is better understood as a borderland or frontier. These tributary systems and territories are under the influence of the central government, but not necessarily directly.

Third, the nomadic paradigm further highlights the fluid nature of territoriality. Territory becomes a function of the flows that take place across it. The flow enablers and flow drivers, such as railways, harbors, airports, cyber-nodes, or financial centers, define the territorial extension of the flows. These territories belong to the hub-and-spoke structure of the liberal economic order, in which connectedness is a key characteristic, without which the territoriality of the connected political communities is hard to understand.

Finland looks different from these three advantage points. It has historically been a border land of the Swedish and Russian empires. During the Cold War, the Finnish position was understood through its traditional geographic location. Though an oft-repeated truism, in the words of Finnish president Juho Kusti Paasikivi, "The recognition of facts is the beginning of wisdom." This referred to Finland's geographical position next to a great power, and the presumed implications of this proximity for Finnish foreign policy. After the collapse of the Soviet empire and after Finland acquired EU membership, it emphasized integration and interdependency, especially through opening up of its borders to economic flows of people, goods, and capital. Membership of the eurozone further accentuated this integration. The wider structural forces brought about by the globalizing economy and the information technology revolution started to define

Finnish territory through these global flows of data, raw materials, and goods. The annexation of Crimea signaled the re-emergence of older imperial Russian ideas concerning its special role, influence, and status in the region.

This multiplicity of territorial understandings leads to a need to re-evaluate the concept of Finnish security. The location of Finland is not as fixed on the map as previously thought, with the result that the recognition of "facts" is not as unambiguous either. Finnish security and resilience are diffused and scattered. The political geography is fundamentally transferred from the traditional map into the level of systemic interactions. In a sense, the nomadic understanding of the map is gaining increasing accuracy. At the same time, traditional geopolitics still lures. However, this interpretation can lead to state-centric overstretch, since no single actor—in Helsinki or even in Kremlin—can manage the complexities, scale, and force of the nomadic world of flows.

It is possible to argue that the three types of territoriality have their distinct scenarios of security. The classical state-based paradigm envisions a sovereign territory that is able to absorb possible crises and shocks by being relatively self-reliant in terms of resources—as, for example, in terms of energy. Here, sovereignty is often perceived as avoiding too deep an interdependency so as to stop it from turning into asymmetric interdependency or outright dependency. The imperial model highlights the need to comprise an economically viable entity that has access to all strategic resources either directly or indirectly. The nomadic scenario turns security from national need into a more global systemic characteristic. Dependencies are taken for granted, and the main attention turns to securing access to the global supply chain and to making the flows as steady and resilient as possible. One way of framing the difference between the intertwined paradigms is the idea of strategic resources. For a state-centric model, strategic resource is defined as a spectrum of resources needed to be self-reliant. For an empire, strategic resource has been the influence over choke-points and areas that allow for the high ground of control over a system of tributaries. In the nomadic model, strategic resource is defined by the ability to tap into the networked resources—the secured access points to flows.

Finnish security can be seen as a hybrid overview scenario in which all three models provide inputs. To a degree, Finland's self-perception is still that of an island among an archipelago of similar sovereign states. Finnish defense planning is for the whole territory of Finland. There is a need to secure this sovereign entity against different types of supply disruptions by having critical supplies at hand for necessary lengths of time. At the same time, Finland is a part of a larger entity, the EU, whose overall viability is seen as important for national security. Also, the EU is important in managing economic dependencies. Both of these spheres of security act as the backdrop for the more nomadic framing of Finnish security. Finnish and European security of supplies are often seen as being increasingly based on more global dynamic interdependencies. For example, the critical infrastructure connecting Finland and Europe to global energy flows needs to be secured on a sustained basis.

The more imperial model is present in the Finnish discussion concerning its location on the border with Russia. This debate is old and still very controversial. It manifests itself also in arguments that see Russian trade as a cornerstone of the Finnish economy. On the other hand, the vast Russian markets and its rich natural resources have created concerns about security of supply, especially in the fields of natural gas and oil. However, the biggest asymmetry is mental: it has to do with viewing Russia as a possible source of future prosperity. Economic growth in Russia was high for several years. At the same time, the Finnish economic outlook has not been very rosy of late. This leads to the popular idea, for example, that the Arctic—which is closely connected with Russia—is the new Nokia for Finland. This hope of economic benefits from close connections with Russia holds much currency in Helsinki. This scenario also provides Russia much leverage in Helsinki. It fits well into Russia's more imperial strategies.

The use of economic leverage for political gain is part of the Russian tool-kit. It may be combined with forms of positive—for example, charm campaigns, high-level visits, and promise of lucrative deals—and negative reinforcement—for example, implicit threats and disinformation campaigns. Russia uses the whole spectrum of soft and hard power tools from economic and cultural to military.[9] Resisting them would

---

[9]A. Simonyi and J. Trunkos (2014), "How Putin Stole our Smart Power," June 18, 2014. The World Post. http://www.huffingtonpost.com/andras-simonyi/how-putin-stole-our-smart_b_5504985.html.

require stronger European and Western unity. To a large degree, Vladimir Putin's spectrum of power tools is specifically aimed to cause disarray and disunity among the West. The key to Western strength has been the alliance itself. This is something that Russia lacks.

Beyond Finlandization

The security policy of Finland—a smaller state in the vicinity of imperial soft and hard ambitions as well as intensifying global flows—begs the question of its actual effective agency. It seems that such an actor undergoes a re-contextualization when the nomadic flow paradigm and security-as-resilience become more widely adapted. The agency of Finland is transformed into one of strategic ability to adapt to structural changes and being able to provide for collective forward-looking resilience. Ideally, Finland would develop capabilities which are unique and which other actors would seek in asymmetric interdependence. This approach would guarantee that other actors develop relations of trust and loyalty with Finland and that they would have a stake in Finnish security.

The beginning of such strategic contributions can be seen in different measures of adaptation to the changing world. Several studies and measures have lately placed Finland close to the very top in global development. These results indicate that Finland has quite a number of elements of power that matter in the contemporary world. Learning to use these strategic elements in the right combination to build different forms of resilience—for example, immunity to the Russian power tool-kit—could offer the key to positive Finnish contribution to the Western community.

Many in Finland draw lessons learned from the years of "successful" "Finlandization". This thinking represents contemporary Finnish exceptionalism. However, this anachronistic lesson learned looks increasingly like just one policy option among many. The solution for neighboring Estonia has been to gain leverage by joining a bigger alliance that has some agency in the geopolitical map. Estonian security policy has focused on being a model participant and active member of NATO in the belief that the Alliance would compensate for its relative lack of power to influence its surroundings. The belief is that

NATO provides the anchor that allows Estonia to compete more securely in the geo-economic sense. In essence, the Estonian solution accords with the traditional small state balancing model. It has found some leverage in NATO to deal more securely with its Russian-speaking minority and with neighboring Russia. At the same time, Estonia is innovating with new territories such as cyberspace. Its success in detaching itself from the post-Soviet trajectories of some countries is based on adapting to the newer realities of global flows and on building trust in networks where vital Estonian security and resilience capabilities reside.

Finland's national security strategy, on the other hand, has been based on the evaluation that Russia will integrate with the Western paradigm and that the likelihood of military conflict is so small that any choice between bandwagoning and balancing is a needless starting point. It seems that the solution thus far has been the general transformation away from the geopolitical map into the map of global economic and technological interdependence. Before Ukraine, this rather successful future-oriented resilience-building focused on the world-class and competitive modalities of an agile and adaptive small state. Security has been seen as a broader theme. Emphasis has been on human and societal security. This has led to the development of a functioning and highly-regarded educational system and innovation economy. The strategic idea has been to create an open user-defined environment that would be as connected as possible to the main global arteries of prosperity. Now in the aftermath of Ukraine, the focus is on how to secure this open state architecture from expansionist Russian influences. By remaining fully open to Russia's influence, Finland runs the risk of being associated with Russian power games and undermining its own strategic flexibility in integrating with the global system, which is based on the liberal values of open markets and free and transparent economies.

The open Finnish state platform developed largely as a way out of the basic security dilemma. If Finland became a world-class state in adapting to growing interdependencies, it could move itself away from its geopolitical bind with Russia. Integration into the global markets and technological framework could also allow Finland to develop more symmetrical dependencies and be less dependent on asymmetric vulnerabilities, such as Russia's energy sector. This escape attempt from the geopolitical bind took place in the context where much of the strategic planning in Finland was based on the belief that Russia would have to adapt to a general integrationist model. The paradigm was that either Russia would remain weak or it would adapt to the same equalizing rules to which Finland was adapting. The scenarios opening after Ukraine were not foreseen and there was no preparedness to plan for them. The strategy of Estonia was, in hindsight, based on a more realistic assessment of the situation.

Putin's victory speech after the annexation of Crimea gave an ideological direction for future Russian action. It was not merely rhetoric. The speech made it clear that Russia would use its military means to destabilize states in the past realms of the Soviet and Russian empires if they acted against its economic and political interests. The instinctive reaction in Finland has been a return to the key myth of its historical lessons learned. This return to the neutral past has been emphasized by three main factions. One bloc sees Finland as an exceptional state in the sense of sensitively understanding Russia's great power interests and knowing how to negotiate the asymmetries of the relationship. Value is placed on the acknowledgement of Russian interests and on Finland's presumed virtuosity of coping with its neighbor. The second line of thinking highlights Finland's exceptional qualities in the area of independent and self-reliant national defense. It is seen that Finland is an island that has to be able to defend itself against Russia on its own, and its capabilities should not be directed to a more collective defense of states other than itself. The third argument highlights the economic necessity of Russian trade for Finland. Some in Finland see new Nokias in the Russian Arctic, or in Russia itself, that are essential for the economic prosperity needed to maintain the special Finnish welfare system. There is an expectation of lucrative deals if Finland does nothing to harm Russian interests. The main arguments against balancing with and against NATO are usually a combination of these three schools of thought and of the background interest groups.

It can be argued that the main fuel for resisting the Estonian model of balancing interests is fear. This fear of Russia's possible reactions limits discussion on NATO because mere mention of it raises the specter of an open conflict with Russia. The anti-NATO circles often co-opt this fear in a double rhetoric: on the one hand, Russia does not present a danger to Finland and, on the other hand, if Finland takes a wrong step—for example, considers NATO membership—Russia will react in an adverse way. For many in Finland, there is a desire to make the existing Finnish comfort zone as plush as possible by attributing discomfort to all the things that could happen if Finland decides to move out of its traditional foreign policy zone of comfort. The elephant in the room is the fear of Russian reactions in the face of Finland joining NATO. This dominates discussions, and it does not have to be explained. Only references are needed. Many Finns still feel the pain of the traumatic past and instinctively block any policy line that can be seen as leading to confronting what is feared.

Conclusions

The overall mapping of Finnish and Nordic–Baltic security has to locate the relevant actors in the wider map of the dynamic international order. The changing nature of the region in interdependent regional and global flows has changed the nature of soft and hard power as well as the resulting spectrum of possible insecurities. The debates concerning the shape of the international order, the future role of the United States in it, and the nature of rising illiberal states have been catalyzed by the Russian position on Ukraine. Some view China's and Russia's recent actions as a formidable challenge to the liberal world order and American leadership. They foresee an era of returning geopolitics and a loosening of the web of Western-dominated interdependence. However, interdependence may not yet be done with, though, in recent years, it has become increasingly apparent that it also carries with it risks and challenges, which need to be managed so as not to put the liberal world order in jeopardy. The actions of rising illiberal states may be explained by these risks and challenges, as interdependence increasingly takes the form of a competition, not foremost in geopolitical but rather in geo-economic terms—for markets, resources and technology.

The U.S. government has also shifted accordingly. It has come to focus on the management of the key institutions that govern this inter-state competition in the economic and technological spheres. This shift—seen by some as weakness or withdrawal—is, on the one hand, logical, but, on the other hand, begs the question concerning the future shape of power and order. In relation to this, and as regional powers seem to be reasserting their spheres of influence using geo-economic vulnerabilities to their strategic benefit, the relationship between the new modalities of world order and regional security is also undergoing transformations. The regional security contexts—especially those surrounding the illiberal state-capitalist actors—offer more detailed evidence for the present health and future direction of the liberal world order. This chapter focused on how illiberal Russia is using its geopolitical and geo-economic capabilities for its strategic benefit and the consequences of its actions in the regional security context.

The first conclusion is that the balancing possibilities for Finland depend on the staying power of the Western-led liberal world order. This basic logic is often bypassed in the Finnish debates that tend to focus on trying to find continuation in the Finnish foreign and security policies. Many in Finland try to rediscover the "deeper" meaning of the "Finlandization" policies of the Cold War years. For others, Finland is neutral, not because of ideological non-partisanship, but because of the historical fact that Finland has to survive on its own and because it has always been left alone. This Winter War-related national sentiment runs deep. At the same time, the euro crisis has led to a sentiment that too much interdependence is bad for the future of Finland. There is nostalgia for the times when Finland was able to survive and secure itself on its own. Such sentiments and nostalgia could translate badly into productive strategic actions in this changed new world where Russia's position, power, and tool-kit are different from those of the erstwhile Soviet situation.

Second, the region is increasingly defined by the emerging and strengthening force of global flows. This entails a strategic shift of balance away from traditional geopolitics focused on relatively self-reliant territorial sovereign states towards taking into account more dynamic geopolitical interdependencies. The approach recommended here entails a growing emphasis on the importance of various flows (for example, of goods, finance, people, information) and their stability, reliability, and security (or lack thereof)—which rely on and use the high seas, airspace, space and cyberspace. All actors are reliant on global flows to a growing degree. These flows have changed the meaning of territory and favor those places and the actors therein who have secured connections to the main arteries of the global world. The localities become re-contextualized as parts of the emerging global hub-and-spoke structure, rather than in their traditional national or regional context.

Third, Finland should continue along its main strategic path of developing an open, connected, yet secure, society and state platform. The success in this "statecraft" provides best practices and examples for others in the region. Finland should more actively look into different combinations of hard and soft power tools that are relevant to the stability of the global flows on which its prosperity depends and to immunizing itself and others from the uses of illiberal power by Russia.

Fourth, Finland should gain better situational awareness of the sources of its own strengths and contribute these tools for the use of other actors. Societal resilience in Finland is based on a well-educated society which often scores very highly on the indices of freedom from corruption, equality, stability, competitiveness and press freedom, to name a few of the key attributes. Furthermore, it has been able to manage with Russia in both peaceful and, now, more turbulent times. Its society is relatively immune to Russian non-linear practices. Because of low corruption levels, some of the long tentacles of the Russian state capitalist strategies have not yet taken strong hold in Finland. Also, Finland has taken the initiative to develop its society towards an open state platform that is very open to the access points of global flows. These secure access points can be used to develop partnerships that strengthen and secure the flows and make them as resilient as possible. The partnership has to pool and share resources between national—for example, Finland, Sweden, and Estonia—and private actors—for example, companies maintaining energy and cyber flows.

Fifth, on a more practical level, Finland should focus on developing NATO's security of supply mechanisms through the partnership program and further participating in and strengthening key institutions such as the Energy Security Center of Excellence. Finland should also use its considerable private and public experience in cyber security to actively participate in NATO's Cooperative Cyber Defense Center of Excellence. It should develop its own national cyber center in close collaboration with the Tallinn center. Furthermore, Finland should be active in the development of new partnerships in new areas that cut across different flow domains, as, for example, how the cyber domain is connected with shipping activity with possible security implications in the Baltic and Arctic Sea regions. These inter-domain interactions remain relatively uncharted and the new Russian doctrine, taking advantage of asymmetries and a non-linear relationship, should be countered by situational awareness and contingency planning in these hitherto unmapped realms.

Chapter 14

U.S.-Nordic Defense Industry Cooperation: Adding Value to the Transatlantic Partnership

Michael Mohr and Erik Brattberg

The evolving security situation in Europe has underlined the importance of transatlantic defense cooperation. The ongoing ambitious initiative to boost transatlantic trade links—the Transatlantic Trade and Investment Partnership (TTIP)—has so far excluded "defense" from the negotiation mandate. Defense industrial relations are, however, a core component of the transatlantic partnership. The time has therefore come to use the momentum for enhanced trade to include deepened defense industry cooperation in the transatlantic agenda. Here, the Nordic region, with its open and liberal defense industry, can play a crucial role. For the United States, the Nordic case is worthy of special attention. U.S.-Nordic defense cooperation has the potential to strengthen Nordic-Baltic defense capabilities, regional energy security and maritime security in the Arctic as well as U.S.-European security in general. Forging a stronger U.S.-Nordic defense industrial partnership could also be seen as a vehicle for promoting transatlantic defense integration.

Nordic Defense Industry Cooperation: Slowly Moving Forward

Though regional military cooperation dates back decades, the main vehicle for Nordic cooperation on defense issues today is the Nordic Defense Industry Cooperation (NORDEFCO). Following the seminal 2009 Stoltenberg report, Nordic defense ministers agreed to set up a new comprehensive structure to replace the previously regional collaborative arrangements. At its essence, NORDEFCO aims to strengthen Nordic defense capabilities by promoting synergies and effective common defense solutions between Denmark, Finland, Norway and Sweden.[1]

---

[1]NORDEFCO website: http://www.NORDEFCO.org/facts-abou/aims-and-o/.

The rationale for regional collaboration is simple: there is a growing regional recognition that Nordic cooperation is essential for retaining existing military capabilities and developing new ones in the region. By seeking to harmonize defense capabilities and, thus, reducing costs, NORDEFCO provides a tool for the Nordic states to pool resources together and increase efficiencies. The fact that the Nordic countries share many similarities in terms of size, geography, language and culture and have far-reaching historical cooperation makes this collaboration easier.

Due to the small-sized defense forces, maintaining sufficient military development and procurement levels is difficult. Nordic defense can be strengthened by increasing cooperation in common education and training, co-location of military units and common equipment for force contribution. The strategic imperative of Nordic defense cooperation has been heightened, not least following the ongoing crisis in Ukraine, but also because of the long-standing trend towards shrinking defense budgets in Europe.

Though still in its infancy, NORDEFCO has already generated some notable results.[2] NORDEFCO can, therefore, be viewed as a positive example of regional defense collaboration in Europe.[3] Both NATO and the European Union are currently promoting the concept of "pooling and sharing" of defense capabilities. NORDEFCO illustrates that practical military cooperation between NATO and partnership countries is possible.

But, despite the potential NORDEFCO boasts, progress has been lacking in some areas, particularly in defense industrial cooperation. Divergent Nordic industrial policies and national regulation procedures hamper regional cooperation in defense industrial issues. To help remedy some of these shortcomings, defense industrial associations in Denmark, Finland, Norway and Sweden signed a Memorandum of Understanding (MOU) in November 2013, strengthening regional collaboration in defense industry matters.

----

[2] See NORDEFCO Annual Report 2013. Available online at: http://www.NORDEFCO.org/files/NORDEFCO%20Annual%20Report%202013.pdf

[3] Ann-Sofie Dahl, "NORDEFCO and NATO: Smart Defense in the North?" *Research Paper No. 101*, NATO Defense College, Rome, May 2014.

As a part of this agreement, it was decided to establish a Joint Nordic Defense Industry Cooperation Group (JNDICG) in order to strengthen mutual cooperation between the Nordic industries, provide interface with Nordic government bodies involved in Nordic defense cooperation and to enhance regional and international competitiveness. This takes place in close collaboration with the NORDEFCO Policy Steering Committee (PSC). So far, efforts have been focused on enhancing the industry's role and on strengthening its dialogue with political leadership. These efforts have resulted in the inclusion of Nordic defense industry associations in NORDEFCO PSC meetings.

NORDEFCO's industrial dimension must be strengthened further by enhancing cooperation with the Nordic defense industry to ensure joint Nordic military capability procurement programs involving two or more regional states. A more coherent Nordic defense industrial cluster would also provide the region with a stronger voice within the European defense industrial base. Given the open and liberal nature of the Nordic defense industry, this could help reduce the European defense industry's heavy protectionist tendencies.

Deepening U.S.-Nordic Defense Industrial Ties

The United States has become increasingly supportive of Nordic defense cooperation.[4] For Washington, the Nordic region represents an open defense market with market-oriented industries and an internationally competitive industry with unique technological niches in certain areas. As NATO currently tries to promote "pooling and sharing" of European defense resources under the auspices of the Smart Defense, Nordic countries demonstrate how to do this in practice. The Nordic region is unique because it includes both NATO and non-NATO countries.

For the above reasons, Washington should engage Nordic countries more closely on defense industrial issues. This includes strengthening both bilateral and multilateral cooperation. Such closer U.S.-Nordic defense industry cooperation would benefit the United States

---

[4]Toumas Forsberg, "The Rise of Nordic Defense Cooperation: A Return to Regionalism?" *International Affairs*, vol. 89:5, pp. 1161-1181.

and Nordic countries alike and could be used as a vehicle for further strengthening of the transatlantic defense ties more broadly. Of course, greater U.S. participation in the Nordics should also come with greater Nordic participation on the U.S. defense market.

On the multilateral level, efforts should focus on including the United States in NORDEFCO collaboration initiatives. Given the slow progress made under NORDEFCO when it comes to defense industrial issues, American engagement in NORDEFCO's multilateral capability development efforts should be welcomed, as it would infuse some well-needed energy into the regional dynamics. U.S.-NORDE-FCO initiatives would fit well within NATO's Smart Defense initiatives and inject it with a well-needed dose of "transatlanticism."[5] Strengthening U.S.-Nordic cooperation would therefore add value to the transatlantic link.

Practical examples could include U.S. participation in procurement of weapons platforms and enablers and military research and development. Cyber security is one obvious area where more U.S.-Nordic cooperation could bring added value. Nordic countries are at the forefront of many cyber issues and have plenty to offer there as well. A joint U.S.-Nordic cyber project could also serve as a forerunner for future common projects in other areas. Another industry sector with high potential for U.S.-Nordic collaboration is maritime security, an area that also relates directly to the High North.

Cooperation with the United States is also important on a bilateral level. For instance, Sweden has strong defense industrial ties with the United States. Sweden's high technical competence makes it an attractive partner for U.S. industry. Today Sweden is a major exporter of defense equipment to the U.S. armed forces. Notably, Saab has actively sought to increase its footprint on the U.S. defense market over the past few years—so far with some success. At the same time, the United States is one of the largest foreign suppliers of defense equipment to Sweden. Cooperating bilaterally with the United States offers advantages and serves as an important complement in multilateral U.S.-Nordic cooperation.

---

[5]Ian Brzezinski, chapter in Kurt Volker and Ieva Kupche, eds., *Nordic-Baltic-American Cooperation*, Center for Transatlantic Relations, Washington DC, May 2012.

"Transatlanticism:" the Missing Ingredient in European Defense

The outlook for the European defense industry is uncertain. Since the end of the Cold War, European defense spending (as a percentage of gross domestic product) has fallen significantly. This is the case despite the presence of economic growth and active European contributions to ongoing operations in places like Afghanistan.[6] As a result, the United States now accounts for about three-fourths of overall NATO defense spending, which is increasingly unsustainable. But European states not only spend too little on defense, they also spend it too inefficiently. This is primarily due to a lack of integration of the European defense market, which remains heavily protectionist and subject to well-guarded national self-interests.

To address these issues, NATO has launched the Smart Defense initiative to pool and share military capabilities in Europe. The European Union (EU) has also promoted a similar concept though it's European Defense Agency (EDA). However, the results have so far been insufficient. The European defense market remains highly fragmented on the demand side. The reason defense material is so costly is because there is simply not enough free trade and competition.

What is also missing is a strong transatlantic dimension: even though European and American defense contractors are major competitors, it makes sense for them to become more integrated. Opening up the U.S. and EU defense markets to competition from suppliers on both sides of the Atlantic would promote further competition. This would be a win-win for the European Union and the United States alike.

In times of declining budgets, it makes sense for governments on both sides of the Atlantic, who today spend too much on defense, to further integrate their markets. Opening up the transatlantic defense market would secure its position vis-à-vis the rest of the world. Most European defense industries already use non-European components in their products and systems. For example, the American-made content in the Swedish-produced Jas 39 Gripen fighter jet is approximately 40%.

---

[6]EDA Data. Available online at: http://www.eda.europa.eu/info-hub

But while European and American defense companies are already quite integrated at the product level, there is much more that can be done. For European defense industry, the U.S. market is an opportunity for further growth and for continued collaboration and technological development as well as continued exports and imports. The United States currently spends about 500 billion dollars on defense annually, which is more than double what EU countries spend combined.[7] But for this to take place, remaining trade barriers must be discarded. A major opportunity to promote transatlantic defense integration is the current negotiations over the Transatlantic Trade and Investment Partnership (TTIP).

TTIP—A Missed Opportunity to Strengthen Transatlantic Defense

TTIP was launched in June 2013 by the European Union and the United States to further strengthen the world's largest trade and investment relationship. TTIP's primary objectives are to eliminate tariffs and improve market access, enhance regulatory convergence and adopt rules that will set the global standard. According to official EU estimates, TTIP would bring an additional 120 billion euro to European economies annually.

It is strategically imperative to strengthen economic relations between the United States and the European Union through completing TTIP, especially after the crisis in Crimea and Russian aggression towards Ukraine. Both sides realize that only by scaling up economic cooperation will the transatlantic political and security dimension be reinforced, so that they can face external challenges such as Putin's increased hostility towards the countries and regions bordering Russia and the West. TTIP can be instrumental in that domain. If the recent crisis in Ukraine has taught us one clear message, it is this: policy unity between the United States and the European Union is absolutely essential. TTIP has generated considerable debate and discussion around the geopolitical and geostrategic dimensions of

---

[7] *EU-US Defense Data 2011*, European Defense Agency, September 2013. Available online at: http://www.eda.europa.eu/docs/default-source/news/eu-us-defence-data-2011.pdf

increased transatlantic economic cooperation. Several U.S. officials have hailed TTIP as an "economic NATO."[8]

Excluded from the TTIP, however, is the defense sector. The reason for this is that "defense procurement" is viewed as a subject that is too sensitive and unique to national and special interests. Many large European defense industries believe that including "defense" in the TTIP negotiations would force them to open up their domestic markets to American defense contractors without ensuring the same level of access for European suppliers to the U.S. market. A lobby campaign led by French and German defense industries and based on European protectionism, forced the European Commission to remove "defense" from its negotiation mandate.

However, the exclusion of "defense" from the TTIP agenda does not mean that the sector will remain unaffected by a potential trade agreement. On the contrary, a number of defense and security industry products will be impacted. In today's defense market, dual-use products increasingly blur the lines between the defense and civilian sectors.[9] A large number of defense products involve essential civilian components and technology. Moreover, even if TTIP succeeds in removing tariffs on these products, other non-tariff barriers would still remain in place. For example, the "Buy American Act" and the International Traffic in Arms Regulations (ITAR) restricts many foreign companies' access to the U.S. defense market. However, the Obama administration's Export Control Reform initiative is shifting many defense items formerly controlled under the ITAR to the export control jurisdiction of the Commerce Department. While such items will still require a commerce export license, under the Commerce Department regulations, many (if not most) of those items may benefit from a license exemption called the Strategic Trade Authorization (STA). Almost all European Union members qualify for the STA license exemption, although there are some qualifications.

---

[8]David Ignatius, "A Free-Trade Agreement With Europe?" *The Washington Post*, December 5, 2012.

[9]Daniel Fiott, "No TTIP-ing point for European defense?" European Union Institute for Security Studies, March 2014.

Using the TTIP Momentum to Discuss Transatlantic Defense Integration

Given the ambitious time-frame set for the TTIP negotiations, the already mounting number of challenges facing negotiators and the resistance from several EU member states, it seems that "the train has already left the station" when it comes to re-introducing "defense" into the negotiation mandate. However, there is rationale for using the momentum described above to put the issues of deepened defense cooperation on the general agenda. The defense industry can use this as an opportunity to spearhead an industry-based initiative.

The conversation about transatlantic defense integration must continue, so that when TTIP is finalized, progress will have already been made. The goal should be to set up an industry-led parallel track that would produce a "shadow TTIP" agreement for the defense sector. The United States should, therefore, work to identify potential front-runners in Europe—countries that are open to transatlantic defense integration and that already have a strong bilateral relation with the United States. Nordic countries are perfect partners in this aspect.

Conclusion

Lacking a large domestic market, Nordic defense industries are almost by definition more liberal and open than other European industries, which tend to be much more protectionist-oriented. For Nordic countries, the United States is a very important partner and export market. Stronger U.S.-Nordic cooperation would infuse new dynamics into the established multilateral regional cooperation framework, NORDEFCO. For the United States, a closer cooperation with the Nordic region also has advantages; Nordic defense industries have unique technological niches in certain areas that could be of interest to U.S. industries.

Ultimately, the goal should be greater transatlantic defense industry integration. TTIP is a test and a vehicle to discuss bigger transatlantic defense market issues. The United States, together with the Nordic countries, must recognize this and take concrete steps to strengthen U.S.-Nordic cooperation, as this would serve as a precursor to greater transatlantic cooperation.

Chapter 15

Nordic-Baltic Defense Trade: An American View

Greg Suchan

It is too late to deter Russia's aggression against Ukraine, although the Ukrainians themselves may yet salvage most of their country's territory. We should be thinking about what the West can do to deter future aggressions, particularly using Russian ethnic minorities in other countries as a fifth column to provide a rationale for Russian pressure and intervention.

Deterrence depends upon threatening costs that outweigh the benefits of aggression. The sanctions the West has implemented so far regarding Ukraine are clearly inadequate to the task. But significantly enhancing U.S. defense industry cooperation with the European democracies is something Moscow would certainly want to avoid if at all possible, for military, political, and economic reasons. It also has the benefit of being a mutually beneficial initiative in its own right.

Of course, greater U.S. defense industry cooperation with all the European democracies would be the most effective response and would impose the highest costs on Russia. However, this is not likely to be possible for a variety of reasons, including because those European countries with large defense industries (no need to mention names) have an incentive to keep the U.S. defense industry out of Europe as much as they can, in order to capture as much of the European defense market for themselves as possible. A current example is that European government officials have recently told their U.S. government counterparts that "some" European Union (EU) members are trying to use the European Commission Directive 2009/81/EC to block government-to-government arms transfers, specifically the U.S. Foreign Military Sales (FMS) program. This argument is, to put it charitably, as silly as the plot of a ballet. They could hardly fail to notice that Article 12(f) of the directive explicitly excludes from its scope "contracts awarded by a government to another government relating to: (i) the supply of military equipment or sensitive equipment."

However, the Ukrainian crisis has caused the governments of Nordic and Baltic countries to give a higher priority to their security concerns, not least because more than a million Russian-speakers still live in Estonia, Latvia and Lithuania. Increased U.S. defense industry cooperation with the Nordic and Baltic governments and their defense industries could therefore be a visible response to Russia's aggression in Ukraine, and the prospect of more such cooperation, extended in duration and scope, might make a contribution to deterring future Russian bullying.

Arms transfers have military and economic benefits but are essentially a political act. That is why since the Neutrality Act of 1935 instituted America's first peacetime export control system all U.S. arms transfers have been conducted under the primary authority of the Secretary of State. Increased U.S. defense cooperation with the Nordic and Baltic states, therefore, would constitute a significant political signal to Russia that its actions in Ukraine have real political (and military) consequences.

What form could increased U.S. defense trade cooperation with the Nordic and Baltic region take? As shown in the table at the end of this article, U.S. defense industry cooperation with Denmark, Estonia, Finland, Latvia, Lithuania, Norway and Sweden is already significant, particularly with the Nordic countries. Norway and Denmark are partners in the F-35 program (formerly the Joint Strike Fighter). Estonia, Latvia and Lithuania receive modest amounts of security assistance funding from the United States. (Apart from Israel, Egypt and one or two other countries that may vary from year to year, no country receives more than few million dollars in U.S. security assistance, which does not go very far when shopping for military equipment.) The United States ratified in 2010 defense cooperation treaties with the United Kingdom (UK) and Australia, but this does not seem an appropriate model for countries in the Nordic and Baltic region (neutral Sweden and Finland might balk at such treaties), even if such agreements prove effective (and the jury is still out on the UK and Australia treaties).

To be effective, an initiative for enhanced U.S. defense trade cooperation should come from the Nordic and Baltic governments themselves. Nordic Defense Cooperation (NORDEFCO) may be one focal point for developing such an initiative, although NORDEFCO does not include Estonia, Latvia and Lithuania, which are the countries most at risk in the post-Ukraine environment. (Michael Mohr's article in this compendium discusses NORDEFCO and its role in defense industrial cooperation at length, so there is no need to repeat that here. It is also noteworthy that Henrik Breitenbauch's article in this book proposes that Estonia, Latvia and Lithuania become members of NORDEFCO.) An effective initiative should involve all seven countries (or as many of them as possible), with the Nordic countries probably providing financial support for the participation of Estonia, Latvia and Lithuania. The focus of the initiative should be on something that addresses the security needs of all seven countries, and something that Moscow will regret seeing them undertake.

One possible area for consideration might be unmanned maritime systems (UMS). Unmanned systems are (within reason) the current fashion in military technology development, and a recent study on unmanned military systems by the Center for Strategic and International Studies[1] (CSIS) found that "The most significant advances or changes to existing force structure involving substitution of unmanned systems in the near term will likely come on the ground, at sea, and undersea." The Baltic Sea is, moreover, the defining geographic feature of the region. UMS are envisioned for such missions as mine clearing (a mission that fits the unmanned systems paradigm of "dull, dirty and dangerous"), as well as anti-submarine warfare. Such UMS are on the drawing board in the United States,[2] but as the CSIS study points out, "as with all the other services, there is no money in the Navy's current future years defense program (FYDP) to produce and field such a next-generation system."

An initiative from the Nordic-Baltic governments, therefore, for joint development of an unmanned maritime system that meets the security needs of the region may find a receptive audience in the United States. Such an initiative might take into account the particular features of the Baltic Sea, such as its relatively shallow depth (aver-

---

[1]Sustaining the U.S. Lead in Unmanned Systems: Military and Homeland Considerations Through 2025, February, 2014.

[2]See US Naval Sea Systems Command (NAVSEA) presentation to the Sea-Air-Space Symposium, April 9, 2014 http://www.navsea.navy.mil/Media/SAS2014/UUVs.pdf.

age: 180.5 feet) and its highly variable salinity levels. The multinational Joint Strike Fighter program has had its problems, but no one seriously argues that those problems result from the international nature of the program. And unlike the Unmanned Aircraft Systems (UAS), international cooperation on UMS would not run up against the multilateral Missile Technology Control Regime, which has raised significant obstacles to transfers of UAS, particularly those with a range in excess of 190 miles and a payload of 1100 pounds.

What would be the advantages to the Nordic-Baltic governments? A joint initiative at this time could benefit from a more cooperative technology transfer environment on the part of the U.S. Department of Defense (DOD), which usually has the final say on technology release to foreign countries. Moreover, a pattern of cooperation with the United States on a focused project like joint development of UMS might lead to increased willingness on the part of the U.S. technology release community to work with the Nordic and Baltic governments on other development projects, so that starting with one joint development project now could set a pattern for additional cooperative ventures in the future. More importantly, a joint development project could produce new and significant military capabilities that could contribute to regional defense.

What would be the advantages for the United States? As the CSIS study on unmanned systems makes painfully clear, the major restraint on the United States moving ahead in development of promising technologies is the lack of available funding. Despite an international security environment that seems to become more threatening with each day's headlines, DOD budget austerity is likely to be with us for the foreseeable future (alas). Having other friendly governments contribute financially and technologically to a joint development program could make it possible for DOD to move forward with a promising program, such as UMS, that might not otherwise make the budget cut. Moreover, Denmark, Finland, Norway, and Sweden have a good record of protecting U.S. defense technology (which is more than can be said of some U.S. allies one could name) and would be partners with which the U.S. technology transfer community would be relatively comfortable. Also, if some governments in the EU are working to freeze out U.S. defense exports to Europe, to the extent they can, a pattern of increased U.S. defense cooperation with the six Nordic-

U.S. Arms Transfers to Nordic and Baltic Countries

(Thousands of U.S. dollars)

	2008	2009	2010	2011	2012
Denmark					
FMS	64,314	28,780	46,586	67,735	26,911
DCS (defense articles)	136,169	98,396	68,526	66,458	182,383
DCS (defense services)	159,808	202,861	254,139	194,821	353,771
TOTAL	359,291	330,037	369,014	329,014	563,065
Estonia					
FMS	5,531	9,108	2,055	3,657	2,309
DCS (defense articles)	6,258	4,955	749	2,694	5,035
DCS (defense services)	0	4,635	0	5,500	871
TOTAL	11,789	18,698	2,804	11,851	8,215
Finland					
FMS	33,448	455,304	53,439	68,750	201,297
DCS (defense articles)	57,066	74,923	188,996	234,900	172,119
DCS (defense services)	644,580	139,852	64,975	186,658	159,052
TOTAL	735,094	670,079	307,410	490,308	532,468
Latvia					
FMS	2,736	4,402	4,982	1,352	3,601
DCS (defense articles)	7,190	4,418	4,088	35,055	9,717
DCS (defense services)	0	3,000	0	0	45,000
TOTAL	9,926	11,820	9,070	36,407	58,318
Lithuania					
FMS	2,614	7,900	1,113	1,226	5,273
DCS (defense articles)	2,697	0	2,221	2,667	2,193
DCS (defense services)	0	0	285	0	10,751
TOTAL	5,311	7,900	3,619	3,893	18,217
Norway					
FMS	262,709	91,388	107,128	174,003	349,753
DCS (defense articles)	195,429	336,970	152,343	213,182	237,208
DCS (defense services)	930,109	575,032	201,616	1,573,518	973,273
TOTAL	1,388,247	1,003,390	461,087	1,960,703	1,560,234
Sweden					
FMS	13,478	11,931	9,451	524,094	23,862
DCS (defense articles)	179,542	202,590	115,160	282,069	204,679
DCS (defense services)	379,578	542,606	419,492	413,976	452,278
TOTAL	572,598	757,127	544,103	1,220,139	680,819

Baltic countries that are EU members (all but Norway) can help the United States cultivate defense industrial allies within EU councils on such issues.

Most important for the United States and the Nordic and Baltic governments, initiating a joint defense technology development program with friendly governments in a region that is under renewed threat from Russia would send a significant and unwelcome message to Moscow that its aggression in Ukraine comes at a price that goes beyond preventing some Russian officials from using their Master Cards during their summer vacations at Disney World.

Chapter 16

High North–Increasing Tension?
A Nordic Perspective

Leiv Lunde

All Nordic countries are key Arctic stakeholders. Collectively they constitute more than half of the members of the Arctic Council and also make their voices heard clearly in broader multilateral bodies with Arctic relevance such as the International Maritime Organization (IMO) and the United Nations Convention on the Law of the Sea (UNCLOS). As of August 2014, they all face a new and serious Arctic challenge, brought upon by Russia's stand-off with Europe and the United States over Ukraine. While not an immediate victim of soured Western relations with Russia, the Arctic is inevitably drawn into a deepening crisis as Western sanctions bite into Russia's Arctic oil sector and many Nordic Arctic communities suffer from Russian's retaliatory sanctions against European food exports. Only the future can tell, but suddenly the fundamental credo of Nordic-Arctic narratives: *high north low tension*—has come into question. Will the Arctic again, after 25 years of peace and growing East-West partnership, see strategic military mobilization and confrontation? If so, what will such a malign Arctic geopolitical theater look like, how will Asia's Arctic entry make a new confrontation different and what options do Nordic countries have for furthering their national interest in choppy Arctic waters?

These questions are addressed in this chapter, which first sets out to briefly describe the five Nordic countries' Arctic policy profiles. Then, commonalities and differences between them are discussed in order to understand their Arctic interests and scope of action both individually and as a seemingly strong collective entity. Finally, challenges to the Nordic countries emanating from the new Russia crisis are assessed, as well as the potential new role of China and other Asian countries in future conflict prone Arctic scenarios.

The Arctic Footprints of Nordic Countries

Norway is by most definitions the most important Nordic-Arctic country, trailing only behind Russia in global Arctic significance. Mainland Norway includes considerable land, coast and ocean areas that reside north of the Arctic Circle, and Svalbard, an archipelago far north and halfway toward the North Pole, adds to the country's Arctic identity. Norway already extracts large volumes of oil and gas from Arctic waters, and Norwegian oil and oil service companies are active on Russia's Arctic continental shelf. Ice melt in the polar region opens new opportunities for the world's fourth-largest shipping nation, explaining why Norway is a leading explorer of the Northern Sea Route. Since 2005, the Arctic has been singled out as Norway's highest foreign policy priority, reflecting the region's economic importance for the country's energy and shipping sectors, as well as fishing, research and development (R&D) and tourism. Climate change is also an important part of the Norwegian Arctic narrative: the Arctic is seen as a venue for climate research as well as a catalyst for action to mitigate climate change.

Denmark is indirectly the other Nordic Arctic coastal nation, with its autonomous territory Greenland almost making up a continent between Iceland and Arctic Canada in itself. Denmark proper is located far south of the Arctic Circle, and its main non-Greenlandic Arctic interests are related to shipping, trade, climate change and management of natural resources. The country is also active in EU Arctic policymaking. Because of Greenland, however, Denmark is perceived as a major Arctic coastal nation, given the former's huge land and coastal areas as well as natural resources onshore and likely offshore. Denmark's Arctic credentials would, thus, be challenged if a gradually more independent Greenland were to succeed in finding and developing major petroleum or other mineral resources and opt for full independence. Greenland's limitations lay with its small population of only 70,000 and lack of relevant education opportunities and expertise. Nonetheless, independence remains a difficult and divisive issue, and relations between Greenland and Denmark will likely sour if the former ever votes for full independence.

Finland has started mobilizing its significant Arctic credentials in anticipation of its Arctic Council presidency in 2017 (Finland follows the United States, which takes over from Canada in 2015). The country launched a comprehensive Arctic strategy in 2013, stressing mineral development, shipping, shipbuilding, investment in Arctic knowledge and sustainable development, among other goals. Finland has no Arctic coast itself, but the Baltic Sea compensates for that. The fact that large parts of the northern Baltic Sea remain frozen in winter has spurred technological and commercial advances by Finland, which now boasts world-class icebreaker technology. Finland's identity and significance as an Arctic country are reinforced by the industrious population in northern Finland, its ambitious Arctic infrastructure plans and its long border and comprehensive economic and political interface with Russia. The latter is both a source of strength and vulnerability, as will be discussed in light of current growing geopolitical tensions between Russia and Europe.

Sweden presided over the Arctic Council from 2011 to 2013, oversaw the signing of important protocols on search and rescue cooperation and oil spill management and effectively managed the process of incorporating Asian countries as formal observers. Its economic interests in the region include mining in Arctic Sweden, and shipping, shipbuilding and icebreaker technology. Sweden also shares a periodically frozen Baltic Sea with Finland. Promoting sustainable development and curbing climate change are other important priorities in the Arctic strategy launched under Sweden's leadership in 2011. Although these are common Nordic interests, Sweden is among the countries stressing the strongest emphasis on environmental concerns in Arctic governance. Some argue that this environmental focus reflects Sweden's relatively modest economic interests in Arctic waters, and it may also explain the country's quite active involvement in EU Arctic policymaking. The latter has generally emphasized the need for strong environmental precautions in the Arctic, including by calling for an embargo on Arctic drilling after the Macondo accident in 2010 in the Gulf of Mexico. This policy has been toned down recently, however, as a result of lobbying by the United Kingdom, Norway and Denmark, and as we will see below, due to the new crisis with Russia over Ukraine, which again leads Brussels to look to the Arctic for energy security.

Iceland is a small and marginal player in international politics, including in the Arctic region. It resides just south of the Arctic Circle, which explains why it is not an Arctic coastal state in the formal sense.

Iceland has managed, however, to put itself on the front row of the global discourse on the Arctic. This is partly due to its president giving high priority to Arctic politics and governance and to branding the country as a meeting place for Arctic debate—for example, by organizing the inaugural Arctic Circle conference in Reykjavík in the fall of 2013. Iceland's economic interests in the Arctic include fishing, shipping and recently oil and gas development. Regarding the latter, one of the first petroleum bidding rounds in Icelandic waters took place in early 2014 and saw China National Offshore Oil Corporation winning one of the licenses.

What is Common and What is Different?

There are commonalities as well as differences in the Nordic countries' Arctic interests. The commonalities are most striking: history, geography, culture, trade and politics today knit them closely together so that they cooperate intimately in Nordic as well as international institutions. Sweden and Norway fought a brief war in 1814 and were on the verge of war as recently as 1905. Yet despite this history, as well as their different experiences during World War II and varying security alliances, Nordic countries enjoy strong and peaceful cooperation along virtually every thinkable dimension.

Yet, one of the surprises for international observers now turning their attention to Arctic waters is the relative lack of a formal Arctic identity in the Nordic region. Arctic politics are decided in the capitals located far south of the Arctic, and there are no Arctic budgets or regional planning units in national ministries. Even the small minority of indigenous peoples in the high north (mainly the Saami people) pay their taxes to the national governments, and the majority of the Arctic-Nordic populations view themselves primarily as national citizens rather than Arctic citizens in any significant sense.

Nevertheless, the Arctic matters a lot to Nordic countries, increasingly so in the wake of growing global attention in the region's affairs, and in light of the current Russia crisis. A potentially important difference between these states stems from the fact that Norway and Iceland are not members of the European Union (EU). Back in May 2013, for example, the admittance of the five Asian countries to the

Arctic Council hung in the balance partly due to a spat between the EU (also an applicant for a formal observer role) and Canada over seal hunting. Canada was furious at the EU for boycotting Canadian seal-skin production, which is seen as a traditional custom and important business opportunity in Canada's Arctic region. Although EU's Nordic members found this spat frustratingly difficult and were skeptical of some of EU's reasoning, they aligned with Brussels. For this and other reasons, Norway became a major broker in Kiruna, ensuring that a decision was made. Asian countries, along with Italy, were accepted as formal observers, while the EU still must wait in the wings for some hard-won concessions from intransigent Canada—the current Arctic Council president.

The differences among the Nordic countries—which again are moderate and should be seen in a holistic context—are mainly due to three factors:

- *Geography*: Some Nordic countries are Arctic coastal states, while others are not. This influences their relative willingness to allow for multilateral decision-making in the Arctic region, with Norway and Denmark/Greenland on the skeptical side.
- *Economy*: The level of economic activity and interest in the Arctic differs significantly among the Nordic countries. This is likely to shape perceptions of trade-offs between resource harvesting and environmental protection.
- *Political and security alliances*: Norway and Iceland are outside of the EU, while Finland and Sweden remain outside the North Atlantic Treaty Organization (NATO).

Arctic Implications of the Current Russia crisis

With the future of Arctic cooperation structures hanging in the bal-ance, Norway in particular, but also the other Nordic countries, are likely to feel the squeeze between aligning with U.S. and EU sanctions on the one hand, and their inclination to keep multilateral coopera-tion with Russia going as long as possible in order not to block any channel of dialogue on the other. Twenty-five years of enhanced cross-border cooperation has made previous monolithic enemy images evaporate and fostered a fertile ground for cooperation on Arctic issues, not least within the framework of the Barents Cooperation structure, a "bottom-up" Norwegian-Nordic-Russian-Arctic institution specializing in cross-boundary people-to-people dialogue. In the longer term, Russia stands to lose even more than Nordic countries from a breakdown of multilateral Arctic cooperation, though that is not likely to be among Russia's main concerns in the current political environment.

The growing tension between Russia and the West over Ukraine provides a timely starting point for closer scrutiny of Nordic countries' Arctic interests. Many would hold Norway to be particularly vulnerable to deteriorating relations with Russia. This is partly a function of Norway's strong economic interests in Russia-relevant areas of the Arctic that now find themselves threatened by sanctions, and partly because Norway's highly prioritized Arctic strategy relies heavily on continually strengthened cooperation with Russia. The high point of this cooperation was the 2011 ratification by parliaments in both countries of the maritime delimitation deal between Russia and Norway in the Barents Sea, which involved 40 years of often protracted negotiations. But bilateral relations since 1990 exhibit a broad range of cooperation initiatives across cultural, economic, scientific and political frontiers. Many even date back to Cold War years, such as Arctic fisheries cooperation between Norway and Russia which has worked conspicuously well for more than 40 years.

Many of Norway's key Arctic priorities would be challenged if Russia continues to distance itself from cooperation with Europe. Indeed, Norway, with major economic interests in the Arctic, would often find it more relevant to approach key Arctic issues together with Arctic super-power Russia rather than with other Nordic countries. This makes a lot of sense when the geopolitical sailing is smooth, but makes Norway vulnerable in more choppy Arctic waters. Economically, Norwegian oil and oil service companies are deeply engaged in the Russian Arctic and are already feeling the heat from sanctions. Salmon exports to Russia in 2013 earned about 1 billion dollars. Politically, Norway has seen Russia's active involvement in the Arctic Council as evidence of Russia's seriousness in working with Nordic and other Western countries on Arctic affairs. Indeed, Russia's active participation is often cited as a success factor for Arctic Council performance. In the absence of Russia, the largest and most important Arctic country, Arctic cooperation will be dealt a heavy blow. It is too early to judge, however, how freezing Western-Russian relations would influence the workings of the Arctic Council and other multilateral structures with Arctic relevance. Canada, the current Arctic Council chair, and the United States have already boycotted an official level Arctic Council meeting in Moscow.

The Nordic Arctic, NATO and the EU

Among the Nordics, Finland arguably faces the most fundamental challenges with deteriorating relations between Russia and the West, while the Arctic dimension of the new turbulence may be less pronounced than for Norway. About 15% of Finland's trade is with Russia, and economic sanctions will hurt Finnish interests. Meanwhile, the EU's stronger security policy draws Finland closer and closer into European and Western security spheres. The crisis is bound to further fuel discussions of whether Finland should also join NATO. Finland's 2013 Arctic strategy holds that military conflict in the Arctic is highly unlikely and emphasizes soft security dimensions such as maritime security and improved structures for search and rescue operations. It touches on Nordic security cooperation, stresses the importance of Barents Rescue where army units are engaged and recommends Nordic countries look to Baltic cooperation, such as Coastnet, for relevant lessons.

One of the interesting Finnish Arctic infrastructure ideas takes on enhanced significance if Russia drifts away from Europe. Several stakeholders are exploring opportunities to open up a north-south corridor for transport and trade of petroleum and electricity from Arctic waters to the Baltic Sea, through Finland and further to the Baltic countries, Poland and even further south. Ideally, Russia would be a key partner in such a project. Alternative routes can be also conceived through the Norwegian Arctic and southwards. It is too early to tell whether this can be one of many greatly needed approaches to enhanced energy security and energy independence from Russia. It deserves, however, a place in this broader discourse that also includes the building of Liquefied Natural Gas (LNG) terminals in the Baltic Sea and potential targeted petroleum exports from the United States to vulnerable European regions on Russia's border.

Sweden has been the most vocal critic of Russia's endeavor in Ukraine, as it had been throughout the Georgia crisis in 2008. But Sweden and Denmark's interface with Russia has less salient Arctic dimensions than those of Norway and Finland. And Swedish debates on their relationship with NATO are expected to intensify in accord with the intensity of Russia's stand-off with the West. Generally, the coming months and years are likely to see important but challenging Nordic discussions on how to handle Russia in Arctic cooperation forums. Based on Arctic interests touched on in this chapter, there is a strong expectation that Sweden will lead the arguments for confronting Russia, and threats to relegate Russia to the margins of Arctic cooperation, while Finland and Norway may more actively explore options for continued cooperation. Finland will be more bound by EU policies than Norway, but Norway is not expected to break significantly with EU policy.

Nordic NATO members Denmark, Iceland and Norway have generally favored a soft, if any, explicit NATO footprint in the Arctic, in order not to militarize or in other ways unnecessarily provoke Russia and risk undermining the overarching "High North low tension" strategic approach. Canada has also for long been skeptical and seen potential NATO Arctic involvement as infringements on Canadian sovereignty. New Norwegian NATO head Jens Stoltenberg may ironically come to preside over the first real NATO Arctic strategy discussions since the Cold War. Nordic countries are likely to caution against any drastic policy changes beyond the soft security focus on defense cooperation in order to improve search and rescue facilities and related maritime security functions in Arctic waters. But Norway has for some years already advocated stronger NATO focus on the Euro-Atlantic region. Norwegian officials have proposed that NATO serve as an arena for building situational awareness and knowledge among allies, provide capabilities in surveillance and protect critical infrastructure on allied territory. The premise until 2014 has been, however, that such mobilization develops with at least some level of understanding with Russia. With the emerging breakdown of military—and related cooperation between the West and Russia, Norway and the other Nordic countries face a new reality with potential trade-offs and far more difficult decisions ahead.

Will We See a New Sino-Russian Arctic Alliance?

With Arctic tensions threatening to rise in the wake of the Ukraine crisis, there is a new factor to consider that was not present in the Cold War days. Even though Nikita Khrushchev offered Mao military bases in the Russian Arctic in return for Soviet bases in China (an offer that was flatly rejected as an insult by Mao), China and other Asian countries' interest in the Arctic is a recent phenomenon. But with China, South Korea, Japan, India and Singapore accepted as permanent observers to the Arctic Council since 2013, Asia has come to the Arctic to stay. Asian countries are already significantly engaged in Arctic research, telecommunication, mining, oil and gas, shipping and shipbuilding as well as emerging as major tourism players in the Arctic. Nordic countries have welcomed Asian countries to the Arctic table, given the inherently global nature of a range of Arctic challenges, and also since the Asians have made it very clear that they understand and respect the United Nations Convention on the Law of the Sea (UNCLOS) and the inherent rights and privileges of Arctic coastal states.

Thus, the new Asian-Arctic embrace has been peaceful and conciliatory and rested on the promise of a High North low tension philosophy promoted by Arctic states. The new crisis between Russia and the West may, however, change that dynamic. Not least given the salience of energy geopolitics in current Western-Russian tensions, observers have started speculating whether the conflict is the impetus needed to really make Russia and China succeed in realizing their hitherto unfulfilled cooperative potential. Many historical, structural and political barriers to Sino-Russian rapprochement remain, but few are cast in stone and the Arctic stands out as one of the new and promising areas of both commercial and political cooperation between Beijing and Moscow. It is far too early to judge how China will balance its geopolitical bets between Russia, on one hand, and Europe and the United States on the other. Nordic countries are mainly spectators to such a global power play, but have solid stakes in their political outcomes. Will Obama or his successor be as successful as Nixon and Kissinger in driving a strategic wedge between Russia and China? Will the EU manage to convince China that Europe constitutes a far more important market than Russia? Or will we see the contours of a new and historic Sino-Russian alliance with the Arctic as one of its most important strongholds? Aiming to predict future developments in a new Russian-Western conflict scenario is bound to be highly speculative.

In conclusion, a natural Nordic-Arctic perspective would be that on we have to be realistic, not naïve, and start planning for more dire Arctic matters, while also acknowledging that the Arctic may still provide a venue for dialogue and cooperation between Russia and its Arctic neighbors. After all, if there is one common understanding among both established and new Arctic stakeholders (including Asian countries), successful exploitation of the rich Arctic resource base requires peace and stability. Military confrontation in the Arctic would create nothing but losers.

Chapter 17

Nordic-Baltic-American Cooperation in the Arctic: A United States View

Lawson W. Brigham

The 21st century Arctic is dominated by change and complexity. Globalization, climate change, regional politics and indigenous people's issues (and voices) intersect at the top of the world. And yet, the Arctic remains one of the world's most stable and peaceful regions, where international cooperation has been the norm among the eight Arctic states with sovereignty over much of the region. Even the 'international high seas' within the central Arctic Ocean, a once remote marine area beyond the jurisdiction of the coastal states, is governed by an international treaty, the United Nations Convention on the Law of the Sea. Greater marine access, a result of profound Arctic sea ice retreat, and new linkages of Arctic natural resources to global markets are influencing Arctic states to develop their northern lands and seas and reap the benefits of this potential wealth. However, the Arctic states individually and cooperatively as members of an intergovernmental forum (the Arctic Council), are challenged to devise effective strategies and measures to protect their indigenous peoples and the Arctic environment.

The development of a set of safety and protection measures for the Arctic marine environment involves key international bodies such as the United Nation's International Maritime Organization (IMO) and the International Hydrographic Organization (IHO). Within IMO, Arctic states have worked to achieve unified approaches to Arctic-specific rules and regulations for the global maritime industry, which tackle operating in remote, polar waters. The IHO has formed an Arctic Regional Hydrographic Commission to address the needs and large gaps in hydrographic services and charting in the Arctic Ocean. Other international specialized bodies, such as the World Meteorological Organization for Climate and Weather Issues, are playing increasingly influential roles in Arctic affairs. The Nordics and the

199

United States are prominent players within these bodies and there is an increasing need for the partners to cooperate on unified and coordinated positions related to Arctic infrastructure, maritime safety and environmental protection issues.

Most observers of current events would agree that the Arctic cannot be decoupled geopolitically from the globe for a host of critical economic, security and climatic change reasons. But how do the Arctic states continue to cooperate in Arctic affairs when one of their major partners, Russia, is involved in destabilizing actions in Crimea, Ukraine and elsewhere? How does the Arctic Council maintain its focus on key environmental and development issues and engage Russia in a range of decision-making policies regarding the future of the Arctic? A strong, focused U.S.-Nordic relationship can enhance this cooperation within the Council, while maintaining a united posture with regard to broad geostrategic issues and challenges. Outside the Council, how do the Nordics and the United States engage the three Baltic nations as meaningful partners in Arctic affairs? Closer cooperation in maritime and naval affairs may be one practical way to enhance regional resiliency and bolster Arctic security.

U.S. National Interests in the Arctic

U.S. Arctic policies and interests in the National Strategy for the Arctic Region (May 2013) focus on three broad priorities and objectives: advancing U.S. security interests, pursuing responsible Arctic regional stewardship and strengthening international cooperation. Table 1 includes the key elements of each of these priorities. This list highlights the diversity, complexity and interwoven nature of U.S. interests in a region undergoing rapid environmental and economic changes. While a key focus of U.S. international Arctic cooperation is the Arctic Council, many other bilateral and multilateral approaches at the international level are pursued to meet specific U.S. objectives in the region. The U.S.-Nordic-Baltic partnership is a key relationship that can add significantly to the Arctic dialogue from inside *and* outside the Arctic Council framework since the partners have a host of intersecting national interests. The broad nature of U.S. Arctic interests provides opportunities for cooperation and innovative arrangements among many public and private organizations.

U.S. Arctic security interests include the fundamental importance of preserving freedom of navigation in the Arctic Ocean. Building up infrastructure especially in the U.S.-Arctic maritime Arctic and developing enhanced Arctic domain awareness are significant security issues that will require large investments in infrastructure for the U.S. Federal Government to meet its broad responsibilities in the region. Expansion of offshore hydrocarbon exploration and development in the Alaskan Arctic is consistent with overall U.S. energy security interests. A focus on responsible Arctic region stewardship involves the use of science, traditional (indigenous) knowledge and integrated management approaches to achieve a balance among economic development, environmental protection and the cultural values and heritage of Arctic indigenous peoples. A national interest includes specific mention of charting the Arctic marine regions, which is in recognition to the fact that there can be no safety net for marine operations without adequate hydrography and charting.

Elements of U.S. Priorities and Objectives in the Arctic Region (National Strategy for the Arctic Region, May 2013).

I. *Advance United States Security Interests*
- Evolve Arctic Infrastructure and Strategic Capabilities
- Enhance Arctic Domain Awareness
- Preserve Arctic Region Freedom of the Seas
- Provide for Future United States Energy Security

II. *Pursue Responsible Arctic Region Stewardship*
- Protect the Arctic Environment and Conserve Arctic Natural Resources
- Use Integrated Arctic Management to Balance Economic Development, Environmental Protection, and Cultural Values
- Increase Understanding of the Arctic through Scientific Research and Traditional Knowledge
- Chart the Arctic Region

III. *Strengthen International Cooperation*
- Pursue Arrangements that Promote Shared Arctic State Prosperity, Protect the Arctic Environment, and Enhance Safety

- Work through the Arctic Council to Advance U.S. Interests in the Arctic Region
- Accede to the Law of the Sea Convention
- Cooperate with other Interested Parties

U.S.-Nordic Engagement in the Arctic Council

The Arctic Council's mandates of environmental protection and sustainable development provide abundant challenges and opportunities for strong cooperation by the U.S.-Nordic partners. It is important to remember that this partnership represents six of the eight Arctic states (Canada and Russia being the other voting members) in a forum that requires consensus on all new initiatives. Two key Council working groups, Protection of the Arctic Marine Environment (PAME) and Emergency Prevention, Preparedness and Response (EPPR) focus on the development of policies for Arctic marine environmental protection and on the practical aspects of dealing with Arctic emergencies. Norway, Finland, Iceland and the United States within the partnership have been particularly active in PAME, forging recommendations for the Arctic Ministers on a range of strategies and marine policies on maritime safety and environmental protection. The work of EPPR attracts delegations from the maritime organizations of all U.S.-Nordic partners. Through close cooperation, they can develop enhanced capacities and a regional resiliency to address the many challenges of expanding Arctic marine operations such as large commercial ship transits, cruise ships sailing in remote waters and offshore hydrocarbon exploration.

The Council's Sustainable Development Working Group (SDWG) has focused on a wide range of projects involving human development, human health, renewable energy and maritime-aviation infrastructure. Experts from the United States and the Nordic States have worked in close cooperation on many of the SDWG studies, in particular two Arctic human development assessments. Two science-based working groups that leverage the research capacities of the United States and the Nordics include the Arctic Monitoring and Assessment Programme (AMAP) and Conservation of Arctic Flora and Fauna (CAFF). Under AMAP, the United States and Norway funded and led major studies on climate (the Arctic Climate Impact Assessment) and oil and gas development (the Arctic Oil and Gas Assessment). Both AMAP and CAFF, using key U.S.-Nordic funding and expertise, have produced pioneering assessments on Arctic Ocean acidification and Arctic biodiversity.

U.S. Arctic national interests focus in part on integrated management, Arctic research, Arctic environmental stewardship and engagement with the private sector. Ongoing initiatives in the Arctic Council where close cooperation with the Nordic states can realize our shared national interests include:

Ecosystems-Based Management (EBM): The Council's experts group is strongly supported by the United States and Norway. Experts from Finland and Sweden could also share their experiences in managing the Baltic Sea ecosystem. EBM is an integral part of integrated Arctic management that the United States has special interest in applying to the U.S. maritime Arctic from the northern Bering Sea to the Beaufort Sea.

Arctic Research Agreement: The Nordics and the United States all have key national interests in mind when supporting ongoing discussions to develop a circumpolar agreement on Arctic research. Enhancing marine and terrestrial access to all regions of the Arctic for the conduct of research is a central element of the current debate. U.S.-Nordic solidarity on this critical issue is essential, for example, to future Arctic marine research on the seabed of the Arctic Ocean and future monitoring of regional climate and marine and terrestrial ecosystems. Land and sea-based monitoring sites are critical to ground validation of data from satellite and other remote sensing systems.

Arctic Marine Oil Pollution Prevention: Development of prevention strategies for oil from ships, offshore development and onshore-coastal marine infrastructure requires cooperation from a host of public and private maritime stakeholders. The United States and the Nordic States at IMO and collectively among their own maritime agencies should develop unified strategies and communicate their best practices to the Council's ongoing task force.

Black Carbon and Methane: Methane releases from permafrost and emissions of black carbon from Arctic ships are challenging issues in need of Arctic climate change research and policy formulation. The

Council's task force requires the latest scientific information from the Nordics and United States on these issues, which is important for developing appropriate mitigation and adaptation strategies. Funding and developing effective monitoring of methane and black carbon releases are integral to taking a holistic, circumpolar approach to these new challenges.

Engagement with Industry and the Business Community: During the Swedish Chairmanship of the Arctic Council (2011-2013), the concept of a Circumpolar Business Forum was conceived to better link the work of the Council with private industry whose investment, technical expertise and strategic planning are driving a new era of Arctic globalization and natural resource development. Having industry experts contribute to Council studies and to Arctic sustainable development, as was the case during the conduct of the *Arctic Marine Shipping Assessment* (released in 2009), provides unique perspectives and experiences that are invaluable to an otherwise Arctic state dialogue. The Forum has been renamed to the Arctic Economic Council and the group will foster business development in the Arctic as well as bring a business perspective to all of the Council's work. U.S.-Nordic support for this initiative can be enhanced by encouraging their industries that are moving into the Arctic to be contributors to the Council's dialogue focused on sustainable development.

Maritime Operations and the Baltic Sea

The Arctic Council's Arctic Marine Shipping Assessment (AMSA) was conducted under PAME and led by Canada, Finland and the United States during 2005-2009. One of Finland's key contributions was a case study on the Baltic Sea and its relevance to cooperation in the Arctic dialogue on developing a framework for maritime safety and environmental protection. The Baltic Sea, with some of the densest marine traffic in the world, has adopted a shipping regime where operational and strategic cooperation has become the norm. Also, as a seasonally ice-covered regional sea, the Baltic represents a regional sea that is most similar to Arctic coastal waters. Winter commercial ship traffic is facilitated by a multi-national fleet of icebreakers to ice-covered ports throughout the region, which extends to the northern coast of the Gulf of Bothnia (between Sweden and Finland) and to the eastern shore of the Gulf of Finland near Saint Petersburg. Significantly all the ports in Finland are ice-covered in winter making marine access a key, national economic security issue. The Baltic Icebreaking Management (BIM) system includes ten partners: Denmark, Estonia, Finland, Germany, Latvia, Lithuania, Norway, Poland, Russia and Sweden. Winter navigation assistance is tightly coordinated by the partners.

Intergovernmental cooperation in the Baltic Sea is founded on the Convention for the Protection of the Marine Environment of the Baltic Sea Area with a governing body, the Baltic Marine Environment Protection Committee (HELCOM). This region has several features of interest to Arctic maritime safety and environmental protection: 89 Baltic Sea Protected Areas, compulsory ship reporting, traffic surveillance (providing comprehensive domain awareness) and 15 traffic separation zones. An integrated information system provides mariners with traffic information, weather, wave heights and ice information in winter. Coordination of incident response especially with an oil spill is conducted by joint operations of the partners with enhanced cross-border facilitation.

The U.S.-Nordic-Baltic partners can use the Baltic Sea regime to discuss useful applications to Arctic maritime safety and environmental protection. Particularly relevant is the handling of operational information including a comprehensive, common marine traffic picture. Enhancing domain awareness in the Arctic is a new challenge and the Baltic Sea system is a model for information transfer between states and users of the waterways. Regional coordination of search and rescue, environmental response and the Baltic Sea system of protected areas and waterways management (through surveillance and traffic schemes) are approaches that have direct relevance to emerging Arctic requirements and marine infrastructure investments. Maritime cooperation in the Baltic Sea is relatively integrated among national and local governments and the partners can discuss how the Arctic might adopt the cooperative features of such integration.

A U.S.-Nordic-Baltic Arctic Agenda

The Artcic region holds unique national and international interests for the Nordics and the United States. The Baltic states, located in northern Europe and on a regional sea with heavy commercial marine traffic, hold key maritime security and environmental interests that have good synergism with an evolving maritime Arctic. The Arctic Ocean is similar to the Baltic Sea in that both are waterways that should be made safe, secure and open to all for trade.

An "Arctic agenda" for the relationship focusing on practical, maritime safety and naval operational issues, as well as Arctic Council opportunities, could include the following components:

Arctic Council Continued Focus on Environmental Stewardship: As the Chair of the Arctic Council 2015-2017, the United States should in its leadership role place continued Council focus on Arctic environmental stewardship. The United States should promote the International Maritime Organization's mandatory Polar Code for ships operating in polar waters during its implementation phase following agreement in spring 2015. The Polar Code is a maritime instrument and new regulatory regime for the Arctic (and Antarctic waters) that will significantly enhance marine safety and environmental protection, central objectives in the Council's work. The Nordic countries and United States should further develop the new Arctic Economic Council with a focus on sustainability issues. Agreement should also be sought among the Arctic states to share marine traffic information among its maritime agencies to enhance Arctic maritime domain awareness. Traffic data passed in real-time among the Arctic states can reduce the risks of potential incidents and facilitate maritime response while also providing an integrated, circumpolar view of Arctic commercial marine operations. Such an initiative, supported by close U.S.-Nordic cooperation, can foster greater engagement with Russia and its long-term development strategies for the Arctic.

Baltic Sea Cooperation: Enhanced maritime cooperation in the Baltic Sea should be a priority in the U.S.-Nordic-Baltic relationship. As a seasonally ice-covered regional sea, the Baltic Sea holds a number of similarities to Arctic coastal waters. A full range of joint operations and exercises (for example, coastal naval operations, maritime law enforcement, search and rescue and environmental response focused on oil spills) can be held with full participation of the three Baltic states, Finland, Sweden, Denmark and the United States. One collaborative research program that would have applications to the Arctic could be a study of the Baltic Sea as an effective ship emissions control area. A cooperative research effort, given the winter conditions in the Baltic Sea, could be focused on understanding oil spills in ice and the challenging aspects of winter cleanup in extreme cold environments. Knowledge of cold regions marine operations gained through joint exercises can enhance the regional readiness of the maritime agencies and coast guards and provide operational experience of value to future Arctic state responses.

Strengthen Unified Approaches within International Forums: The U.S.-Nordic-Baltic relationship can prove fruitful within the International Maritime Organization (IMO), the World Meteorological Organization (WMO), the International Hydrogaphic Organization and other bodies. A number of institutions are increasingly focusing their attention on the Arctic as an emerging region tied to global markets and the global environment. All affected actors are maritime states and strong supporters and contributors to the work of the IMO. Unified approaches to a broad range of emerging issues can provide significant leverage with the global maritime industry. With regards to the Arctic, the IMO is developing measures to enhance Arctic marine safety and environmental protection, including a mandatory Polar Code mentioned previously in an Arctic Council context, and future Arctic-specific initiatives (such as special area designations, marine routing and ship emissions controls). A strong U.S.-Nordic-Baltic partnership can help shape IMO's agenda and can influence WMO's work on global and regional climate change, where the Arctic is viewed as a bellwether of current and future warming on the planet.

Enhanced Arctic Maritime and Security Operations: A range of joint Arctic maritime operations can focus on joint search and rescue, emergency response and law enforcement. In selected operations, which are closely related to civil functions, Russia can be engaged directly. Search and rescue exercises have already been conducted under the auspices of the Arctic Council's Working Group on Emergency Prevention, Preparedness and Response with the experts of the eight Arctic states fully participating. Joint law enforcement exercises, for example related to future Arctic fisheries and offshore oil and gas developments, could be conceived and conducted by the coast guards of the Arctic states. Such cooperation engaging Russia can be done under the umbrella of the Arctic Council or outside of this intergovernmental forum, but the Nordics and United States should foster the creation of this form of close maritime cooperation as a way to build regional resiliency.

Coastal Arctic naval operations (perhaps conducted on a smaller scale than full NATO deepwater operations) could be planned using the substantial capacities of the Nordic and Baltic states coupled with various U.S. Coast Guard and Navy air and ship units. Leveraging this combined capability in Arctic littoral waters and perhaps on the waters of the Baltic Sea, provides enhanced competency and expertise in cold regions war-fighting and possible future enforcement actions. Iceland might be one ideal operating base for such an exercise and Greenlandic or northern Norwegian waters should also be considered for hosting joint operations. Joint testing of new technologies, for example the use of unmanned underwater vehicles for coastal mine laying operations in Arctic conditions, would benefit all of the partners. Using the icebreaking capacity of Finland, Sweden and Estonia in joint training exercises would be a unique contribution to understanding real-time operations in ice-covered waters.

Future Head of State Arctic Meeting: The possibility of a Head of State Arctic meeting was suggested by the United States in the May 2014 implementation plan for its National Strategy for the Arctic Region. Such a meeting or 'summit' was thought to be a possibility for the U.S. Chairmanship of the Arctic Council, perhaps to be held as early as 2016 at the 20th anniversary of the signing of the Ottawa Declaration, establishing the Council. Whether this meeting remains feasible in the current geopolitical climate in Europe-Russia-United States relations is unknown. Discussions in the United States will hopefully continue and the concept of having such an historic, high level Arctic gathering should not be dismissed for the near future or delayed indefinitely. If not the United States, then the next Arctic Council Chair, Finland in 2017-2019, might be able to orchestrate a meeting of the leaders of the eight Arctic states. The Nordic States and the United States should make a part of their collective agenda strong support for a Head of State Arctic meeting to be held near-term within the broad framework of the Arctic Council. Key objectives would be to sign a new agreement (one such binding agreement could be related to Arctic research) and communicate to the world the cooperative nature and positive relationship among the Arctic states in regional affairs. A meeting of leaders would reinforce the view that the Arctic states are committed to protecting Arctic people and the environment and also maintain the region as a safe, stable and peaceful place, where sustainable use is the foundation for a future Arctic. A global audience is watching how the Arctic states will communicate their shared interests and future vision for a peaceful Arctic. The U.S.-Nordic partners have a prominent role in making this clear message a reality and one visible, effective action is through a meeting of the Arctic state leaders.

Uncertain Arctic Future and Long-term Vision

Uncertainties are the norm in the emerging Arctic. Future unknowns include the rapid rate of regional climatic change, the pace of natural resource developments, the rate of public and private investments and evolving security challenges presented by Arctic and non-Arctic states alike. Engaging successfully in Arctic affairs requires a long-term vision where broad cooperation, flexibility and adaptation are critical to maintaining regional stability. The U.S.-Nordic relationship will be central to maintaining such a stable and peaceful Arctic region. This close relationship especially at the Arctic Council will be influential in shaping environmental security in the region and structuring a workable relationship with Russia on a range of practical needs and issues related to environmental protection and sustainability. Outside the mandate of the Council, a U.S.-Nordic-Baltic focus on shared maritime interests and joint marine and naval exercises in littoral waters can forge a highly constructive network of capacity and resiliency. Developing a stronger relationship today will prepare the partners for a complex set of future Arctic environmental, economic and military security challenges that are beginning to emerge early in the 21st century.

Chapter 18

Don't Retrench on Me:
Why and How the United States Must Engage

Daniel S. Hamilton

2014 marks the 25th anniversary of the opening of the Iron Curtain; the 75th anniversary of the beginning of World War II; and the 100th anniversary of the beginning of World War I—all important milestones shaping America's relationship to Europe, a relationship that over a century has been marked by cycles of U.S. engagement and retrenchment.

Today, as Americans appear both preoccupied and paralyzed by problems at home, and as some world regions beckon and others threaten, there is considerable temptation to retrench from Europe— to ask why Europeans can't tackle their own problems, why America is still needed, whether Europe matters as it may have in the 20th century, why Europe's challenges should be more relevant and pressing than problems at home or elsewhere in the world.

Not only are these temptations understandable, it is not unreasonable to think that such questioning might even be more acute when considering America's relations with its many close friends and allies in northern Europe—a stable and prosperous part of the world with a tradition of pragmatic cooperation, where human rights, democracy and the rule of law are respected and international responsibilities are largely acknowledged. Why should these countries command greater attention from U.S. policymakers than a multitude of others? What's the problem? Why should we care?

For the sake of the transatlantic relationship it is important that Europeans are able to answer these American questions. But it is equally important that Americans understand their own enduring interests in Europe, interests that endure beyond the attention demanded by periodic crises, threats or opportunities.

Simply put, I would suggest that U.S. interests in northern Europe and its surrounding neighborhood derive from three enduring U.S. interests toward Europe itself.

First, the United States has an enduring interest in a Europe that is hospitable to freedom. Over many decades it has acted on that interest, including through support of democratic allies across the continent, support for European reconciliation and integration, and support for European efforts to create an open, pan-continental Single Market.

In this regard, the U.S. has an enduring interest in consolidating the democratic transformation of Europe—working with its European partners to extend as far as possible across the European continent the space of democratic and economic freedom where war simply does not happen. To the extent those parts of Europe not yet part of this space can be included, the United States has an interest in working with others to advance those goals. Because the United States engaged with its NATO allies, and supported its EU partners, in their courageous decisions to open their institutions, 100 million more people in the Euro-Atlantic area now live in freedom, democracy, relative prosperity, and fundamental security than 25 years ago.

This transformation is not complete. To see it through the United States must not only engage, it must enlist support. The Nordic-Baltic states are among the strongest proponents of this vision, having profited so greatly from it themselves, and together with the United States and other European partners can help sustain a transatlantic commitment to the continued spread of freedom and democracy throughout all of Europe.

The sheer existence of the Baltic states as independent sovereign countries is testimony to the power of this ideal and the significance of these shared interests. Each of the Baltic states has immediately relevant experience with the transition from dictatorship to democracy and from state-run to market economies. Each exists today primarily because of the will and determination of its own people, but also in part because of the engagement and support of the United States and other European partners—particularly those in northern Europe. Together the Nordic and Baltic states have significant expertise in the hard work of anchoring democracy, and continue as important value-added partners to the United States to tackle unfinished business.

Second, the United States has a related interest in a European continent that is at peace with itself. The American people would be the first to cheer if Europeans proved capable of resolving European conflicts on their own. Unfortunately, this has not proven to be the case, as demonstrated by the Russian-Ukrainian and Russian-Georgian conflicts, the Balkan wars of the 1990s, and in U.S. peacekeeping and efforts at reconciliation and reassurance that—at European invitation—continue today.

Nonetheless, particularly after the Balkan wars there was a generalized sense in Western capitals that the natural state of the "post-Cold War" era would be European peace and stability. In good Yankee jargon, many Americans spoke of Europe as being "fixed;" the horrors and divisions of 20th century Europe seemed destined for the history books and of growing irrelevance to Europe's—and America's—future. The corollary was that Europe would be less demanding of American attention.

Continued turmoil and violence in European regions beyond the EU and NATO, however, suggest that the more useful historical frame to understanding Europe's future security challenges is less the "post-Cold War era" than the "post-Soviet succession"—a far more turbulent, uncertain and longer-lasting reshuffling of relationships among and within European societies and among states than many would care to admit or acknowledge. The "post-Cold War" frame implies that Europe's 20th century earthquake has ended, things have stopped shaking and the ground is stable. The "post-Soviet succession" frame implies that the earthquake is ongoing and can be dangerous. The ground is still shaking, and the landscape is still likely to change.

The collapse of the Soviet Empire necessitated a re-ordering of Russia's relations to its neighbors; relations among the post-Soviet successor states; and a restructuring of societal relations within all the countries across this vast space. This re-ordering is certainly not complete. Vast swaths of wider Europe are still beset with historical animosities and multiple crises, including a number of conflicts that in some way affect all of Europe. Tensions over Transniestria, Nagorno-Karabakh, Abkhazia and South Ossetia, which some euphemistically label "frozen conflicts," are in reality festering wounds that absorb energy and drain resources from countries that are already weak and poor. They inhibit the process of state-building as well as the development of democratic societies. They generate corruption and organized crime, and can be breeding grounds for trafficking, terrorism and nuclear smuggling. They foster the proliferation of arms and a climate of intimidation. They are a major source of instability within these countries and the broader region. Belarus remains a dictatorship. Ukraine is impoverished, insecure and in turmoil. Moreover, Vladimir Putin has demonstrated clearly and forcefully that he intends to treat parts of wider Europe as Russia's own special preserve. As a result, wider Europe is significantly less democratic, less secure, and less at peace than it was at the beginning of this decade. And in a Europe without walls, if stability does not spread eastward, instability is almost certainly likely to spread westward—in fact, it already has.

The epicenter of the post-Soviet succession earthquake, of course, is Russia itself. Vladimir Putin feels the tremors. His response has been to challenge directly the notion of a "post-Cold War" European security order and to question openly the sovereign integrity of a number of European states. Moscow has engaged in a determined effort to improve its capacity to mobilize and deploy large forces quickly, and has demonstrated itself both willing and able to conduct effective asymmetric operations inside the sovereign territory of other countries. European insecurities have been fueled by Russia's illegal annexation of the Crimean region of Ukraine; its active support for Ukrainian separatists; launching of missiles from Russian into Ukrainian territory; deployment of tens of thousands of troops on the Russian-Ukrainian border and many into Ukrainian territory itself; cyber attacks in Estonia; provocative military activities towards the Baltic states, Finland and Sweden; efforts to intimidate European energy consumers; violation of the 1987 Intermediate Nuclear Forces (INF) Treaty and the 1994 Budapest Memorandum on Security Assurances against threats or use of force against the territorial integrity or political independence of Ukraine, among other activities.

While these security challenges affect all Europeans, it is unlikely that Europeans will be able to resolve them on their own. Moreover, many Europeans look to the United States for assurances of security. Moscow's defiance of Europe's prevailing security order, together with continued turbulence in wider Europe, challenge U.S. interests in a

Europe at peace—and whenever Americans have ignored the in-between lands of Europe, they have always paid a higher price later. Successful reforms in wider Europe could resonate significantly across the post-Soviet space and into the broader Middle East. Failures risk destabilizing competition, confrontation, and conflict.

In short, the United States and its allies and partners are again challenged to engage on challenges to security in Europe, after having focused for more than a decade on security challenges far from European shores. Here again the Nordic and Baltic states offer considerable added value. The Baltic and Nordic states, each in its own way, have been forthright in their defense of the European security order, the inviobility of borders, and the right of small countries to determine their fate. They are important partners when it comes to protecting this goal. As neighbors to Russia, the Nordic and Baltic states offer valuable perspectives and have substantial stakes in managing relations with Moscow and engaging Russian society.[1] The Nordic-Baltic states cannot change Russia on their own— but they can contribute to building more coherent EU and NATO policies toward Russia.

The Nordic-Baltic states offer additional value by demonstrating that deeper cooperation can often generate greater political influence and better advance national interests than can disparate individual efforts. The Nordic-Baltic countries present a cohesive group of democracies that have long shed national rivalries and who present exceptional models of multinational military cooperation, despite the fact that they do not all share the same alliances or institutional memberships.

Third, the United States has a keen interest in Europe as a partner with which it can work to deal with transnational challenges that no nation can tackle effectively alone. Europe not only plays that role already in areas such as peacekeeping and development assistance, and is even more engaged in other areas such as confronting climate change, it has the potential to do far more. The United States thus has an interest in a confident, capable, outward-looking Europe, not one

---

[1]For valuable insights into U.S.-Nordic-Baltic cooperation, see Kurt Volker and Ieve Kupce, eds., *U.S.-Nordic-Baltic Engagement in a Globalized World* (Washington, DC: Center for Transatlantic Relations, 2010); and Damon Wilson and Magnus Nordenman, "The Nordic-Baltic Region as a Global Partner of the United States," Atlantic Council of the United States, 2011.

so best by turmoil or so focused on instability along its periphery that it cannot play this broader role.

This reinforces the U.S. stake in working with European partners who reflect this outward-looking perspective and who are willing to act on it. Northern European countries are exemplars of this outward-looking approach and can be leaders within and beyond Europe to work with the United States for more effective democratic governance grounded in the rule of law, progress against corruption and trafficking, peaceful resolution of conflicts, secure energy production and transit, and more confident and prosperous market economies. They are widely regarded as "honest brokers" in the world's hotspots.[2] They offer substantial expertise and experience in areas ranging from development assistance and reconciliation efforts to peacekeeping and maritime operations. Sweden, a non-ally, took part in NATO's Libya operation and has played a major role in Afghanistan. Norway and Denmark have been vigorously engaged in a range of NATO out-of-area operations. Lithuania, Latvia and Estonia each stepped up to contribute to Afghanistan, showing a commitment to an outwardly engaged transatlantic community, even though their resources are small.

An Agenda for Enhanced U.S.-Nordic-Baltic Engagement

These enduring interests help to explain why the United States should resist the urge to retrench, why it should in fact double down on its engagement in Europe, and why it should pay particular attention to ways it can work with Nordic and Baltic partners and allies. The Nordic-Baltic states are value-added partners when it comes to core U.S. interests toward a Europe that is hospitable to freedom, is at peace with itself, and that can act as a partner on a range of regional and global challenges. The values and vision that drive their security policies, their demonstrated capabilities, and their capacity for multinational collaboration make them valuable allies and partners of the United States. Precisely because the Nordic-Baltic region is stable, prosperous, financially sound, growing economically, and peaceful, partnership with the United States can magnify each country's ability

---

[2]See Ian Brzezinski's contribution to Volker and Kupce, *op. cit.*

to advance its goals and protect its interests.[3] And perhaps the best way to retain U.S. engagement in Europe is to be able to point to European allies and partners who are not simply consumers of security but value-added contributors.

This sets the context for an agenda for enhanced U.S. engagement with its Nordic and Baltic allies and partners. This agenda includes respective efforts within broader multilateral frameworks as well as initiatives by the United States directly with the eight Nordic-Baltic states.

Boost NATO's Role and U.S. Engagement

First, with regard to NATO, the U.S. and its Nordic-Baltic allies share an interest in developing an Alliance with a full spectrum capability to address Article 5 threats; be more resilient to strategic surprises and disruptive shocks; and able to deal with new types of challenges such as energy and cyber security. They each have an interest in ensuring that NATO maintains a focus on missile defense and that NATO's Readiness Action Plan is implemented to equip the Alliance with the capacity to counter across the spectrum of contingencies, from hybrid attacks to rapid mobilization. They share an interest in making sure that the NATO Response Force, which was originally focused on out-of-area operations, now places more emphasis on collective defense, deterrence and reassurance. They should also push for using NATO infrastructure funds to sustain Host Nation Support (HNS) arrangements in the Baltic states that can facilitate a rapid Allied response to unforeseen and quickly unfolding events. They should ensure that military equipment, fuel and lubricants, as well as different kinds of ammunition, are pre-positioned to raise the deterrence threshold and to bring Allied troops faster into their operations areas. They also share an interest in engaging in regular exercising to test NATO's contingency plans for the collective defense of the Baltic states and Poland, and to structure such efforts so as to maximize U.S.-Nordic-Baltic military cooperation.

---

[3]See Wilson and Nordenman, *op. cit.*

In this context, the 2014 NATO Summit decisions were a step in the right direction. But more will need to be done, including by the United States. Specifically, the United States should not only enhance its participation in such NATO exercises, it should maintain a persistent force presence in the Baltic states and Poland. The Obama Administration's $1 billion European Reassurance Initiative should be used to create a few new highly visible initiatives to highlight U.S. engagement in northeastern Europe, and to fund U.S. participation in broader Alliance efforts. Baltic air policing, F-16 training for Poland, and NATO AWACS flights should continue, but more needs to be done. Forward Operating Bases, with prepositioned equipment, could be created in each of the Baltic states. U.S. forces should help maintain a NATO Reception Center based in Poland, with prepositioned stocks, to ensure rapid reinforcement in times of crisis. A fully operational, jointly operated Pershing Air Defense capability could be established in the region. A U.S. naval vessel should be present in the Baltic Sea at all times. The American presence should be bolstered at the NATO Cyber Center of Excellence in Estonia. EUCOM should participate more vigorously in the NATO Response Force, with its adapted mission as suggested earlier.

Russia's asymmetric tactics in Ukraine should prompt NATO to prepare itself better to counter possible asymmetric operations on NATO territory, especially in the Baltic states. This will require a comprehensive approach including special operations forces, police and border guard training, and agreement on political as well as military responses. It highlights the need for the U.S. and its allies and partners to make "resilience" a new common focus for security cooperation—more on that later.

The United States should also encourage the Nordic countries to extend NORDEFCO to the Baltic states as a way of cementing the prominent role of Sweden and Finland as premier partners of NATO; strengthening the NATO aspect of Nordic-Baltic security; enabling greater interoperability among regional forces; facilitating security cooperation with Washington; and opening opportunities for greater cooperation with Poland, Germany and other allies.[4]

---

[4]For more, see Henrik Breitenbauch's chapter in this volume.

Create a New Partnership Model

The most straightforward way to strengthen Nordic-Baltic defense capabilities and to enhance security throughout northern Europe would be for Sweden and Finland to join NATO. Each country would be more secure as a full NATO member, and NATO would be better with Sweden and Finland as members.

Short of such a step, however, Sweden and Finland should press the Alliance to reexamine its model of partnerships.

Northern Europe can be the proving ground for a redefinition of NATO's partnerships. How this could work requires us to first step back and look at the relevance of current partnership models. More than twenty years since the creation of the Partnership for Peace, the Alliance's current partnership framework has run its course. The challenges of both European and global security have evolved considerably—as have the nature, needs and opportunities of partnership.

NATO's various partnership arrangements have been predicated on a basic hub-and-spokes model. Partners are each linked to NATO, but are not always optimally linked to each other. Different partners have different aspirations with regard to the Alliance. Some want to be members, others want to be interoperable, still others prefer little more than dialogue. The current partnership framework does not address such differences well. Over the course of operations in Afghanistan and elsewhere, some partners have proven themselves more capable than some allies. Yet the current framework does not enable the Alliance to extract full benefit from such value-added partners. NATO also does not do particularly well when it comes to partnering with institutions, yet its own comprehensive approach to security is predicated on such ability.

Many partners around the world are attracted to NATO's model of interoperability, which is becoming the global gold standard. Partners have demonstrated great readiness to learn from NATO practices when it comes to what one might call the "hardware" of interoperability. Operations far from NATO territory, however, have demonstrated that NATO may have something to learn from its partners when it comes to the "software" of interoperability, such as understanding differing cultural contexts, patterns of relationships, differing civilian-military relations, societal mores and customs. The hub-and-spoke model is essentially a one-way partnership model; there is opportunity for NATO to gain from making partnership a two-way venue for learning, particularly when it comes to the "software" of partnership.

With these experiences in mind, NATO partnerships should evolve from a hub-and-spokes model to a non-hierarchical network of part-nerships linked via five nodes or clusters. A first basic cluster of part-ners would engage in political dialogue with NATO to improve mutual understanding, avoid misconceptions, and find common areas of interest. This could constitute the entry point for new partners. A second cluster should consist of NATO working with partners who wish to develop their capabilities and their interoperability, in order to be able to contribute to peace support operations and other activities. A third cluster should be a special track for those countries that have declared their intent to join the Alliance. These countries are intent on understanding the requirements of membership, and have declared their willingness to meet those standards. They should be on their own track to accomplish these goals. A fourth cluster would consist of international organizations partnering with NATO.

The fifth cluster would hold special significance for U.S.-Nordic-Baltic cooperation. It would build on decisions taken at the 2014 NATO Summit, including Swedish and Finnish MOUs with NATO that provide, among other things, for NATO to make use of Swedish and Finnish territory and installations. But a revised model would go even further. It would consist of Premier Interoperable Partners (PIP)—countries not currently seeking membership yet willing and able to contribute to NATO efforts beyond the PfP norm. Countries such as Sweden, Finland or Australia, for instance, have in recent years formed deep partnerships with NATO. They have a serious mil-itary track record on par with many of the most capable NATO allies, and are already largely interoperable with NATO. NATO recognized this at its Summit in Wales, and set in place a new enhanced interop-erable platform for such countries. This is all positive. Yet more can be done.

NATO should go beyond its 2014 Summit decisions by offering Sweden and Finland a new role as Premier Interoperable Partners

(PIP) via an opt-in model[5] that provides for structured and regular consultations at the political, military and intelligence levels with the North Atlantic Council (NAC), the Military Committee, the International Staff and the International Military Staff. This would occur routinely on all levels, including ministerials and summits. These would not be plus-one arrangements, but a practical and regular part of doing business at NATO headquarters, the Supreme Headquarters Allied Powers Europe (SHAPE) and at the Allied Command Transformation (ACT) in Norfolk. Consultations would cover all relevant matters related to operational connectivity, capability development, capacity building as well as prevention and thematic issues of political significance; offer early involvement in policy discussions relevant to operations, a role in planning and decision shaping relating to exercises, education and training, and full access to NATO Smart Defense programs and to the Connected Forces Initiative; offer opportunity to participate in the NATO Response Force, which would be used as a facilitator for continued interoperability and force integration; offer opportunity not only to participate, but to have a role in planning related to force rotations and related operations; offer opportunity to opt-in or opt-out of exercises, education, training and operations and to make recommendations for exercises, training and education and even for potential operations.

At the 2014 NATO Summit, allies in fact offered capable partners a new Interoperability Platform. But the opt-in model, linked to a Premier Interoperable Partner status, goes further and should be considered as the next step beyond the Summit decisions.

Lift and Extend the E-PINE Agenda

The Enhanced Partnership in Northern Europe (e-PINE) is a unique and useful vehicle for the United States and the 8 Nordic-Baltic countries to discuss regional and global issues. Yet e-PINE could be better utilized.

E-PINE discussions are typically carried out twice a year among political directors from respective foreign ministries. The original

---

[5]See the chapter by Hans Binnendijk, Debra L. Cagan, and Andras Simonyi in this volume. Elements of their proposal are presented again here to clarify the concept and relate it to my recommendations about an overall revision of partnerships.

222 ENHANCING U.S.-NORDIC-BALTIC SECURITY COOPERATION

frame for these discussions was the Northern European Initiative launched by the Clinton Administration. At that time deliberations focused primarily on ways to facilitate Baltic inclusion into Euro-Atlantic institutions and to advance the vision of a Europe whole and free. Once the Baltic states entered NATO and the EU, the focus of discussion shifted to how the 8-plus-1 format could be better utilized with regard to other countries in transition in central and eastern Europe. E-PINE has offered added value to shared efforts to promote human rights, market reforms, and democratic practices of governance across this region.

Given the stakes involved in Ukraine and other countries in wider Europe, it is important to reanimate the vision of Europe whole and free and to use it to drive the e-PINE agenda. Without such a vision-driven agenda, e-PINE's relevance could fade. The most effective counter to Russian intrusion into Ukraine, for instance, is to work with Ukrainians to make their transition to a more representative, effective and prosperous democracy a success. Baltic states offer relevant experience in open society transition; Nordic states and the United States offer extensive expertise in championing democracy and human rights around the world. Practical cooperation can show public opinion in transition countries that closer partnership can do real things for real people; and can reassure government leaders that reforms can be worth the political risks involved. E-PINE meetings should not just take place in e-PINE country capitals, but also in places like Kyiv and Chisinau. Consideration should also be given to lifting current e-PINE discussions by considering annual or biannual consultations at Foreign Minister level.

E-PINE should not focus solely on "out-of-region" concerns, however. Attention should also be paid to exchange of good practice on common issues, drawing in relevant officials from other agencies, research directorates and societal actors. It would be particularly useful to consider practical projects that could facilitate U.S. engagement in regional Nordic-Baltic projects, or to initiate new forms of cooperation, especially related to energy, cybersecurity, e-governance, issues of societal diversity and inclusiveness.[6] As Lawton Brigham outlines in

---

[6]See Michael Polt's chapter in this volume.

his chapter, U.S.-Nordic-Baltic cooperation could focus on maritime cooperation in the Baltic Sea, including lessons for other regions, such as the High North.[7]

Given the changing nature of common security challenges, the e-PINE countries might again break new ground by pioneering new approaches to societal resilience, including possible new forms of diplomatic, intelligence, economic, and law enforcement cooperation; customs, air, and seaport security; data protection and information exchange; bio-resilience; critical infrastructure protection; and greater cooperation among special operations forces.

Transboundary arteries carrying people, ideas, money, energy, goods and services criss-cross modern societies and contribute significantly to economic growth and prosperity. They are essential sinews of open societies, daily communications, and the global economy. Yet this dynamism also creates vulnerabilities that can lead to intentional or accidental disruption of such critical functions as transportation, energy flows, medical services, food supply chains and business systems, communications, cyber links and financial networks. Governments are accustomed to protect their territories; now they must protect their society's critical functions, the networks that sustain them, and the connections those networks bring with other societies.

These developments call for private-public partnerships and close interactions among governments, the private sector, the scientific community, and non-governmental organizations.

As leading democratic knowledge economies, the United States and its Nordic-Baltic partners are at the forefront of efforts to forge greater societal resilience in the face of such challenges. They have both opportunity and need to exchange good practice and to explore more creatively new approaches to societal security.

Since most of these networks are owned by the private sector, the e-PINE partners should consider, as one example of such new approaches to security, a public-private Global Movement Management Initiative (GMMI) to align security and resilience with commercial imperatives in global movement systems, including shipping, air

___
[7]See his chapter in this volume.

transport, and cyberspace. Such an effort could improve cooperation among public and private stakeholders and serve potentially as a precursor for a more ambitious transatlantic cooperation.[8]

There is an additional reason why societal resilience resonates with the e-PINE format: each of the e-PINE countries has an interest in ensuring the societal resilience of other countries, particularly on their borders, since strong efforts in one country may mean little of neighboring systems are weak. By pioneering new approaches to societal security among themselves, the United States and its Nordic-Baltic partners should also be able to "project resilience forward" to others. E-PINE partners should make a concerted effort, together with other NATO and EU allies as appropriate, to work with Ukraine and other Eastern Partnership countries to improve societal resilience to corruption, psychological warfare, and intentional or natural disruptions to cyber, financial and energy networks and other critical infrastructure, with a strong focus on prevention but also response. A Forward Resilience Initiative would build on respective U.S.-Nordic-Baltic strengths; give practical content to the broader vision of a Europe whole and free in the context of new security challenges; and provide tangible support to transition countries in need of such assistance.

Finally, given e-PINE's potential as an incubator of good policy and practice, both among governments and societies, consideration should be given to the creation of a joint U.S.-Nordic-Baltic Center—virtual or actual—that would connect experts of the nine countries for purpose-specific tasks and solutions.[9]

---

[8]This suggestion is adapted from IBM Global Business Services, "Global Movement Management: Commerce, Security, and Resilience in Today's Networked World," and "Global Movement Management: Securing the Global Economy," available through www.ibm.com/gbs/government. For more on the international aspects of resilient networks, see Daniel Hamilton and Mark Rhinard, "All for One, One For All: Towards a Transatlantic Solidarity Pledge," in *The U.S.-EU Security and Justice Agenda in Action* (Paris: EU Institute for Security Studies, 2012); Daniel S. Hamilton, Bengt Sundelius and Jesper Grönvall, eds., *Protecting the Homeland: European Approaches to Societal Security—Implications for the United States* (Washington, DC: Center for Transatlantic Relations, 2005); Bengt Sundelius, "Beyond Anti-Terrorism: Ensuring Free and Resilient Societies," in Daniel S. Hamilton, ed., *Shoulder to Shoulder: Forging a Strategic U.S.-EU Partnership* (Washington, DC: Center for Transatlantic Relations, 2010).

[9]I share the views of Linas Linkevicius as expressed in his chapter.

Advance a U.S.-Nordic-Baltic Arctic Agenda

The U.S.-Nordic relationship will be central to maintaining such a stable and peaceful Arctic region. The Baltic states, located on a regional sea with heavy commercial marine traffic, also have key maritime security and environmental interests that are synergistic with an evolving maritime Arctic. The Arctic Ocean and the Baltic Sea are waterways that should be made safe, secure and open to all for trade. Lawson Brigham and Leiv Lunde outline practical steps for cooperation in their respective chapters; I need not duplicate their good recommendations here.

Push Early Conclusion and Ratification of TTIP

Economic prosperity is one of the greatest guarantors of a Europe whole and free. Strong economic performance underpins U.S. and European capabilities and commitments to common security. The Transatlantic Trade and Investment Partnership (TTIP) currently being negotiated by the United States and the European Union promises to unleash significant opportunities to generate jobs, trade and investment across the Atlantic. But TTIP is far more than a free-trade agreement. It is about creating a more strategic, dynamic and holistic U.S.-EU relationship that is more confident, more effective at engaging third countries and addressing regional and global challenges, and better able to strengthen the ground rules of the international order.[10]

TTIP is likely to have an outsized positive impact on U.S.-Nordic-Baltic cooperation, offering significant geopolitical potential as a values-based, rules-based initiative. TTIP is likely to strengthen Western economic and social cohesion and contribute to greater attractiveness of the Western model. While it is not an "economic NATO," it can offer a second transatlantic anchor to NATO, stimulate U.S. investment and reinforce the U.S. commitment to Europe. It has the potential to spark greater links among U.S.-Nordic-Baltic knowledge economies.

TTIP is becoming particularly important in the context of changing transatlantic energy security. More effective energy cooperation was not an original impetus for the talks, but should now be incorpo-

---

[10]For fuller elaboration of TTIP's geopolitical implications, see Daniel S. Hamilton, ed., *The Geopolitics of TTIP* (Washington, DC: Center for Transatlantic Relations, 2014).

rated to facilitate U.S. energy exports to Europe as part of a more strategic transatlantic approach to energy cooperation.

Recent events in Ukraine and Russia have made clear that creating a transatlantic energy market is about more than economic efficiency. Energy cooperation has become an indispensable pillar of the Western community. Today the EU produces only a small portion of its energy needs, importing about 80% of its oil and about 60% of its gas. More than a third of this oil and 30% of the gas is of Russian origin. Some EU member states are 100% dependent on Russian energy supplies.

Over the past few years America's oil and gas boom has rendered the United States over 80% self-sufficient in energy production and use. It will soon become an exporter of natural gas and surpass both Russia and Saudi Arabia to become the world's largest producer of oil and liquid natural gas.

A successful TTIP would enable the United States to export gas to Europe, since U.S. law prohibits such exports (or requires onerous licensing procedures) except to countries with which the United States has a free trade agreement. In essence, members of the TTIP and the Trans-Pacific Partnership alike should be eligible for waivers to DOE licensing requirements. In addition, TTIP could enable the United States and the EU align standards in areas such as e-mobility and energy efficiency, reduce tariff and non-tariff barriers to clean energy goods and services, and create mechanisms for mutual recognition of regulatory processes regarding energy innovation. It also offers a mechanism for the United States and the EU to agree on basic normative principles that could have important global repercussions. One example is mandatory access for third parties to pipelines in the hands of a monopoly. Both U.S. and EU law provide for this, but if extended more broadly as an international norm it would have significant impact on countries such as Ukraine or those in Central Asia.

U.S. gas exports to Europe could alleviate European dependence on unpredictable suppliers; just the prospect has forced Russia to break the link between oil and gas prices and to negotiate better terms with a number of European customers. Moscow's efforts to assert a new sphere of influence over its neighborhood, including over some EU member states, have galvanized European efforts to chart a new energy future, where possible with the United States.

By reducing European energy dependency on Russia, both the United States and Europe will be better able to defend and promote their values, while capturing the immense gains from greater economic integration between the world's two largest markets. Much of this goes beyond TTIP, of course, but TTIP could play a catalytic role. Lifting U.S. export restrictions would be a first step, but so too would speeding up infrastructure development, especially for liquefied natural gas.

Some critics are skeptical that substantial U.S. energy could flow to Europe anytime soon, given the fact that appropriate new infrastructure could take years to build. But likely investors are deciding *today* on such multi-year projects, and thus a strong U.S-EU political signal of intent to build a more strategic energy partnership, including through TTIP, can in fact influence such investment decisions, even as it sends a strong message of transatlantic solidarity in the face of Russian troublemaking.

TTIP presents a huge challenge to the Kremlin's efforts to divide Europeans from Americans. It offers something that the Kremlin cannot match: a transparent, mutually beneficial agreement which creates a rules-based framework for international cooperation. A reinvigorated transatlantic marketplace among highly-connected, highly-competitive democracies, whose people enjoy greater economic growth and rising standards of living, would challenge the Kremlin's version of "managed democracy;" render Russia's own one-dimensional natural-resource-based economic model increasingly unattractive; and consign its rival economic project, the Eurasian Economic Union, to irrelevance.[11] Greater U.S.-EU energy cooperation would strike at the heart of Russia's monopolistic approach to European energy markets. And if such benefits extended to non-EU neighbors, particularly Ukraine, Russians themselves are likely to ask why their own country can't be better run.

For all these reasons, the Kremlin is conducting "active measures" in Eastern Neighborhood countries and in the EU itself, including tactics of pressure and intimidation, to derail the TTIP. The West should push back while indicating a readiness to engage with Russia economically on the basis of the very rules and procedures being advanced

---

[11]See Edward Lucas, "TTIP, Central and Eastern Europe and Russia," in Hamilton, *op cit.*

through the TTIP. The message is not that the West is excluding Russia, but that Russia is excluding itself from this promising dynamic.

Conclusion

Despite challenges at home and elsewhere in the world, the United States retains enduring interests in Europe that cannot be secured by disengagement and retrenchment. Europe has entered a new security reality; U.S. commitment is as necessary now as it has been in the past. Europe is also important to U.S. interests in other parts of the world. Cooperation with Nordic and Baltic states can magnify the impact of U.S. engagement, just as U.S. action can enhance the security of countries in northern Europe. A practical agenda for U.S.-Nordic-Baltic cooperation, as outlined here and as suggested by the various authors in this volume, can make a difference.

The times they are a-changin'. We must keep our eyes wide.[10]

---

[10]With apologies to Bob Dylan.

About the Authors

Mika Aaltola is the Director of the Global Security Research Program, Director of the Center for U.S. Politics and Power at the Finnish Institute of International Affairs and Professor of International Relations at Tallinn University. He is a Senior Visiting Fellow at the Center for Transatlantic Relations at the School of Advanced International Studies at Johns Hopkins University, Fellow at CERI Sciences Po and Visiting Professor at the University of Minnesota. His published works include *Sowing the Seeds of Sacred: Political Religion of American Era* (2008), *Western Spectacles of Governance and the Emergence of Humanitarian World Order* (2009), *Understanding the Politics of Pandemic Scares* (2012) and *The Challenge of Global Commons and Flows for U.S. Power* (2014). His current research focuses on understanding the impact of global flows on global security, resilience and power.

Hans Binnendijk is a Senior Fellow at the Center for Transatlantic Relations at the School of Advanced International Studies at Johns Hopkins University, and at RAND. Until 2012, he was Vice President for Research and Applied Learning at the National Defense University and Theodore Roosevelt Chair in National Security Policy. He previously served on the National Security Council staff as Special Assistant to the President and Senior Director for Defense Policy and Arms Control. He also served as Principal Deputy Director of the State Department's Policy Planning Staff and Legislative Director of the Senate Foreign Relations Committee. He has received three Distinguished Public Service Awards. In academia, he was Director of the Institute for the Study of Diplomacy at Georgetown University and Deputy Director at London's International Institute for Strategic Studies.

Erik Brattberg is a a Fellow at the Center for Transatlantic Relations at the School of Advanced International Studies at Johns Hopkins University, Resident Fellow at the Brent Scowcroft Center on International Security's Strategic Foresight Initiative, and a Research Associate at the Swedish Institute of International Affairs in Stockholm. He has published widely on transatlantic and European security, including in *The Huffington Post*, *The Washington Post*, *European Voice* and *The National Interest*.

Henrik Breitenbauch is a Nonresident Fellow with the Center for Transatlantic Relations at the School of Advanced International Studies at Johns Hopkins University and a Senior Researcher at the Centre for Military Studies, University of Copenhagen. He focuses on international aspects of defense and security policy in Denmark, NATO, Europe and the United States as well as on strategy and strategic organization. He served as Lead Writer for the Defence Command Denmark on NATO Allied Command Transformation's Multiple Futures Project and has since been involved in ACT's long-term defense planning projects.

Lawson W. Brigham is Distinguished Professor of Geography and Arctic Policy at the University of Alaska Fairbanks and Senior Fellow at the Institute of the North in Anchorage. He is currently a Commissioner on the Alaska Arctic Policy Commission and a member of the Council on Foreign Relations and the World Economic Forum's Global Agenda Council on the Arctic. Previously, he was a career U.S. Coast Guard officer who commanded the polar icebreaker *Polar Sea* on Arctic and Antarctic expeditions. He served as Chair of the Arctic Council's Arctic Marine Shipping Assessment (2004-2009), Vice Chair of the Council's working group on Protection of the Arctic Marine Environment, Research Fellow at Woods Hole Oceanographic Institution, faculty member of the U.S. Coast Guard Academy and the Naval Postgraduate School, and Alaska Director of the U.S. Arctic Research Commission. His chapter reflects his personal views as an academic and researcher at the University of Alaska Fairbanks.

Debra L. Cagan is a career State Department officer with over 30 years of domestic and international experience advancing U.S. national security interests. She is currently the Senior State Department Fellow at the Center for Transatlantic Relations at the Paul H. Nitze School of Advanced International Studies (SAIS), Johns Hopkins University. She has also held assignments as Deputy Assistant Secretary of Defense for Coalition Affairs in Iraq and Afghanistan, diplomatic and political advisor to senior U.S. and NATO military officials, Director for Strategic and Nuclear Policy for Europe and Eurasia and lead negotiator for nuclear and nonproliferation agreements. The views expressed are the author's own and not necessarily those of the Department of State or the U.S. government.

Heather A. Conley is Senior Fellow and Director of the Europe Program at CSIS. Prior to joining CSIS, Ms. Conley was Senior Adviser to the Center for European Policy Analysis, Executive Director of the Office of the Chairman of the Board at the American National Red Cross (2005-2008), Deputy Assistant Secretary of State in the Bureau for European and Eurasian Affairs (2001-2005) and Senior Associate with an international consulting firm led by former U.S. Deputy Secretary of State Richard L. Armitage (1994-2001). She began her career in the Bureau of Political-Military Affairs at the U.S. Department of State, where she served as the State Department liaison for the U.S. Department of Defense's Global Humanitarian Assistance Program (HAP). Following this assignment, she was selected to serve as Special Assistant to the coordinator of U.S. assistance to the newly independent states of the former Soviet Union.

Daniel S. Hamilton is the Austrian Marshall Plan Foundation Professor and Director of the Center for Transatlantic Relations at the Paul H. Nitze School of Advanced International Studies, Johns Hopkins University. He also serves as Executive Director of the American Consortium on EU Studies, designated by the European Commission as the EU Center of Excellence Washington, DC. Recent books include *The Transatlantic Economy 2014*; *The Geopolitics of TTIP*; *Atlantic Rising: Changing Commercial Dynamics in the Atlantic Basin*; *Open Ukraine: Changing Course towards a European Future*; *Europe's Economic Crisis*; *Transatlantic 2020: A Tale of Four Futures*; and *Europe 2020: Competitive or Complacent?* He has served in a variety of senior positions in the U.S. State Department, including as Associate Director of the Secretary of State's Policy Planning Staff and as Deputy Assistant Secretary of State, including responsibility for NATO, OSCE and U.S.-Nordic-Baltic relations. He received the State Department's Superior Honor Award for his work negotiating the U.S.-Baltic Charter and co-authoring the U.S. Northern European Initiative. Various awards include Sweden's Knighthood of the Royal Order of the Polar Star.

Pauli Järvenpää is a Senior Research Fellow at the International Center for Defense Studies (ICDS) in Tallinn, Estonia, where he focuses on the security of the Baltic Sea and Nordic regions ("Mare Nostrum") and on issues related to NATO, the EU and transatlantic cooperation. He most recently served as the Finnish Ambassador to Afghanistan (2010-2013). Before that he was Director General of the

Defense Policy Department at the Finnish Ministry of Defense (2002-2010) and the Defense Advisor at the Mission of Finland to NATO in Brussels (1999-2002). He was educated at Harvard and Cornell.

Linas Linkevicius is the Lithuanian Minster of Foreign Affairs, a position he has held since December 2012. He has an extensive diplomatic and security experience having served as Ambassador to Belarus (2012), the Permanent Representative to NATO (2005-2011), Minister of National Defence (2000-2004), Ambassador and Head of Mission to the WEU and NATO (1997-2000), and Minister of National Defence (1993-1996). He was also member of the Seimas (Parliament) (1992-1996) and Deputy Chairman of the Seimas Committee on Foreign Affairs, Head of the Seimas delegation to NATO (1992-1993) and Chairman of the Council of the Lithuanian Labour Youth Union (1992). His decorations include the Order of Three Stars, Third Class (Latvia) (2001); Cross of Commander of the Order of the Lithuanian Grand Duke Gediminas (2003); Cross of Commander of the Order of the Cross of Vytis (2004); Order of the Cross of Terra Mariana, Second Class (Estonia) (2005); and Order of Honour (Georgia) (2011).

Leiv Lunde was appointed Director of the Fridtjof Nansen Institute (FNI) in 2012. He has worked as Researcher and Policy Analyst with FNI and ECON Analysis (1990-1997; 2000-2005), as Norwegian Deputy Minister for Foreign Affairs (1997-2000; 2005) and as Policy Developer in the Norwegian Ministry of Foreign Affairs (2006-2011). In this capacity, he launched the Norwegian Oil for Development program and served as principal energy envoy to the foreign minister. His current research interests include the geopolitics of energy, energy and climate change, energy governance, determinants of energy developments in the Arctic region, Asia's role in the Arctic and comparative analysis of foreign policy organization and performance.

Michael Mohr has served as Vice President and Head of Public Affairs at Saab AB, Sweden's leading security and defense company, since 2011. For a number of years, he served as the Secretary General of the Swedish Security and Defence Commission, coordinating the Commission's proposals for the reform of Sweden's military defense, as well as Sweden's overall security and crisis management structure. He served as Special Attaché to the Swedish Embassy in Washington, DC (2006-2010), coordinating U.S.-Swedish bilateral homeland security relations. He was also involved in the creation of a Swedish Cyber Defence, serving as both the Secretary General of the Swedish Cyber Security Committee and the Chairman of the Cabinet Office Working Group on Information Operations.

Michael Polt is Senior Director at the McCain Institute for International Leadership in Washington, DC, where he leads the Institute's signature Next Generation Leaders Program and teaches foreign policy. He assumed this position in 2012, after concluding a distinguished 35-year diplomatic career serving six presidents and eleven Secretaries of State. Among his many high-level diplomatic assignments was service as U.S. Ambassador to the Republic of Estonia during the Obama administration, Ambassador to Serbia and Montenegro during the Bush administration and Principal Deputy and Acting Assistant Secretary of State for Legislative Affairs in the Powell and Clinton State Departments. The author's views are his own and do not represent the opinion of the McCain Institute for International Leadership or its affiliates or those of the U.S. Department of State or the U.S. Government.

Johan Raeder is Director General for International Affairs at the Ministry of Defense in Stockholm, Sweden. Prior to this, he served as Director General for Political Affairs (2008-2013) and Director for Security and International Affairs (2001-2008) within the Ministry. His chapter reflects his personal views.

Andris Razāns has served as Ambassador Extraordinary and Plenipotentiary of the Republic of Latvia to the United States since 2012. He served as Political Director and Undersecretary of State at the Foreign Affairs Ministry (2010-2012), as Ambassador to Denmark (2004-2009) and as Ambassador at large to the Ministry Policy Planning Group (2009-2010). He has served as Third Secretary and then as Second Secretary at the Latvian Embassy in Copenhagen, Denmark (1994-1997), Head of the EU Policy Division at the Foreign Ministry (1997-1998) and Diplomatic Advisor to the President of Latvia, Vaira Vike-Freiberga (1998-2000). He also served as Deputy Head of Mission at the Latvian embassy in Stockholm, Sweden (2000-2003), Head of the Policy Planning Group at the Foreign Ministry (2003-2004) and as Diplomatic Advisor to the Latvian Prime Minister, Indulis Emsis (2004).

Caroline Rohloff is a Research Associate with the CSIS Europe Program, where she provides research and program support on a range of issues, including security and defense cooperation in northern Europe, the evolution of NATO and transatlantic relations and developments in the Arctic region. Prior to her time at CSIS, she worked with the U.S. Department of State on European Union affairs.

András Simonyi is the Managing Director of the Center for Transatlantic Relations at the School of Advanced International Studies at Johns Hopkins University. He has a long professional career in multilateral and bilateral diplomacy, international non-governmental and governmental organizations, as well as in the private sector. His focus has been the transatlantic relationship. He has held some of the highest positions in the Hungarian diplomatic service, including as Hungary's Ambassador to the United States and to NATO.

Keith Smith is presently Senior Associate at the Center for European Policy Analysis (CEPA). He served as Senior Associate at the Center for International and Strategic Studies (2002-2013). Mr. Smith retired from the U.S. State Department in 2000 after 38 years of service. His last posting was as Ambassador to Lithuania. He has focused on issues involved in Russian-European energy relations. He has consulted governments and several private energy firms in Europe and the United States since 2001. He has written extensively on Russian energy relations, including the politically coercive use of oil and gas exports. His commentary represents his own views and not that of any institution.

Ine Eriksen Søreide is the Norwegian Minister of Defense, a position she has held since October 2013. She represents the Conservative Party and is elected to parliament from the constituency of Oslo. Her parliamentary experience includes: Chair, Standing Committee on Foreign Affairs and Defense, and Chair, Enlarged Foreign Affairs Committee (2009-2013); Head of the Delegation for Relations with the European Parliament, and Head of the European Consultative Committee (2009-2013); Chair, Standing Committee on Education, Research and Church Affairs (2005-2009); and Member, Standing Committee on Education, Research and Church Affairs (2001-2005). Political appointments in the Conservative Party include: Member of the Conservative Party Central Executive Committee (2000-present); Chair, Young Conservatives in Norway (2000-2004); First Vice Chair,

Young Conservatives in Norway (1998-2000) and Chair (2000-2004); and Member, Central Executive Committee of the Young Conservatives in Norway (1996-1998).

Gregory M. Suchan is Senior Associate at Commonwealth Consulting Corporation, a government relations firm in Arlington, Virginia. He retired from the United States Foreign Service in 2007, and his 34-year career with the Department of State focused primarily on political-military issues and included overseas assignments to U.S. diplomatic missions in Mexico, London, NATO headquarters, Pakistan and Denmark. He was Deputy Assistant Secretary in the State Department's Bureau of Political-Military Affairs (2000-2007) and worked on diplomatic support for Operations Enduring Freedom and Iraqi Freedom (2001-2003). He supervised the Department of State's Directorate of Defense Trade Controls (2003-2007). He was Head of the Department of State offices responsible for government-to-government arms transfers under the Foreign Military Sales (FMS) program and Commerce Department export controls.

Mike Winnerstig is currently Deputy Director of Research at the Swedish Defence Research Agency (FOI). He is also in charge of the FOI "Security in the Baltic Neighbourhood" program. His research and publications have primarily focused on transatlantic security, U.S. defense and security policy and Nordic-Baltic security issues. He has formerly been employed by the Swedish Institute of International Affairs and Stockholm University. In 1997-98, he was a Research Fellow at the Belfer Center for Science and International Affairs, Harvard University. He has also held fellowships at the Stiftung Wissenschaft und Politik (Germany) and the Centre for Defence Studies, Aberdeen University (UK).